BLESSING

ALSO BY DAVID SPANGLER

Parent as Mystic, Mystic as Parent

The Call

A Pilgrim in Aquarius

Everyday Miracles

Revelation: The Birth of a New Age

Emergence: The Rebirth of the Sacred

Reimagination of the World
(with William Irwin Thompson)

BLESSING

THE ART AND THE PRACTICE

DAVID SPANGLER

Riverhead Books

a member of Penguin Putnam Inc.

New York

2001

Riverhead Books

a member of

Penguin Putnam Inc.

375 Hudson Street

New York, NY 10014

Library of Congress Cataloging-in-Publication Data

Spangler, David, date.

Blessing : the art and the practice / David Spangler.

p.   cm.

ISBN 1-57322-184-8

1. Blessing and cursing.   I. Title.

BL560.S63   2001   00-068344

291.3'8—dc21

Printed in the United States of America

1   3   5   7   9   10   8   6   4   2

This book is printed on acid-free paper. ♾

Book design by Chris Welch

ACKNOWLEDGMENTS

This book would not exist were it not for the people who became part of my blessing classes, allowing themselves to be my guinea pigs in order to try out this material. Each of you gave a great deal of yourself to explore the possibilities and techniques of blessing. You folks, and you know who you are, are truly a blessing. Thank you all.

I want to offer a special acknowledgment and debt of gratitude to Barbara Finn, who generously transcribed all the tapes from these classes, deciphering nearly inaudible questions and responses recorded under less than professional circumstances and giving up a significant amount of her free time to do so. The resulting transcript proved an invaluable resource for me, particularly in creating the workbook. She made my job very much easier. Thank you, Barbara!

ACKNOWLEDGMENTS

As always, I want to thank my fabulous editor, Wendy Carlton, who transformed the straw of my manuscript into the gold of this book, and my wonderful publisher, Susan Petersen Kennedy, for her continuing support and encouragement. As a writer I feel very blessed by both of you. I also want to thank Venetia van Kuffeler, Wendy's most capable and friendly assistant, for being there for me to answer questions and generally being helpful when Wendy was not available.

This book would not be anywhere near as nice to hold and read were it not for Lisa Amoroso who designed the cover, and Claire Vaccaro and Chris Welch, who are responsible for the layout and overall look of this edition. Thank you. You provide the setting that allows my words to shine. None of these fine people, however, would ever have worked on this book had it not been for my agent, Ned Leavitt, who is both friend and adviser in the intricate world of publishing. Thank you again, Ned!

Finally, I want to especially thank my wife, Julie, and my four children, John-Michael, Aidan, Kaitlin, and Maryn, who are truly the richest blessings in my life!

THIS BOOK IS DEDICATED TO ALL WHO BRING BLESSINGS INTO OUR WORLD. YOU HAVE NEVER BEEN MORE NEEDED AND IMPORTANT.

CONTENTS

BLESSING

PART I

THE PRACTICE
OF BLESSING

Where two or more are gathered

in the name of that which loves,

that which is compassionate, that which

liberates, there blessing is also.

One

GIVE ME A BLESSING

This book was born one evening in the fall of 1965, though I didn't realize it at the time. I was twenty years old. I had harbored ambitions of becoming a molecular biologist, but answering an irresistible inner calling, I had left college and a degree program in biochemistry to cast my fate upon the very uncertain waters of being a lecturer on personal and spiritual development. On this particular evening, after I had finished my regular weekly lecture at a spiritual center in Los Angeles, I was approached by a well-dressed middle-aged woman who said, "Would you please give me a blessing?"

Give me a blessing.

IF WE GAVE voice to the most common wish within each of us, it would probably be this.

We look to the universe, to the world around us, to each other, and, if we are believers, to the invisible world of the sacred, and if we have one basic desire—voiced or not, recognized or not—it is that all these things be on our side. We want life to be our ally: helping us, empowering us, enabling us to be safe and happy. We want good things to come our way: our wounds healed, our loneliness banished, our power restored, our fears allayed. We want alienation to be replaced with belonging, impoverishment with abundance, bondage with liberation, and darkness with light.

We want to be blessed.

And in our better moments, we want to be a blessing for others.

Give me a blessing.

YEARS LATER, I am at an informal gathering of laypeople attending a conference on science and spirituality. During a meal break, we collect in a loose circle and the conference leader asks, "Who would like to give a blessing before we eat?" There is a moment of uncomfortable silence. No one volunteers. Had our host said, "Would anyone like to say a few words before we eat?" a half-dozen voices might have spoken out, but to stand up and give a blessing? It seems presumptuous. Finally, one man speaks a few words, and I can see relief on the faces of others. I feel relief myself. Why? What is it about giving a blessing that makes a person feel uncomfortable?

Give me a blessing.

OVER THE THIRTY-FIVE years I have been in public life, lecturing and teaching about spirituality and spiritual practice, I've given thousands of blessings. I have blessed people, events, buildings, places, even a composting toilet! You would think I'd feel comfortable about giving blessings by now, and most of the time I do. But sometimes, as at that conference, I feel reticent. I may feel it's more appropriate for someone else to do it, someone who is more attuned to the particular event or place. But sometimes I simply feel shy. *Who am I,* I wonder, *to stand in the place of spirit and pronounce a blessing?* After thirty-five years, I can still have my doubts.

Give me a blessing.

I DON'T CALL myself a spiritual teacher, although that name is often applied to me. I feel that each of us has an indwelling spirit— a unique and personal connection with the sacred—which is our true spiritual teacher. What I do is to help people identify and connect with that spiritual side of themselves. I support them in learning to listen to it and embody it in their lives. Because of this, people sometimes see me in a role similar to that of a clergyperson; it is in this context that I am asked to offer blessings. But a blessing is not the function of a particular role. It is the natural expression of the fiery love and inclusiveness of our inner spirit. It is the manifestation of a soulfire, and each of us can be its hearth. To bless is not a prerogative only of ministers, priests, and rabbis; it is not the exclusive domain of saints and holy people. It is a natural human ability, and anyone can do it. But first we must claim that ability.

Give me a blessing.

IF I CAME to you and said, "Please do me a kindness," or "Please help me," you might feel put upon by my request, but at least it would fall within a familiar range of human interaction. You would have an idea of how to proceed. You could, for example, inquire as to just what help or kindness I needed or wished, and then see if you had the resources or willingness to proceed. There is nothing unusual about being asked to help. But you may find it unusual and disconcerting to be asked to give a blessing. The implication is that you have access to a spiritual source capable of making that blessing real. The implication is that there is holiness within you.

This is an identity many modern people are uncomfortable with. We are not like the Irish peasants who, when walking by a farmer's field, could quite naturally and sincerely call forth blessings upon the land and the crops. In our fast-paced, highly electronic culture, we don't feel so intimately connected with spirit anymore. It's easier—and often more believable—for us to call someone on the other side of the world on our cell phone than it is to call upon a creative spirit within. Through technology, we have become connected to each other and to the world in incredible and generally useful ways. But we have become disconnected as well. And it's this disconnection that amplifies the voice within us that longs to call the universe home, that yearns for an unknown wholeness, that looks for allies and support in the world about us, that seeks liberation from a growing sense of alienation.

Give me a blessing.

THE ISSUE OF identity is important. We identify ourselves in so many ways, but most often through our roles, or our possessions, or our social status. We may rarely say, "I am myself. I am spirit. I am soul. There is a holiness in me. Therefore, I am someone who can bless." For blessing is spirit reminding itself of who it is in the midst of its myriad incarnations and manifestations. Blessing is a conversation of recognition between myself, and myself within another. Blessing is a reminder of the love that lies at the core of us, waiting to become our blood and sinew, bone and tissue. If in the "new physics" and the "new cosmology" the stars remind us that we ourselves are made of "star stuff" and therefore kin to the universe, then in a new, holistic spirituality, blessings remind us that we are made of spirit stuff, soul stuff, love stuff—"blessing stuff"—and therefore kin to life and to each other.

When we bless, we are not just doing good. We are remembering this.

Give me a blessing.

WHEN I WAS a child, I was aware that there was a non-physical, invisible, spiritual side to life. It seemed perfectly ordinary that this was so, for it was the world as I experienced it. I did not, however, think much about blessings. Oh, my grandmother would pat me on the head and tell me I was a blessing, but that was what grandmothers did. The only times I heard about blessings were when someone sneezed or we said grace at mealtimes or when I heard the minister invoke blessings on the congregation at church. A popular song encouraged me to count my blessings instead of sheep, but usually I was asleep when my head hit the pillow and didn't have time for either. Giving and receiving kindnesses and helping people out were an everyday part of life, a part of neighborliness, a part of fulfilling one's responsibility as a human being. I didn't think of them as blessings. And when I left college and embarked on a career as a lecturer, I was simply wishing to share the delight, wonder, and empowerment I felt in experiencing a dimension to life beyond our five senses, a dimension filled with spiritual resources for and allies of humanity.

I certainly didn't think of myself as going forth to bless anyone.

- *Give me a blessing.*

"GIVE ME A BLESSING," the woman said. She stood before me expectantly and trustingly, and I knew I couldn't say no to her. I had no idea what I was going to do or how to go about it. I didn't know why she wanted a blessing—much less wanted it from me—but in that moment, it didn't seem right to ask. The correct response was . . . to respond: to meet her halfway, to match her trust in me with my trust in her and in spirit. If I could not approach her in knowledge and experience, I could approach her in love and faith.

But it was hard. Part of me wanted to turn and walk away or suggest she see one of the leaders of the center where I had spoken. They were loving and wonderful people of high integrity whom I knew gave blessings regularly as part of their non-denominational ministry. A moment before, I had been immersed in a flow of spirit as I lectured, feeling inspired, enthused, and magnetic. Now, though, as this member of my dispersing audience stood before me expectantly, I felt empty, ignorant, unprepared, and altogether unsuitable for what she was asking.

What if nothing happens? I thought. *What if it's only words?* In short, I was afraid. I saw with perfect clarity that my image of the kind of blessing I wanted to give was a cartoon. It was an image of a burst of spiritual power, heavenly choirs singing, inner lights blazing, magical bells and whistles going off, with the recipient having all her problems solved, her consciousness raised, her life transfigured. It was pure Hollywood. It was pure ego.

Give me a blessing.

BUT THEN WITH equal clarity I knew that such a display would not be a blessing at all. A blessing had nothing to do with esoteric or spiritual pyrotechnics. It was a whisper, a gentleness, a voice that spoke not of my power but of the power within the recipient. It was not a hurricane of energy but a soft and warming breeze that invited us to open windows and doors to let stuffiness out and new life in. It was an invitation to openness. It was not meant to impress but to touch and to connect. It could take whatever form would make that connection.

I understood then that whatever spiritual forces might flow within a blessing, what was most needed was simple human caring and presence, a mindfulness of being present to the other. It required nothing more magical or grandiose than meeting her halfway, for a blessing, I realized, is a two-way street: not something someone does for someone else, but something we become together in order that a spirit may flow. The principle was deceptively simple but very familiar: Where two or more are gathered in the name of that which loves, that which connects, that which is compassionate, that which liberates, there blessing is also.

I could not have put all this into words. But it was there as a knowing, almost as an instinct rising to the surface. And in that knowing, I simply took her hands and held them, closing my eyes, becoming still, and reaching out to embrace her in my spirit and to be embraced in hers, allowing that connection to invoke what was needed.

As we sat together in this way, there was a warmth that enfolded us, a loving presence that was sweet and unpretentious but seemed to stretch on into infinity. There was a sense of opening out to a vastness. And down my arms and through my hands into hers, there was a sense of something flowing, as if part of that warmth that embraced us had become fluid and was moving from me into her. No bells. No whistles. No radiant rainbow lights flashing about our auras. Just being together, two people acknowledging each other, acknowledging our humanness, acknowledging the presence of the sacred that emerges when human beings gather each other to their hearts in goodwill and caring.

The feeling of this presence lasted for about a minute or so, then receded. We opened our eyes and smiled at each other. She simply said, "Thank you," got up, and left the auditorium.

That was it.

My first blessing.

I never saw her again, never knew why she wanted the blessing, never knew what, if anything, happened as a result of it. And it didn't matter.

She may have asked me for the blessing, but I was the one who was blessed.

For that evening, at the very beginning of my career, I learned something important about spirit and letting go, about our human connection and the power that can arise from it, about love, and about blessing. What I learned was not so much an insight, although certainly insights began to unfold from that experience; it was a deeper stirring and awakening within my own soul. It was a remembering. And over the years, in addition to other influences it has had upon my work, this remembering finally culminated in a series of classes related to the art of blessing, which inspired this book.

Give me a blessing.

WHEN MY CHILDREN were toddlers and we would take them down to the park to play, they would run a short distance out into the world, play for a bit, then run back to touch Julie's or my leg, climb into our laps, and generally touch in, being reassured that we were still there. Then they would be off again, exploring, playing, discovering. Then they would come back again and reconnect. Over the years, the distances they would go and the length of time between moments of reconnection would grow greater, but the cycle was still there. I expect it always will be there, although as they become adults, it will change in the ways it manifests.

In a way, a blessing is just such a moment of reconnection with each other, with the world, and with the source of our being. There is in our world, as I said at the beginning, a desire for that connection, for wholeness, for empowerment, for life. There is a desire for all that a blessing can give. At the heart of the world, in the hearts of each other, a voice speaks out, sometimes softly, sometimes with a shout: *Give me a blessing.*

The essential message in this book is that each of us, you and I, can answer that voice. We can be points of reconnection, points of remembrance, points of love. We can be blessings.

Give me a blessing!

Yes, I will.

Two

TEACHING
BLESSING

I came to be teaching blessing by one of those serendipitous accidents that later we look back on and call inspiration. I was giving
a weekend workshop on connecting with one's inner spirit. My
classes and workshops are always at least half extemporaneous. Although I have a general sense of what I am going to say, I like being
open in the moment to the unique dynamics of each particular
class, allowing them to shape my presentation and draw forth much
of the actual content. It gives a flow and immediacy to the class that
I would never get from having everything scripted.

There are times, though, when inspiration dries up and I'm not
sure what to say next. My traditional response to such a moment is
to be honest about it and call for a break or ask for questions. But
in this particular instance, the blank place came at the end of the

class. There was nothing more that I wanted to say but I felt it was too early to actually end. Simply finishing the class with questions seemed flat, as if it would not honor the feeling we had created together. It would be anticlimactic.

As we finished our final break, I had a sudden image of dividing everybody up into groups of three. I wasn't sure what we would do then, but I've learned to trust images like this, so as everyone came back in, I had them separate into these small groups. When they had done so and were waiting for the next step, it occurred to me that since we had been working on tapping spiritual forces within us, an exercise in sharing those forces with each other would be a good way to end. I realized I would have them draw on their inner energies to give each other blessings.

The procedure was simple. I would have one of the three give another one a blessing, using the insights we'd been working with in class, while the third person held the process silently in a spirit of unconditional support, creating a safe context for the other two. Then after a time, positions would rotate so that every person had a chance to be the blesser, the receiver, and the supporter.

I wasn't sure what to expect from this exercise. As I do after all my exercises, I had everyone take time for personal reflection on whatever they had experienced and then gave them an opportunity to share anything they wished with their two partners, or with the class as a whole. Usually this elicits quite a bit of discussion, but in this case, everyone was very quiet. I wondered if the whole thing had fallen flat.

As everyone was getting ready to leave, though, they came up to me one by one to say how powerful and important the exercise had been to them. The fact that they had little to share was due to not wanting to dissipate the feelings it had generated. They wanted to leave the class on the crest of the wave the exercise had created.

As I talked with them, I realized that for many of the participants, it had been one of the very few times they had been asked to give someone else a blessing. The act of doing so had been a powerful experience for each of them. Furthermore, coming within the context of the class in which I had given them training and suggestions for accessing their spiritual power, they felt they had new insights for making the act of blessing real and not just a recitation of words without much meaning or power.

Far from ending the class on a weak note, the exercise of blessing had taken it in a powerful direction that none of us, especially me, had anticipated. Which, incidentally, is why I teach classes, both for the joy and excitement of unexpected moments like this and because it teaches *me* what I need to know.

I have to admit that I'm hesitant about having people do exercises like this. Working as a teacher in San Francisco during the sixties put me at the epicenter of both the rise of the alternative culture (with the hippies on one side of the Bay and the student anti-war radicals on the other) and the rise of the humanistic psychology movement and the creation of encounter groups. Over the years, I witnessed excellent teachers who used psychospiritual exercises skillfully and precisely to bring new insights to their students. I also encountered people who used those exercises as ways of feeling their own power and manipulating their audiences. Such workshops left a participant riding an emotional high that was the psychological equivalent of (and had about as much spiritual nutrition as) eating too many chocolate Ho Hos. Indeed, I could see that some workshop leaders fed like vampires off the emotional energy they would generate in the participants.

The result of this was that I leaned over backwards in the other direction, hesitant to use any kind of group exercises at all so as to distance myself from the Ho Ho crowd. I relied primarily on lecture and discussion to accomplish my educational aims. And I cut myself off from some perfectly good tools simply because I didn't appreciate how some people used them. So, the effect of this blessing exercise was a revelation to me. It made me excited about doing it again. I looked for other opportunities in other classes and workshops to get people blessing each other. I even did it once at the end of a lecture when it had no relevance at all!

Every time, the result has been the same. To one degree or another—and usually very deeply—people have been moved both by exchanging blessings with someone else, who is usually a stranger, and by what they experience in themselves as they do so. Indeed, it has been the latter—the sense of inner change, flow, and power and the deepening they feel within themselves as they bless—that has been most powerful.

Finally, instead of looking for ways to fit this exercise into other workshops and classes, I realized I needed to create a class that would focus on the art of blessing itself. I decided to use this exercise as a model for exploring both our inner depths and the power of extending ourselves from those depths to others and to the world around us. That class was the foundation for this book. And I was blessed to have as wonderful a group of fellow co-explorers into the art of blessing as I could ever have hoped for.

In this process of teaching a way of blessing, I have realized ever more strongly what I sensed when I gave my first blessing on that long-ago night in Los Angeles. A blessing is much more than just an act. It is an affirmation of our interconnectedness; it is the creation of an opportunity for the power of that connectedness to pour through into our lives and the lives of others. So in practicing the art of blessing, we are really practicing being connected. We are practicing how to discover and express those parts of ourselves that innately understand that connectedness and the wholeness that emerges from it.

In that context, whatever form it may take, blessing is at the heart of any spiritual practice. For ultimately all such practices are about remembrance, connectedness, wholeness, and being a participant in the flow of love that weaves the world together from the most numinous to the most material. They are not about how we may develop ourselves or become holy, saved, or enlightened. Spiritual practices are about how we give of ourselves, sharing our life, our presence, and our substance so that the body of creation may be seamless and the infinite may be reflected in the presence of the finite.

Three

AN ECOLOGY
OF BLESSINGS

Trying to define a blessing is like trying to define a whole ecology filled with myriad plants and animals. There are so many varieties of each, particularly if that ecology is that of, say, a jungle. There the animals and plants come in a multitude of shapes, colors, and sizes from the very simple to the majestic, from the very tiny to the very large, from the plain and unobtrusive to the elegant and colorful. You cannot define the whole ecology by picking out any one animal, bird, or plant.

There is a similar challenge in deciding just what a blessing is. Consider the multitude of ways in which we encounter the idea of blessing in our lives.

A friend writes me a letter and ends it, "With blessings."

We sit down to dinner and ask that our meal be blessed.

A minister stands before her congregation and invokes blessings upon the worshippers.

When I left home, I asked my parents for their blessings.

Before the big game, the coach prays for blessings on the team.

I sneeze, and my daughter says, "Bless you, Daddy!"

Some friends of mine lost everything they had in a fire that destroyed their home. A year later, having started over and found whole new opportunities for work and living opening to them even better than what they had before, they looked back on what had been a disaster and called it a blessing. It had forced them to change, to look at their lives in a new way, and discover new possibilities they wouldn't have noticed before.

Throughout our days, the idea of blessings weaves a melody of connection and caring, but we may never give that much thought. Until, of course, something happens to bring blessings to our attention. Something good happens, someone does something helpful for us (or we for them). We almost always think of blessings as good things, something to be desired. But just as some difficult events, like the fire that destroyed my friends' home, can turn out to be blessings in disguise, some happy event can turn out to be otherwise as time goes on.

A man in our town won the state lottery worth several million dollars. At the time, he said it was a dream come true, a real blessing. A year later he was forced to leave his job and the town, both of which he loved, because he couldn't find any privacy from all the people coming to him for charity or wanting him to invest, or just haranguing him because he had won and they hadn't. He couldn't lead the normal life he had before his windfall. Even close friends began treating him differently. He said the money had become a curse, devastating his life.

So blessings can be ambiguous. There's a famous joke about this. A man riding in an airplane can hardly fail to notice the beautiful woman sitting next to him. He also can't help but see a very large, very expensive-looking diamond ring she is wearing. So in order to strike up a conversation, he asks her about the it.

"Oh," she tells him, "this is the famous Sawyer Diamond, named after my husband."

"I see," he replies. "You must be very pleased to own it."

"Oh, yes," she replies. "It's a real blessing."

"But why is it famous? Is it one of those diamonds with a curse on it?"

"Why, yes, it is."

Intrigued, he asks, "And what is the curse?"

"Mr. Sawyer."

We call these "mixed blessings," these things we're not entirely sure are good things. I recently suffered from a kidney stone. At the time the pain was so excruciating, it did not seem like a blessing at all. However, when after a couple of weeks it did not pass, the doctor performed surgery to remove it, only to discover that a small tumor was growing in my bladder. Catching this cancer at such an early stage, it was easy to remove, and I have had no recurrences. But had it not been for the pain of the kidney stone, I would never have discovered the tumor was there, as by itself it was not causing me any symptoms. So the kidney stone turned out to be a blessing indeed.

Then there are also things that are a blessing to us, but not so to others. Just as one person associates a jungle ecology with lions and tigers and elephants while someone else thinks of exotic birds or colorful flowers, we don't all think of the same thing as a blessing. A Mexican meal is a delight for my children; for me it's an evening of heartburn and indigestion. A friend gives me a book, and I feel blessed. But if I gave him a book, he would thank me politely and then give it away to someone else because he is not a reader.

For some people, blessings come from God, but others see blessings as coming from people. Indeed, people experience blessings whatever their image of the sacred may be, even if they have no image at all or don't believe in a god. The feeling of the blessing might be the same, but people with different religious backgrounds could disagree as to its source.

A blessing can be a request that God give grace and happy, prosperous circumstances to someone. It can be an invocation of spiritual presence. It can be a wish that someone's life be expanded or augmented in some way. It can be an act that creates wholeness, healing, or protection. It can be a desire that good things be made manifest. It can be a moment of connection with another that opens new possibilities for a better life.

A blessing can be seen as a sign of divine favor or of a person's inner spiritual quality. It can be seen as the result of a life well lived or of work well performed. A blessing can be the fruits of a happy relationship; it can be the events and memories that spring forth from a shared presence of love.

And blessings need not be actions or events at all. They can be subtle influences that embrace us, moving invisibly in our lives to empower, support, and nourish us. These especially are the kinds of blessings I like to explore in my classes.

There are as many ways in which a blessing can be asked for, invoked, or transmitted as there are kinds of blessings. It can be done through words or through silent prayer and visualization. It can be done through ritual. It can be done with an embrace. It can be accomplished by a laying on of hands, a gesture, a look, a mental attitude, or an empathetic projection of feeling. It can be a gift crafted with skillful effort and hard work. It can spring from a spontaneous, impromptu expression of goodwill.

Blessings enter our lives in many guises for many reasons and create various effects, all of which in some way leave us more capable or whole than we were before. There is no doubt that however they may manifest and whatever they may be, blessings make the world a lovelier, happier, and more creative place to live in. They enhance our capabilities, awaken us to new possibilities, and generally open a space for us in which something new and potentially transformative can emerge.

It is a good ecology to have in our world. And like an ecology, there is a niche for every possible type of blessing.

Furthermore, adding to the ecology of blessing is not fundamentally hard to do.

At heart, giving a blessing is really quite simple. We innately know how to do it, precisely because it comes from the heart, from a sense of caring and helpfulness. Every time you create safety and reassurance where before there was fear, you are giving a blessing. Every time you perform an act of kindness, providing money where there was poverty, shelter where there was vulnerability, food where there was hunger, love where there was loneliness, comfort and encouragement where there was despair and depression, you are being a blessing. There is no special technique other than having an open, generous heart and a loving, aware mind. You don't have to possess any particular gift in order to embody goodwill or to be kind and helpful.

In fact, being a source of blessing is a natural human attribute. It's an expression of those impulses we have to create community and to support life. That we have negative impulses, too, that take us in opposite directions in no way diminishes the potential we have to bless. It only demonstrates that we are complex and paradoxical beings, and that in all areas of our lives we need to make choices about how we will act and the effect we wish to have upon our world. Certainly there are times when giving a blessing comes more naturally. Blessing is easiest when it's simply the overflow from a joyous heart. But it's when we are able to make the choice to bless even though everything in us wants to curse and strike out that we demonstrate the power of the human soul to choose what builds life and creates wholeness.

Within each soul is a passion: an inner fire born of love and of an intelligence profoundly immersed in the wholeness of all creation—therefore, an intelligence burning with compassion. A blessing is this very soulfire made manifest. When our angry and hurt heart chooses to bless in spite of its pain, then we ourselves become the kindling that enables this fire to release its light into the world.

If I think of a whole ecology, I can be overwhelmed and awed by the multiplicity of forms that life can take within it. Or, I can be filled with a sense of wonder at life itself and with a realization that I, too, am a manifestation of that life. Similarly, in thinking about blessings, I can be overwhelmed by the multiplicity of ways they can appear and be created and be defined. But that misses the point. Like life, all blessings come from a single source: the soulfire of an intelligent love and compassion willing to give of itself. Whether they're simple or complex, obvious or subtle, planned or spontaneous, blessings happen when this soulfire is released and shared.

Blessing happens when a heart opens and we find all of us there within it.

Four

SHARING BLOOD, SHARING BREATH

Whenever I want to understand something, I either go to my wife—who is all-knowing and all-wise—or to my *Unabridged Random House Dictionary of the English Language,* which, while not as beautiful as she or as fun to talk with, nevertheless knows more words. Within its pages I feel like an archaeologist tracing the origins of words and trying to picture the kind of experiences and images from which they arose. Sometimes you find interesting reversals in which a word has come to mean its exact opposite. (Did you know that *silly* once meant "wise"?) Sometimes you find something less benign than you were expecting,

Such as: Blessing has a bloody past.

Blessing comes from the Old English *bledtsian,* which means "to consecrate." That's fair enough and about what I expected. But further reading shows that *bledtsian* itself comes from an earlier word, *blod,* which means "blood." From this, the dictionary concludes, *blessing* originally meant "to consecrate with blood."

For centuries, religious rites were often conducted using the blood of sacrifices, either animal or human, for of all the parts of a creature or person, the blood was the most holy, the most powerful, the most magical. Blood was the carrier of life.

We see this idea carried on in the Christian tradition in which blood plays a significant sacramental role. It was the spilling of Jesus' blood during the Crucifixion that is considered the salvific act, the blessing that redeemed the world. I can still remember being accosted on my college campus by members of the evangelical Campus Crusade for Christ and being asked if I were washed in the "Blood of the Lamb."

Likewise, one of the most solemn oaths of childhood is the blood oath. I remember seeing a Western movie with a good friend in which a white man and a Native American proclaimed their bond of friendship by becoming blood brothers. They sliced their palms with a knife and then clasped their bleeding hands together. Inspired, my friend and I got out my father's hunting knife, which seemed more manly and official than a bread knife from the kitchen. However, when the moment came, we decided that blood was blood whether it came from a slashed palm or a pinprick in the finger, and we opted for the latter, less painful method. Not knowing my religious history, I never realized that in consecrating our friendship in this way, we were giving each other a blessing!

Of course, blessings by pin, knife, or sacrifice are fortunately less common these days. Instead, we have come to see blessing as a sharing of the vitality and animating force rather than the blood of life: a consecration through an endowment or sharing of spirit. Which brings up another trip to the dictionary.

Spirit, as I might expect, is defined as the vital principle animating our bodies—in effect, our life energy. And the origin of this word is in the Latin *spirare,* which meant "to breathe."

This is no surprise. In countless creation stories God, or the gods, give human beings life by breathing into them. In such stories, it's this breath of the sacred within us that enables us to live and, even more significantly, connects us to a transcendental reality.

Blood and breath. Without them, we could not live. They are absolutely fundamental to our existence, so it's no wonder they are so intimately woven into our ideas of blessing and spirit. What better way to consecrate something, making it special, than to add to its life force, enhance its being, increase the impact of its presence?

But blood and breath suggest another important image when it comes to blessing. Both perform their life-giving task by flowing, circulating, and connecting. Our blood circulates, bringing oxygen and nourishment to our cells as well as chemical messages and information that connect the community of our body. In a similar way, our breath circulates between us and our world in an exchange of gases that ultimately become the flesh of plants and the flesh of humankind as well, connecting us to the community of life on earth.

Surely a blessing is also a flow of life force between ourselves and others or between ourselves and the sacred. It's an act of connection. It restores through love a circulation of spirit among us that may have become blocked, forgotten or overlooked. It reconnects us to the community of creation.

A blessing is much like a transfusion or an act of resuscitation in which new blood and new breath—a new sense of presence and life—is given to us so that we may be empowered, restored, or re-vitalized.

A blessing is the passing of spirit between us. It's a slash in the flesh of the ego so that the blood of the soul may be exchanged and we may become life brothers and life sisters. It's the breathing of the soul so that a nourishment of love and compassion, caring and support, may circulate between us.

In the act of blessing, we consecrate each other. We give of ourselves to each other. Our souls breathe and bleed upon each other, so that we might enter together into the larger circulation of life and spirit within creation.

Five

BEYOND
KINDNESS

A good friend of mine, Andy Smallman, the director of the Puget Sound Community School, teaches a class on kindness. In Andy's class, he has his students do acts of kindness for themselves, for family members, for strangers, for people they like, and for people they don't. They explore ways in which one may do a kindness, and then they record and share the results of those acts, what it felt like doing them, and so forth.

I teach a class on blessing. In my class, I have the participants explore what it's like to bless themselves, each other, people in their lives, and the world at large. We explore ways in which blessings can be given, and I have them take note of what it feels like to bless and what the results may be.

Aside from the difference in terminology, might these not be essentially the same class? And if not, what is the difference? What, if anything, is the difference between a blessing and a kindness? And as the late anthropologist Gregory Bateson used to ask, is it a difference that makes a difference?

One brisk winter afternoon I was out shopping. With the Christmas season approaching and downtown parking at a premium, the store I was visiting had had problems with shoppers parking in its lot and then going to nearby stores, taking spaces away from its own customers. So it had hired a parking attendant to stand outside and make sure that only those who intended to visit the store could park.

It was one of those windy, damp days that blow down on Seattle in December, a drizzly day carrying with it the distant promises of arctic snows from the north of Canada. I could see that the parking attendant was feeling the chill. So I went up to him, asked him if he'd like a cup of coffee and what kind, then went into a nearby Starbucks to get it for him.

The attendant was surprised and grateful. I was grateful as well for an opportunity to do something nice for someone. I've always been an advocate of the bumper sticker that reads: PERFORM RANDOM ACTS OF KINDNESS.

The question is: Did I perform a blessing?

If I am the recipient of an act of kindness, it may make no difference to me. If my life is made a little easier, I may certainly feel blessed even if the other person was only, in their minds, performing an act of neighborliness. In my gratitude, I am unlikely to quibble over semantics. It's certainly possible to say that all the ways in which human beings can be helpful, compassionate, kind, and generous to each other are blessings. If so, then certainly we might as well say that kindnesses and blessings are the same thing. Whatever we call them, the world is certainly a better place because of such acts.

But is a blessing only something that makes me feel good, secure, happy, or nourished? Is it only something that makes me feel taken care of in some manner? Or is there something about a blessing that makes it more than just an ordinary act of kindness?

It has been my observation that people often think of a blessing as something more than just a kind act. It's a kind act with an extra something added. It's a good deed on steroids.

I see a blessing as an act that incorporates a specific spiritual element. It's an act in which I open myself up to allow a deeper, fuller part of me to flow, extending and affirming the circulation of life and spirit within the world. It's a sharing of blood and breath.

When I brought the parking attendant a cup of coffee, I simply wanted to make a cold and wet situation less uncomfortable for him. I had no intention of sharing blood or breath, literally or metaphorically. I wanted to give him a cup of coffee, not my inner life force.

Here are two stories to more fully illustrate the difference between a blessing and a kindness. Back in 1966 in Los Angeles, some months after I'd had that first experience of giving a blessing to the woman at my lecture, I had reached the end of my financial rope. My lecture series had come to an end, and nothing had arisen to take its place. In fact, every job opportunity I explored fell through. As it turned out, I needed extra time at that point to pursue a kind of spiritual apprenticeship in support of my inner calling, and spent hours each day in study and meditation. And a growing number of people began to come to me for spiritual help and guidance. This was helpful to me as well, for it provided a form of training to sharpen my skills of inner awareness. For that reason, I felt I couldn't charge them for my time or service. I viewed their coming as a gift from the universe to help my development.

But as the weeks went by, my savings dwindled. Then I received an invitation to go to Salt Lake City and teach a series of classes that promised to restore my finances. The only problem was that I couldn't afford to get there. By that time, I was literally down to fifty cents in my pocket.

Then, out of the blue, one of the people I had been counseling invited me out to dinner. We talked about a variety of things, and as dessert was being served, he thanked me for the help I had given. Although he knew I didn't expect it, he wanted to make some payment in return. He gave me a check for fifty dollars, which, as it turned out, was exactly enough gas and food money to get me to Salt Lake City.

Once I reached Salt Lake, I gave a series of successful lectures that replenished my bank accont. But the more important gift came from a woman who had sponsored me. She was a sweet lady who was old enough to have been my grandmother. She was shy and self-effacing. She had a deep interest in alternative and esoteric spiritualities, which she kept private from her Mormon neighbors in her very conventional suburb.

Yet, she went beyond her shyness to help organize my trip to Salt Lake. And in order to keep me from having to spend money on a hotel (which I couldn't have afforded, though she didn't know that), she offered to put me up in her home. She told me years later, though, she'd been worried about what her neighbors might think, seeing a young man coming and going from her house. But in spite of her concern, she made me feel very welcome and comfortable, and in fact did all she could, not only to facilitate my stay, but to be supportive about my work as a whole. We would have tea together in the afternoon, and she would draw me out to discuss my life, my vision, my dreams and aspirations. She was unfailingly encouraging.

I was there a little over a week. And when I left, this time for the San Francisco area, where another series of lectures had been arranged for me, she unexpectedly handed me a check for a thousand dollars, calling it a contribution towards my future work.

That stay in Salt Lake was a turning point for me. It renewed my confidence in what I was doing. The money I was given, as well as the money I earned, went a long way to getting me established in the San Francisco Bay area, enabling me to build my reputation and clientele there without immediate financial pressure. But even more important was the inner support I was given by my new friend. That made a difference.

Thinking back now on my student and my sponsor, they were people who each did me a kindness and met a need. Both were helpful financially at a time when I needed help. Both gave me precisely what was needed to make my next step possible. One was not more helpful or more kind than the other. I was (and still am) grateful to both of them.

To the man in L.A., his help was in effect a payment for counseling services I had provided. His gift arose from friendship but also from a desire to fulfill an obligation he felt. It was a kindness. It was helpful and generous, but it went no further than that. Like giving coffee to the parking attendant, there was no sense of blood or breath in his gift.

By contrast, my friend in Salt Lake indeed gave of her self. She could easily have had me stay in a hotel, let me do my talks, and then said good-bye when I left, and it would've been perfectly appropriate. Instead, she reached out to me not just as a visiting lecturer but as a whole person. She gave to me as David, not just as a counselor, or lecturer, or someone who had helped her in some way.

That is why I felt helped by my Los Angeles friend but blessed by my friend in Salt Lake. She gave me something beyond money or a place to stay; she shared her spirit.

There is another side to this story too. For, in overcoming her own fears and opening to new possibilities, my friend in Salt Lake felt blessed as well. She felt liberated from old thoughts and images that had constricted her life. She became more active in a number of ways, and over the years I knew her, I watched with pleasure as her whole personality lightened up.

That is a hallmark of blessings: They overflow the specific act through which they are transmitted. It's hard to bless without being blessed. I can perform a kindness, like bringing coffee to a parking attendant on a cold day, and the act is complete in itself. But a blessing often evokes hidden resonances; it echoes through our lives and the lives of others in unexpected ways.

And unlike buying someone a coffee, giving a blessing cannot be done mindlessly and it cannot be done by habit. Nor does it arise from the *should*'s that many of us subscribe to. In short it cannot come from a superficial place in us. It comes from the depths, and in so doing it takes us into those depths as well.

There are things that we may do for others that arise from a sense of personal or social obligation. I may give money to a beggar because I feel guilty at having while he has not, or because my church or my upbringing says I should. But it can be a cold exchange with little feeling in it or any concern at all for the real person who is that beggar. I've seen people pass by a beggar on the street and, without looking at him or slowing down at all, flip a few bills in his direction and hurry on as if nothing had happened. The money may be helpful to the beggar but it has hardly come with a spirit of blessing. No blood or breath there!

I don't mean this as a criticism, though. In many situations, it's better to give than not give at all. A kindness does not have to be a blessing in order to be helpful or important in its own right. To not perform a kindness just because I'm not sure it will also be a blessing, or because I don't want to give any more deeply than the surface act entails, is to miss the point entirely. There is no hierarchy of values here. We should never underestimate the power of kindness to positively affect our world. Simple kindness is a powerful spiritual force. If we had more of it in the world, we could transform society into a manifestation of compassion, and that would truly be a blessing!

It's also possible to take any example of kindness and trace its roots to the same spirit of love and caring from which blessings emerge. But some plants have shallow roots and some have deep ones, even though they are growing in the same soil. Because I am interested in blessing not only as a way of doing good and being kind but as a spiritual practice, a way of discovering and entering into a place where the roots go down to touch the bedrock of the soul, I choose to make a distinction between acts that are kind and acts that also take us into a fuller relationship with life.

In making that distinction, I understand that the boundary between a blessing and a kindness is fuzzy. Each of us needs to discover just where it runs through our lives and what we are called to do on either side of that line. We use the word *blessing* in so many ways to mean so many things that it can lose its ability to vitalize a spiritual power within us. We can forget there is another side to the boundary between kindness and blessing—a side we can cross over to in spite of our faults or our sense that we are not "spiritual" enough to be a source of blessings.

When *blessing* becomes a synonym for anything that makes us happy or prosperous, no matter how trivial it may be, it creates an attitude that doesn't allow for the depths to which the practice of blessing can take us. Nor does it appreciate that not all blessings come in pleasant packages. Sometimes important blessings emerge from hard and painful times, even from tragedy. We say they are "blessings in disguise," and they may be well disguised indeed. It may be a long time until the day we realize that where there was loss there is now new life, or where there was suffering there is now a capacity to heal.

The truth is, we often prefer kindnesses to blessings anyway. Kindnesses can be like pretty flowers growing in the sunny meadows of our lives, raising our spirits, making us thankful and happy. But blessings, like all things that arise from spirit, can take us from the sunny meadows into dark caverns where we go deeper than we may have expected or wanted to go. Blessings can take us into that darkness that is the birthplace of life and light, like the deep soil that nourishes the seed before it erupts into sunlight. This can be a fertile, energizing place, but it's rarely a comfortable one.

In distinguishing kindnesses from blessings, I'm encouraging us to look more deeply and more precisely so that we don't lose sight of an identity and a way of relating to the universe that goes deeper than our skin, deeper than our thoughts, deeper than our emotions. But in seeking greater precision, I also don't want to suggest that a blessing must look like one thing in particular or meet certain criteria. Since blessings arise from unique human beings and the unique relationships they form with each other, there is no way one can sculpt an image of an ideal blessing and say all blessings must look like this. As I said before, in the blessings zoo, there is room for all shapes and sizes.

In seeking to understand blessing, let us not go from one extreme, where every kindness can be a blessing, to another extreme where a blessing is only a deliberate act. An impulsive act of charity in which our spirit rises to an occasion can certainly be a blessing. A definition is as valuable for what it leaves out as for what it includes, but here we must be careful not to leave out too much. A blessing needn't take place in a solemn, pretentious, or formal way, filled with pomp and ritual. To bless—to share one's spirit with another—is a natural human act. It can be executed with all the delight, whimsy, and spontaneity of which we are capable and still be a moment in which the gift of ourselves flows to another with a depth that only spirit can provide.

In defining a blessing, perspective is important. We should be careful not to define it in a way that makes it so ordinary that it loses its capacity to open us to the depths within ourselves as well as within creation. We don't ever want to lose our sense of wonder, nor do we want to explain blessing in a way that we fail to recognize or appreciate the miraculous.

On the other hand, we can fail to appreciate our innate power to bless if we regard blessing as a force so awesome and special, it must lie beyond our ordinary capabilities. Then there is the danger of losing its humanity and capacity to connect with us in our everyday lives.

So, is there a difference that makes a difference? Yes, though I think it's something we each must discover for ourselves. I wish only to point out that the difference is there so that you will look for it on your own. In my own imagination, I think of a kindness as a blessing in seed state. If it falls on the proper soil, it will blossom into an upwelling of spirit as rich as in the most deliberate blessing. Likewise, I think of a blessing as a kindness with roots through which spirit flows in an act of life-giving circulation. My interest is in following those roots inward to the place from which that spirit erupts.

Andy Smallman teaches a class on kindness. I teach a class on blessing. But at the end of the day, the important thing is not that there's a difference between them; it's that we don't have to choose. We can both be kind *and* bless. When we are, the two merge and become the face of love turned in compassion towards the world.

Six

A BLESSING
IS A GIFT

There are many kinds of gifts. There are gifts that we may be given that are part of a social requirement. Suzie in the secretarial pool is getting married, and I am expected to chip in with my co-workers to buy her a gift. There are gifts given in expectation of something in return. I give a gift to my boss, hoping that he will think of me favorably when it comes time to give out raises or promotions. I give a friend a fancy gift on his birthday so he'll give me something fancy on mine. These gifts are free, but they have a transactional flavor about them. They arise, not out of a response to the recipient and their well-being, but out of a situation—usually one in which I feel a need or an obligation to give. I would call such gifts "presents."

There is no reason why presents can't be wonderful, delightful, and perfectly appropriate. They can certainly grease the social wheel in important ways. And at their best, like kindnesses, they can make the world a happier place.

But what I'm calling a gift in the context of this book is something more. It's not only free. It's also directed at the recipient as a whole person and is meant to be an empowerment or a celebration of that wholeness. In other words, I give to you rather than to your need (or your "want"). My gift may in fact meet a specific need, but it primarily comes with my blood and breath to honor and uplift you.

A blessing is this kind of a gift.

We do not bless as a payment in return for some service rendered. We do not bless expecting anything in return. Those are transactions, and they have their proper place in our world. But it's a different place from where we find blessings. A blessing is not a transaction.

A blessing is a gift given freely.

And this is how it must be, for perhaps the primary effect of a blessing is to liberate us. A blessing gives us something—support, vitality, insight, opportunity—to enhance and expand our lives.

When parents bless their children who are about to enter the world on their own, it's not to reel them back in but to send them on their way upheld and uplifted by the love and spirit of the family.

When I ask God for blessings, it's so I may be enhanced in some way, not limited.

When we sing "God Bless America," we have images of the nation being empowered, not diminished.

A blessing sets us free, not to be irresponsible and disconnected, but to become more of who we are or who we can be.

A gift carries a special quality precisely because it's a gift and not a transaction. If someone gives me a book, it's different from my having bought the book myself. It's not just that I have saved some money. The book comes with the added presence of the giver's thoughtfulness, love, and good feelings towards me. A gift comes with the "blood and breath" of the donor. It's value-enriched.

It doesn't matter how intrinsically valuable the actual gift may be. As I was beginning this chapter, my daughters, Kaitlin and Maryn, returned from a camping trip to the beach with their mother and oldest brother. As soon as they were in the house, they ran up to me with their gifts: small stones they had found on the beach. These were perfectly ordinary pebbles; I could have walked to a nearby park and found the same thing. But as gifts from my daughters, carefully selected from a multitude of pebbles on the beach, they were magical and filled with presence. They were coinage minted from the gold of their love and the silver of their delight.

A blessing, like a gift, carries a feeling of spaciousness. As a true gift, and not a transaction in disguise, it's freeing to both the giver and the receiver. It does not obligate either one.

A blessing, like a gift, has extra impact precisely because it is not a transaction. A transaction is usually bounded by the terms of the exchange. I give you twenty dollars, you give me a book. You give me twenty dollars, I give you a meal. Once I have the book and you have the money, or I have the money and you have the meal, we are complete. Nothing more need be there between us—no blood, no breath. What you see is precisely what you get. A blessing is not bounded in that way. With a blessing, what you get is more than what you can see. It has something extra which cannot be defined or limited by the situation that has called it forth. A blessing is more than a response to a need. It's a response to the whole person.

And therein lies its capacity to liberate us by calling forth from within us possibilities for vision, growth, and life.

An acquaintance of mine founded a very successful youth center in a gang-ridden section of New York City. There were many reasons for its success, but one of the most significant was that only volunteers could serve on its staff. You could only work there if you gave yourself away. So the staff was filled with professionals from many walks of life—doctors, teachers, lawyers, businesspeople, actors and actresses, counselors, cooks and nutritionists—and they all had to give their skills, their time, their energy. There were no transactions of payment for services.

When I asked the founder about this, he said that someone who gives of him- or herself brings a quality and a vitality to the center that no money can buy. It's not just that they may work harder or may be more enthusiastic. They bring a special, discernible kind of caring, born of their gift of themselves. The staff wanted to be there, and that came through to the kids. The kids in turn responded to an environment in which people were there for them, not to fulfill the requirements of a job, but because they desired to be there in spite of any sacrifices this might entail. The power of this commitment greatly facilitated the ease and the willingness with which the young people began to transform and open up, changing their lives in productive, positive ways.

A gift comes with the spirit of the giver. In fact, I might say that the gift *is* that spirit. Sometimes when we give or receive a gift about which we are less than enthusiastic, we say, "Well, it's the thought that counts!" Often this can be a way of covering up our disappointment or our thought that the gift really isn't a very good one! But sometimes, it is a recognition that the tangible form of the gift is not as important as the intangible spirit it expresses. Like my daughter's pebbles, the gift is simply a medium through which love is transmitted. But to someone who can see the flow of spirit involved, it really *is* the thought that counts! And it's the quality and impact of this spirit that enriches our lives in subtle (and not-so-subtle) ways, in addition to whatever benefits the gift may specifically convey.

A blessing is like this too. A blessing is, most basically, the transmission or extension of the spirit at its source. If I receive what I perceive as a blessing from God, what I'm really receiving is the quality and presence of God's spirit in my life. That's where the transformative power resides. If I bless someone, I give them something of my spirit. I'm sharing my life force with them, whatever outer form that blessing may take.

This means that a blessing, like a gift, cannot be forced on someone. I can't make you accept the qualities of my presence or spirit, for if I do, my act ceases to be a blessing. It loses its connection to wholeness and its empowering capabilities, and it becomes instead something manipulative and potentially damaging.

I was invited to dinner by two people whose work paralleled my own to some extent. We'd only met a couple of times, but we all wanted to get to know one another better. This dinner was a step in that direction. I understood from the invitation that there would just be the three of us there. When I arrived, though, I was surprised to find a fourth person there. It was a man whom I'd also met once or twice before who billed himself as a spiritual teacher. But to my perception, there was something "off" about him.

As he was there in my new friends' living room, I was determined to make the best of it. But as we were chatting before dinner, this man suddenly got up and came around behind me. Placing his hands on my head, he announced that he was going to give me a "blessing." This was definitely nothing I had asked for, and as I felt his inner power stirring, every alarm bell I had in me went off.

The quality of presence he was projecting was so unpleasant and creepy that I sprang to my feet and told him to stop. But rather than stopping, he and my hosts tried to convince me to let him go ahead and give me a blessing, which, they said, would be good for me. They even ended up partly chasing me around the chair, trying to get me to sit down again! At this point, as soon as I had positioned myself near the front door so I could leave with some semblance of dignity, I simply thanked my hosts for their invitation, turned around, and walked out.

Later, I discovered that this man had a habit of giving people "blessings" as a way of showing off what he felt were his inner powers. But what he was doing, of course, was not blessing at all. There was nothing giving or wholesome about his actions, as he forced his inner presence upon someone else.

A blessing can't be forced onto someone any more than a gift can be and still remain a gift. When you bless, you're giving your self away—becoming selfless, rather than trying to prove yourself or demonstrate your "inner powers." You're serving the one who is being blessed, not yourself, just as a gift, to be a gift, must serve the recipient and not simply be a way of making yourself feel good. For a blessing to truly be a blessing, there must be a willingness on both sides; indeed, it's probably more accurate to say that a blessing is a co-created event, not a one-way flow from blesser to blessee. It's a dialog, not a soliloquy.

When a friend of mine fell into unexpected and severe financial trouble, I was fortunately in a position to give him several thousand dollars to help the situation. The money was to meet his immediate need, but if all I gave him was money, I might just as well have been a bank. What I also gave him were my love, my concern, my respect for him, a freedom to move ahead without obligation to me, and my ability to see him as a whole person—someone who was creative, powerful, and very giving in his own right—and not just as someone in financial need.

Like a gift in this respect, a blessing addresses our wholeness. It connects with all parts of us, not just those parts that may be (or feel themselves to be) in need. It reminds us that we're connected people, part of a larger whole, immersed in a greater love.

With this remembering comes not an obligation but a responsibility to that larger whole. In this, a blessing is also a kind of a gift. For while a gift is not transactional, requiring a return from us, it lifts us through gratitude and delight into a community of givers who celebrate the love that unites us by discovering what they can offer from their own hearts to keep that love flowing and alive.

Receiving a gift awakens the giver in me. It awakens that part of me who participates in and desires to enhance the circulation of life that flows throughout creation from the heart of the sacred.

A blessing is also a call to remember this circulation, this flow of the blood and breath of creation, and to enter into it. When we do, that is when we become the blessing. That is when we become the gift.

SUPERHEROES

When I was ten years old, I was filled with a desire to make a difference in the world. I wanted to be a force for good, helping people and battling evil. So, inspired by my comic books, I decided to become a superhero.

I asked a younger friend to be my sidekick—a Robin to my Batman—planning that together we would sally forth into the neighborhood in search of evildoers.

We called ourselves "The Do-Gooders." Not as imaginative as "The Avengers," perhaps, but it did have the virtue of being straightforward. We convinced our mothers to sew the letters DG prominently in red thread on the front of our T-shirts, and we fashioned matching masks and capes from old sheets. Finally, appropriately garbed, we felt ready for any bad guys we might meet.

And there *were* bad guys. There was one fellow in particular, the main neighborhood bully whose idea of a pleasant afternoon was to pick on smaller kids. We decided he would be our first target. And as if to prove that heaven truly shines upon the righteous, we had no sooner left my house than we discovered this miscreant actually in the act of bullying a younger boy on a playground nearby. Here was our first chance to Do Good!

There was a reason this fellow got away with his bullying, though. He was bigger and stronger than any of the other kids in our neighborhood, including us. But in the glow of our new identities, we overlooked this crucial factor. Loudly screaming our intimidating war cry ("Do-Gooders to the rescue!"), we simply ran up, pounced on him, and wrestled him to the ground.

It was at this point that imagination collided with reality. I discovered that I had no idea how to fight—and, alas, no superpowers to compensate for this lack. To the extent that I had thought about the action side of superheroing, I think I had expected that, like the Shadow, our very presence would strike terror in any evildoer's heart, causing him to surrender. I don't think I imagined that we would have to do any actual fighting.

Our foe apparently had not read the same comic books I had. Although undoubtedly surprised by our assault, he showed no sign whatever of giving up and proceeded to jab at us vigorously. Luckily for us, though, it turned out that he didn't really know how to fight either, having relied on his size to intimidate his victims. So, having demonstrated our point—bullying would not be tolerated while the Do-Gooders were around—we decided it was time for a strategic retreat, leaving our victim to remorsefully reconsider his crimes.

In short, we ran for our lives.

As it turned out, he not only did not run after us, he actually stopped his bullying. I think he was shocked, and a little frightened, that someone had finally challenged him. So in spite of our ineptness, we achieved something. The dynamic Do-Gooders had made a difference!

There are times in our lives when we would all like to be superheroes, or at least just regular heroes. Of course, our images of what it means to be a hero can be inflated, just as my ten-year-old image was, by flashy images from the media. We can overlook the myriad ways in which we are heroic in the midst of our everyday lives. Whenever we resist the temptation to act at less than our best, we are heroes. Whenever we refuse to settle for mediocrity, whenever we overcome the impulse to strike out emotionally or mentally (or, certainly, physically) simply because we are feeling wounded, we are heroes. Sometimes, just getting out of bed to face another day at a boring job in order to support our families is the most heroic act in the world. Comforting when we would rather be comforted, loving when we would rather be loved, nourishing another when it's we who cry out for nourishment, are all the acts of a superhero. No mask or cape needed, just a loving and caring heart.

On the other hand, when we witness the daily dose of disaster, danger, and despair that parades across our TV screens during the news, it seems that only a superhero can possibly set things right. And there are so many images in movies and in books that portray the hero as possessing some inner or outer power that sets him or her apart from the rest of us. Surely, we need such power, too, if we are to make a difference.

And what of all the spiritual, psychic, and human potential workshops whose ads boldly and attractively proclaim that they can teach us to be powerful? What about all those late-night infomercials that so seductively inform us that through their book, technique, or process we will gain the power to become wealthy, healthy, successful, and wise? In the realm of commerce as much as in the realm of entertainment, the message is that we need to develop a power of some kind.

Blessing is not a power.

It is power*ful*—perhaps the most powerful act in the world because of its potential to *em*power, transform, and restore wholeness. But a blessing is not a magical force that we can wield, or a spiritual ray gun that shoots laser beams of love. It's not a power that allows us to do something. It doesn't give us any ability to manipulate or control our world.

It's something more subtle than that.

Although we *do* something in order to create a blessing, a blessing is not something we do *to* someone. Rather, it's something we *become* with that person. In sharing our blood and breath with another, we discover that we become part of a larger body that contains us both. It's this recognition, and the power inherent in that larger presence, that is the blessing.

When I was fourteen years old, I spent part of the summer with my grandmother in Monterey, California. All my life, I've suffered from chronic asthma, and on the day after my parents arrived to pick me up, I woke up gasping for breath. Alarmed, my parents took me to a nearby doctor, a middle-aged man who reminded me in attitude, if not in looks, of Doc on the old TV western *Gunsmoke*. He checked me over and wrote out a prescription ("Just in case . . ."). But then, instead of passing me out the door to see the next patient, he simply sat back in his chair and talked with me. We talked about what my summer had been like, where I went to school, and what I hoped to do in the future. He shared with me stories of his experiences as a doctor and how he had spent summers when he was a kid.

After about twenty minutes, I discovered that my asthma had gone. My breathing was normal. I felt it was a miracle, and all without having to take any medicine. The doctor had recognized that my asthmatic attack had come on as a result of my excitement at seeing my parents. So he simply acted to calm me down.

In treating me, he didn't do anything special; he certainly didn't do anything "medical." I never did take the medicine he prescribed. He simply sat with me and we talked. We could have been on a park bench together or sitting at a beach. He could have been an uncle, a grandfather, a friend. He related to me, and together we became part of something larger, something spacious in its calmness and ordinariness. And in that open space my emotional and physical constrictions loosened up, expanded, and released. My asthma disappeared like dandelion seeds blown and dispersed on a summer breeze.

I felt myself blessed by this doctor, but he did not use any special power. He did not zap me with some inner lightning bolt. He simply was present in a full and compassionate way. I felt embraced by his heart and invited into a calm space in which we shared our common human adventures. What he did for me didn't come from some secret or special esoteric, occult, or religious knowledge. It came from his ordinary wisdom and his presence as a fellow human being.

If we approach the art of blessing as if we're going to learn some esoteric technique or gain some magical inner power, we may deceive ourselves. For blessing does not reside in power. If anything, it resides in stillness, openness, and vulnerability. The "power" to bless doesn't come from our usual fix-it orientation to life, one that sees problems and attempts to correct them. There is nothing wrong with this orientation, of course. It's very important in a practical sense. And we need to develop the skills and the power to make right things that have gone awry in our world.

But blessing comes from a different orientation. Blessing arises from a state of mind and heart that understands wholeness, that understands joy, that sees what is right rather than what is wrong. It's not problem-solving as much as it's problem-dissolving.

The art of blessing does not require us to be superheroes. It only requires us to be ourselves. A superhero is set apart from the world, distanced in some fashion from ordinary humanity. But to bless, we want to be present. We want that distance to be diminished. How can I enter into the presence of the sacred with you, how can I join with you in a circulation of life, how can I share blood and breath if we are separated? How can we become that larger body together if you or I see blessing as a power I have but you do not because of something I have learned, or because of an ecclesiastical authorization, or a perception of holiness, or any number of other separating images?

In approaching the art of blessing, it's important to understand that we really are entering a territory that is different from the one we navigate through most of our daily lives. We are shifting to a way of looking at the world and at ourselves that is unusual in our mainstream society. This is not a magical or esoteric perspective. It's simply a way of understanding the ordinariness of the sacred and the sacredness of the ordinary.

And part of that understanding is realizing that if I wish to bless and to be a blessing, I don't need a mask and cape to help me out.

Eight

THE IMAGINATION
OF BLESSING

One of my good friends is the actor Richard Chamberlain. He is a sweet and caring man fully committed to following a spiritual path. We met twenty years ago at a conference in California, but we might not have become friends were it not for the intervention of another friend. This was because for me the man wearing Richard's face was not Richard at all but the Count of Monte Cristo, and Aramis, one of the Three Musketeers. He was, in short, the epitome of swashbuckling heroes, and if ever there was someone who wanted to buckle a swash, take sword in hand, and go forth to battle evil, it was me. Richard, on the other hand, had a bit of awe about spiritual teachers—a category in which he kindly placed me, if only because I was on the stage lecturing and he was in the audience listening—and, as he told me later, wondered what it would be like to be one. I represented a desire of his as much as he represented a desire of mine.

Furthermore, in our respective arenas we had both experienced being a celebrity (Richard was a famous, household name and I was, well, a famous name around my household), and neither of us wanted to intrude upon the other's privacy.

So we each had particular images that prevented any relationship from beginning. Given our mutual shyness, it took a friend inviting us out to lunch and basically forcing us to go beyond those images and say hello to each other as people. Which we did quite nicely, thank you, largely by recognizing and laughing about these images themselves.

This is not an uncommon experience at all. It was exaggerated perhaps by the influence of our respective professions, but people experience this kind of reticence everyday as their images and projections arise to obscure their perceptions of others. In fact, most young men and women meeting for a first date spend as much time, if not more, encountering their images of each other as they do meeting each other (assuming they ever really meet each other at all)!

The role of the imagination affects the art of blessing as much as it does our relationships. How we imagine what a blessing is and the way one is given is important. Our images can empower us and liberate us, or they can interfere. They can come between us and others, between us and the greater life that a blessing may awaken.

When we're not practicing with exercises, exploring images is a large part of what we do in a class on blessing, just as it's a large part of this book. We do so, not in a spirit of sorting out right and wrong images, but rather to understand the impact a particular image we hold may have on us. If an image helps me make the kind of connection with another through which a blessing may flow, then that image is useful to me and will remain so as long as it supports that connection.

Flying on airplanes is not my favorite thing in the world to do. My work, however, often requires me to travel to lecture or give classes. The compensation is that I get to visit wonderful places and work with outstanding people. On one such trip east I had to take a 5:15 A.M. flight out of Seattle in order to make my connections. Unfortunately, I had badly pulled a muscle in my back the day before. I was in pain and definitely not looking forward to six hours or more sitting in narrow, cramped seats.

As I boarded the plane, I automatically wandered back into the economy section looking for my seat, which on my ticket said "2A." But the economy seats started with row 10, so where was row 2? Feeling as I did that early morning, I was not thinking clearly. For a moment, all I could imagine was that someone had ripped eight rows of seats out of the plane. I was about to ask a stewardess about this when it suddenly dawned on me that row 2 was in first class! But how could I be in first class when I had purchased a supersaver, non-refundable, sardine-class fare? I decided I could figure this out later, and hustled back up to the front of the plane to find my wonderfully spacious and comfortable seat. Talk about a blessing!

It simply never registered when I first looked at my ticket that I could be in first class. I never travel first class. But this time, for some unknown reason, the airline had arbitrarily upgraded me, which was a lifesaver for both my back and my energy. But as I flew to the East Coast in unexpected and unfamiliar luxury, I discovered that I felt like an interloper. Some part of me kept waiting for the stewardess to come down the aisle and point an accusing finger at me. "You, sir, do not belong up here. You are an economy-class person. Return to the rear of the plane, where you belong!" I realized that even if I didn't have an economy-class seat, I still had an economy-class mentality. I didn't feel worthy of being where I was. (In all fairness, I should note that this did not bother me on the way back. By then I had discovered a capacity to adapt to luxury when called upon to do so.) What was amusing about this incident for me was that in working with individuals who are exploring their own spirituality, I often need to help them move beyond attitudes of unworthiness. In one way or another, many of us have an economy-class mentality when it comes to spirituality.

This is particularly true when it comes to blessing. Most people don't have any problem doing good deeds for others. Being kind doesn't usually create a crisis of self-worth or identity. But blessings, many of us feel, come from the domain of "spiritual first class." People give kindnesses, but it's God who gives blessings.

Most of us see ourselves in economy class with other ordinary folks. To give a blessing is a spiritually powerful act, and it's not unusual for a modern person to feel he or she doesn't measure up to what is needed. In fact, I've even known clergypersons who are uncomfortable giving a blessing, unless they're reading from an official book of prayers.

Being helpful is part of our normal everyday repertoire; being "blessingful" is probably not. Blessings are associated with holiness, sacredness, spirituality—but do we feel holy, sacred, or spiritual in our everyday lives? Do we feel we can be a source of blessing?

When I begin a class on blessing, this is the first question that must be answered. For if we cannot appreciate our own spirit and the power it contains, how can we go beyond being kind to being a source of blessing? In effect, we have to upgrade ourselves into first class. Or we have to recognize that where blessings are concerned, there are no classes at all.

One way I tackle this issue is to have people simply practice blessing each other. Then they can both experience for themselves a flow of presence, spirit, or energy within, and hear what another has experienced as a result. Sometimes, nothing happens. But over time, as they move beyond images that may be blocking them, people have profound experiences. They realize that as surely as they have blood and breath, they have the ability to share them.

It's also helpful to think about blessing as a sharing of life and the qualities of life with one another in an empowering way. These qualities can be named in various ways: energy, vitality, spirit, wisdom, peace, love, encouragement, enthusiasm, and support. But however we name them, the point is that we all can experience access to at least some of them. They're not foreign to our experience. They're not qualities exclusive to mystics and holy persons. We know these qualities in our everyday lives, and we can share them. And that sharing opens a door through which an unobstructed, connected, holistic presence—a loving, empowering presence—can expand around us, embrace us, and become the blessing.

There is a related issue, one I had to confront early in my career as a teacher. It is the issue of glamor, power, authority, and the tendency of people to put someone who works with spiritual realities on a pedestal (and, unfortunately, sometimes the tendency of such a person to want or to allow that to happen). This is a major issue all by itself, with ramifications of ego, manipulation, and the abuse of trust and power that go far beyond the scope of this book.

Where the art of blessing is concerned, the many problems this issue presents are boiled down to one: cutting off the co-creative relationship from which a blessing emerges. It can postulate a false hierarchy of who has the right or the ability to bless and who does not. And it treats blessing as something that someone does to someone or something else rather than as a relationship that all parties enter into equally.

When I first began lecturing, I was nineteen years old and still in college. From the beginning of my public work, there was a glamor that attached itself to me largely because of my age (I was younger by far than anyone else on the spiritual lecture circuit!), but also because I could see into and interact with what the Austrian mystic and scientist Rudolf Steiner called the "supersensible worlds"—an ability for which I could claim as much credit personally as I could for having eyes and ears, which is to say none whatsoever.

As a consequence, people often pushed pedestals towards me for me to climb onto. An early experience taught me just how destructive to one's inner work such a pedestal can be. I was invited to meet with a small organization of spiritual seekers, to give a talk, and then have a meal together afterwards. This gathering was set up by a wonderful woman who sparkled with wit and a sense of joy in her life.

On the day appointed, I went to this group and gave my talk. I felt it went well, but there was a curious strain in the atmosphere of the room. This strain was more pronounced afterwards when we all sat down to eat, as if a heavy mantle of formality had fallen upon us. Even the woman who had invited me was subdued and exhibiting none of her usual humor. So I decided to lighten things up a bit.

Now, it may not fully come across in a book like this (or perhaps you might feel it comes across too much!), but I am a very humorous person. Granted, the quality of my humor is a subject of lively debate among all who know me, but that I like to laugh is not. And when I feel something is stuck in the atmosphere of a meeting or place, my instinct is to turn to humor to get the momentum flowing again.

So, I began to joke with my friend to get some witty repartee going, but she reacted with even more distress. So I stopped. Later, when I caught her alone, I asked her what was the matter. To my astonishment, she told me the leader of the group had informed them all that I was a spiritual adept and that because of my "high spiritual station," I was to be treated with respect. In particular, humor was to be avoided because it wasn't "reverential"! So naturally, after that I began laughing and teasing the whole lot of them, seeking to dispel this particular myth. My friend enjoyed it, but I was never invited back to speak again.

The real point of this story is that I could feel something blocking the flow of energy and spirit among us, though I didn't know at first what it was. But when my friend told me what the situation was, I knew immediately what had happened. I had been separated from these people by an image. And when the outward flow of my spirit is blocked in that manner, I cannot connect except in the most superficial way.

Pedestals and the images they create get in the way of blessing for everyone involved. They separate us. They can reinforce the idea that blessings can only be given by the people on the pedestals while the rest of us can only hold out our hands and receive. Such an image can certainly come between people. And, to the extent it represents egotism, assumptions of superiority, and pride, it can come between a person and God.

Unfortunately, blessings are often presented as things that happen to us, usually by the grace of those on the pedestals. We think of blessings from the standpoint of the recipient, not from the perspective of a donor or a creator. We're asked to count our blessings as things we have or things that have been done to or for us. Why not count the blessings we have created or given as well?

Perhaps we feel that there's something egotistical about naming the blessings we do or claiming to be a source of blessings for others. But while humility and modesty have an appropriate place in any spiritual path, they should not end up disempowering us or robbing us of any sense of our participation in the blessing process. In life, we are receivers *and* we are givers. We can be blessed *and* we can bless (and, as we shall see in a later chapter, being the blessee is often more difficult than being the blesser). Blessing is not just the sharing of material resources or the doing of kindnesses. It's an act of sharing spirit, an act of invoking, inviting, and involving a spiritual dimension. We all can do this. It's our innate heritage as human beings.

While doing classes on the art of blessing, I have discovered that sometimes participants do not feel they can bless because they don't feel holy. In their minds, blessing comes from holiness. I agree that blessing is a holy action. And I agree that there are people around whom the light and fire of spirit seem to burn with a clear presence. When I am in the presence of such people, I feel embraced and connected with spirit, not separated from it because I am made to feel less holy than they. I feel empowered and valued for who I am, not for who I should be. Holiness includes and connects, for that is the true character of spirit.

But all too often, holiness becomes an image that separates us. Holiness becomes seen as a form of celebrity, and then, as happened between Richard Chamberlain and myself, it keeps us apart from our own spiritual nature. In our imagination it becomes what we may long for but not what we see ourselves as possessing or able to possess.

For me holiness is not a state or a condition, like a special badge or suit of clothes I may wear. It's not like a graduate degree or certificate that I earn through study. It's not even an "energy" or a charismatic presence. It is certainly not spiritual celebrityhood. Holiness instead emerges from relationship. It's dynamic. It's a manifestation of what is happening between me and another in the moment. Was Mother Theresa a holy person treating the poor and the ill in Calcutta, or was she a person who was holy while treating the poor and the ill in Calcutta?

I see holiness as an emergent condition. It arises as a special radiance from conditions in which love prospers, connection may be made manifest, and wholeness regained. It arises where our actions and our presences open doors to an unobstructed universe and to the presence of the sacred—the presence of that which is most real. I see holiness as an embodied blessing.

Far from needing to be holy in order to bless, it's the other way around: I become holy when I bless, each time I bless. If I make blessing my way of life, then that way will be filled with holiness as well.

How I imagine myself plays a significant role in how freely I can bless. When holiness and the innate spirituality of life can be part of this imagination, then blessing becomes a reality for me and not just an experience I must leave to others.

Nine

THE UNOBSTRUCTED
WORLD

Perhaps the most common image of a blessing is that it is a force of love that passes between two people. It is a transmission of well-being, directed by a will to enhance the wholeness of another person's life. Dr. Roberto Assagioli, the Italian psychiatrist and colleague of Jung who created the psychotherapeutic system called "Psychosynthesis," defined a blessing as "a transfer of spiritual energy." In this, he agreed with the description of blessing given by many spiritual teachers throughout the ages.

I can certainly accept this definition, having experienced this flow of subtle energy between myself and others. It can sound mysterious, but it's not. The idea of subtle energies and forces that pass between ourselves and the world is commonplace in many spiritual traditions. In the martial arts, a major element of training is learning to recognize and direct just such a subtle energy, called *chi* or *qi*. A person who is psychically sensitive can see and feel the transmission of an invisible force from one individual to another when a blessing is performed or, for that matter, even when someone simply directs a kind thought or feeling towards another.

However, it is my experience that a blessing is more than just a transfer of spiritual energy. I may be able to "zap" you with energy and make you feel good, vital, and high. But that will no more put you in touch with a deeper sense of life or of yourself than will a great cup of coffee, a piece of fine Swiss chocolate, a night at a rock concert, or a day spent getting psyched up at a motivational seminar. Being zapped by energy is not the same thing as having a spiritual experience, even though the two may go together. For that, we must go beyond a simple experience of energy enhancement into another kind of experience altogether.

Sharing energy is like touching someone. It can be comforting and even exciting, but it's not the same thing as a sharing of self and spirit, blood and breath. Sharing spirit with another is more like experiencing a mutual presence together. If I can enter into a spirit of love and I then direct my attention and intention towards you, a condition is created in which you may enter into and share that state as well. This is a process of induction or resonance. It's very different from beaming you energy like a laser bolt from a ray gun.

The presence that we can share in the midst of a blessing is one of profound interconnectedness, wholeness, and flow in which there are no obstructions to the manifestation of a oneness within us and between us. I think of this presence as the unobstructed world of spirit. A blessing is an invitation from one person to another to enter into and share this world. It is the opening of a door so we can enter this world together.

This unobstructed world can manifest in various ways in our lives quite apart from an act of blessing, although when we experience it we may indeed feel blessed. One of its more common manifestations is through synchronicity or what Carl Jung called "meaningful coincidences."

Two friends of mine had been living in Los Angeles but were moving to the East Coast. They were trying to sell their house before they moved, but the market was slow. So, to speed things up, the wife in particular began working with various affirmations said in the spirit of house-selling. One that she used in particular was "Jesus, please sell my house." Unfortunately, she often got the words mixed up in her mind, so it would come out as "Jesus, please buy my house."

During this time, she came to Seattle to do a theater project that lasted for a couple of weeks. While she was here, she got an overnight mail from her husband. The letter said a buyer had been found, and the realtor needed her signature on the enclosed documents. She was startled and very amused to see that the buyers were a Mexican-American couple, and the husband's name was Jesus.

Jesus *had* bought her house!

Because I teach classes on manifestation—which might be called "the art of creating synchronicities"—I hear a lot of stories like these, many even more wonderful and strange than my friend's. (In fact, I wrote a book about them called *Everyday Miracles*.)

Sometimes the quality of unobstructedness that a synchronicity can display can be astounding, even spooky. Once, while out Christmas shopping, I stopped at a phone booth to call a small hobby shop in Seattle to see if they carried a gift for which I was looking. Before I even put money in the coin slot, the phone rang, startling me. I picked it up and heard a voice asking who was there. I said, "Who is this?" It turned out to be the sales clerk in the very hobby shop I was about to call, whose own phone had rung just a moment before!

Likewise, synchronicities can be more ordinary and trivial. I am thinking of a friend and suddenly he calls. I am driving in downtown Seattle on a busy day, and just as I approach the building I need to go into, a car pulls out of a parking space right in front of the entrance.

In his book called *Synchronicity: The Bridge Between Matter and Mind,* physicist F. David Peat suggests that synchronicities, whether astounding or trivial, are glimpses beneath the surface appearances of our world into a deeper layer of order and relatedness. Our world of everyday encounters and events strives to replicate that deeper wholeness through the connections and coincidences that we experience as synchronicities.

When we experience synchronicities, it's like being part of a masterfully choreographed dance in which we all move precisely in harmony with the music. And in this dance there is an order prescribed by the music and by the type of dance it is. Yet, there's also a sense of freedom and exhilaration as we're transported by the movement and the music.

Synchronicities, when we pay attention to them and to the feelings they engender, have a similar sense of liberating orderliness. It's as if all around us there is a subtle music playing: vast and intimate melodies running through our lives, our activities, our world, connecting us all in unimagined ways. Most of the time we're so preoccupied that we don't hear it at all, but every now and then, we connect with it, consciously or unconsciously. And when we do, we may well feel a sense of power and presence and reality more intensely and intimately than at any other time. We realize that we are really living in the midst of a great dance floor.

I call this dance floor the unobstructed world.

I think of it as unobstructed because I experience it as a condition in which life and spirit flow in an unimpeded way. It connects and unites all beings, much as music gathers all the dancers together into shared rhythm and movement. It's a condition in which we are so aware of our interrelatedness, our oneness, that every being acts on behalf of the well-being of all other beings. Think of dancers executing their steps in a way that enables others to do the same, complementing and blending their movements into a seamless experience.

This state is well known in spiritual and mystical traditions. It's called by many names and is often equated with the presence of God or with the timeless, dimensionless Source whose presence pervades and orders all creation.

Unobstructedness in this context doesn't mean the same thing as being without limits or boundaries. Limits create definition and channel the flow of life or energy. An obstruction simply stops that flow. Unobstructedness must be understood from the point of view of the whole. A river overflowing its bank and flooding throughout the countryside is unobstructed, for the moment at least. But it *is* obstructing and even destroying all the other forms of life that must contend with its raging waters.

The unobstructed world is not a condition in which I can do or say whatever I want, no matter what obstructions I may create for others. It's not a world in which I am limitless in my potential expression, regardless of the consequences. That world is purely a fantasy of the ego. The unobstructed world is unobstructed because, as in a dance, all the participants willingly and deliberately act to ease the way for each other. They empower and enable each other to blend and merge with each other's flow and movement, energy and space, in ways that serve and enhance the whole dance.

There is a word for that kind of activity and perspective. It is *love.*

The unobstructed world is also one of creativity and emergence. To continue the metaphor of the dance, if you can create a new step that enriches the overall performance or even just your own part in it, then I want to support you. And I would expect the same in return.

There is also a word for this kind of mutually supportive interaction that enables something greater to emerge than either of us might be able to create alone. It is *synergy.* In a synergic relationship, the whole becomes greater than the mere sum of its parts precisely because they're relating in a way that allows something new to emerge. There is no obstruction in the flow between them.

Consider a basketball team whose members are interrelating so well that they function like a single organism. In the heightened enthusiasm and spirit of a well-played game, a team rhythm and performance emerges that is more than just the combination of the players' skills. Everything goes right. All their moves flow in harmony. Every pass, every shot, seems to go just where it needs to. Each player feels enhanced, filled with the power of the team's combined energy.

This is synergy in action. From a spiritual standpoint, at its heart is love and trust and a desire to better not only our own performance but that of everyone around us. And with a sense of synergy comes a feeling of belonging, of being part of something greater than ourselves. And at the same time we feel not diminished but rather enriched in our own individuality and personhood. The unobstructed world is certainly more than a state of synergy. But synergy directly points to and reflects the innate quality of profound relatedness and mutual service that emerges from that world.

Another expression of this unobstructed world is found in the psychophysical condition that psychiatrists refer to as the "flow state." It arises from an intense and self-forgetful engagement with the world (again, like holiness, from relatedness). We experience flow when we're intensely enjoying ourselves, or when we're completely caught up in the moment. We seem to cross a line between *doing* an activity and *becoming* that activity. The doing becomes effortless, as if the activity were doing itself through us. In effect, the activity becomes unobstructed.

We have the experience of flow most often in play, or in work that's so engrossing and satisfying that it becomes like play. Perhaps that's another way to think about the unobstructed world: It reflects and embodies a spirit of playfulness within creation, not to mention within its Source. Perhaps that's also a way to think about blessing: as an experience and sharing of the deep play of the universe.

It's not how we usually imagine blessing. We think of a blessing as something wonderful that has happened in our lives, as something that brings us happiness. Or we think of blessing as a special charge of spiritual energy or as a manifestation of grace and divine favor. We may not think of it as a form of play or as a state of flow, though it can lead us to experience elements of either or both.

But my point isn't whether or not blessing may be a psychological flow state. My point is that flow, synchronicities, synergy, and blessings all point to a common state of being, one which cannot be precisely defined but which can be experienced. And when we do, what we experience is being caught up in a spirit of belonging, of relatedness, of spaciousness and empowerment. It's a state of joy, a state of harmony. It's a state in which we are re-membered.

It's the unobstructed world in which there are no barriers between my heart and yours, my soul and yours, my power and creativity and yours. I consider this state to be at the heart of blessing. In fact, I would define a blessing as anything that enables us to experience to any degree this unobstructed world—particularly in a way that enables our openness to that world to grow in us.

To embody the wholeness, power, and flow of this unobstructed world in a way that others may experience it as well is precisely what the art of blessing is all about. It's the "transmission" or sharing of this experience, not just the transmission of an energy or the performance of a kindness, that in my mind constitutes the true spirit of blessing.

Ten

THE GREAT
WORK

This may seem like a silly question at this point in the book, but why learn to bless anyway? If I'm a kind and generous person, if I remember to say "Bless you!" when someone sneezes, and cultivate a sense of gratitude in my life by counting my blessings instead of sheep, isn't that enough? Aren't blessings the purview of the sacred anyway? Surely, it's God who blesses, and my role is to pray for those blessings to be abundantly manifested in our world.

The answer for me is neither that God—or the sacred by whatever name we choose—does not bless, nor that we should fail to invite those blessings through prayer or invocation. My answer is that through a spiritual act like blessing, we learn to discover ourselves in a deeper way, and we become a human source of enrichment for our world. The art of blessing becomes a mode of service, a spiritual practice, and a participation in what the Western mystical alchemical tradition termed the Great Work.

When I first moved to Seattle fifteen years ago, it took me all of five minutes to drive to the grocery store. Now with many more cars on the road that same trip can take me as much as half an hour if traffic is particularly heavy. And I'm lucky. I live in one of the less congested areas of town.

There's a lot of congestion in our modern lives. Far from living in an unobstructed world, some days it seems like everyone and everything gets in our face, blocking us mentally and emotionally as well as physically. Synchronicities or moments of grace, harmony, and flow stand out like oases in a desert of wasted efforts, stymied energies, and stress. To lead a spacious life seems more and more difficult. Speaking as a father in a household of four children from six to eighteen years of age (and a pack rat myself), what will get us all in the end will be clutter!

Looking at humanity as a whole, I'd say that much of our psychological and spiritual energy is stuck. It's blocked by old habits and by images of conflict, separation, and violence. Our fears limit our imaginations. They cripple our will to change, to embody new visions of a more humane and ecologically harmonious world. This image of "stuck energies" isn't simply a metaphor; at a psychic level of perception, it's a very real condition of obstructedness, whatever terms I may choose to describe it.

This obstructedness is not due to the physical nature of our world, as some philosophical teachings might lead us to believe. The idea that we dwell in a dense world that's intrinsically resistant to spirit or the flow of energy, or that somehow our souls are weighted down by the materiality of the earth, is flat out wrong. It comes from a failure to fully experience the zest and power of life, a failure to perceive that every particle of our world radiates with a soulfire drawn from the hearth of the infinite.

No, the experience—and the reality—of obstructedness doesn't inherently come from the earth, but from our own incomplete and still-maturing state of being. It comes from our own thoughts and feelings, our own imaginations and fears. It comes from our own failures to connect. If anything, we obstruct ourselves because we resist being fully present in our world, for each other, and within our own incarnations with all their pains, risks, limits, and challenges as well as their joys, their creative potentials, and their opportunities.

Here I want to reemphasize something I said in the last chapter. Unobstructedness is not the same to me as having no limits. A limit is something that defines us and channels our efforts, giving us focus, but it's not an obstruction. An obstruction blocks; it disperses our focus. It adds nothing to our lives and can even threaten them. A road has limits that indicate where I can drive and where I cannot; if I cross the center dividing line, I become an obstruction—and most likely a deadly one—to anyone driving in the opposite direction.

None of us likes limits. We revel in myths of unbounded, unimpeded power and activity, forgetting that in such a state we can become like the floodwaters in my earlier metaphor. A flood is obviously powerful but it's also dispersed; floods don't drive turbines and create electricity. Only rivers do that. Limits concentrate power in order to create freedom in a different way.

The unobstructed state is not one of license to do whatever we wish; as I said in the last chapter, it's a state of relatedness based on mutual empowerment and respect that enables energy, life, ideas, and power to flow freely between us. Unobstructedness is a shared state, not one I can enjoy irrespective of others. Indeed, what is really unobstructed isn't our actions but our capacity to relate. Think of a relay race in which a baton is passed from runner to runner. The success of the race depends not only on the swiftness of the individual runners but also on the ease and grace with which they can pass the baton from one to another. And in the end, it's not a single runner who wins but the whole team.

In the unobstructed world, we all win or no one wins; there's no partial victory for just a special few. This perspective is beautifully and powerfully embodied in the Buddhist doctrine of the Bodhisattva. This is a person who has achieved enlightenment and, being free from any need for rebirth, could pass on into the mystery of nirvana. But instead, he or she remains in the world to serve others and empower their quests for enlightenment, for he or she knows that until all are free, no one is. Until all are enlightened and unobstructed, no one is.

The effort to bring into our human experience the liberation and creative power of the unobstructed spirit is what has been called the Great Work: the enlightenment of humanity and the upliftment of the world. Sometimes, within a Christian perspective, this Great Work is described as the work of redeeming ourselves and the world. But I like to think of it as a work of reclamation.

Amidst all the tragedies in our world—the pain, loss, and sorrow that parade in an unending march of tears across our nightly TV news—there is one tragedy that seems to sum up the anguish of our obstructed world. This is the tragedy of waste.

The fact that through violence and neglect we waste lives and resources is obvious. But we waste other things that are not so obvious. We waste dreams, efforts, hope, and all the potential of relatedness. We waste opportunities to serve, support, and connect with each other. We waste the creative energy that could be there between us. We waste possibilities for joy and ecstasy. We waste possibilities to know the sacred not as something distant but as a presence at the core of our being, infusing our every action with holiness.

We waste our humanity. It's so visible in our endless conflicts and wars; in the distrusts and suspicions that thwart our relationships; in the arrogance that leads one group to put its race, its religion, its customs and beliefs, above those of any other; in the fear that makes us hide our faces from each other and build walls between us. We waste who we might be. We waste what could be humanly and spiritually possible if we learned how to create unobstructedness with each other, if we learned how to pass batons of love, wisdom, creativity, and energy between us with grace and skill.

And beyond a doubt we waste our world: its breathable air, its drinkable water, its fertile soil, its regenerative forests and oceans. We waste the lives of all the creatures that not only share this planet with us but share our beingness and potential as well. For they hold keys to the unobstructed world that we don't. They're part of the music we dance to. If they disappear, there will be only silence where there once was melody, and we will find ourselves trying to dance to memory and not to the full rhythm of unbroken life.

The essence of the Great Work is the reclaiming of this waste. It's the work of replacing the obstructedness that promotes such waste with a spirit of unobstructedness that allows all of us to experience ourselves and each other in full measure. And it's in this context that the art of blessing is important to me. For when we bless, we extend this spirit of the unobstructed world into our lives and the lives of others. We become participants in the Great Work.

The term *Great Work* does sound imposing, even intimidating. But in fact, the Great Work is really made up of a multitude of individual Little Works. Just as the towering cathedrals of medieval Europe were built one stone at a time, the transformation of the obstructed into the unobstructed takes place one act at a time, one choice at a time, one blessing at a time.

It's a transformation that takes place through an interior alchemy, through our own personal version of the Great Work. That's why the art of blessing may be seen as a spiritual path. For to bring the unobstructed spirit into our world we must ourselves experience that spirit and make it part of who we are, part of our blood and breath. We ourselves must become unobstructing.

This obstructedness is more than just traffic jams on the way to the grocery store or bad weather that forces the cancellation of a sporting event. It's the obstructedness of our attitudes, feelings, images, and habits, whether directed inward towards ourselves or outward towards others. It's these subjective obstructions that can scatter and block our energy.

For example, fear of failure may keep me from accepting a major new assignment at work, thus wasting the potential for a liberating advancement in my career. Envy and resentment may cause me to lash out at someone who might have been a friend, wasting the potential of that relationship. A poor self-image may lead me to denigrate or even hate people who are different from me racially or religiously, wasting the opportunity for gaining new insights that may enrich my own perspective.

All of these attitudes become impediments to living my life in its fullness, and to reaching my potential. But they also lead me to choose obstruction over liberation and a creative relatedness; they lead me to project my own obstructedness onto others. I become a curse, rather than a blessing.

So the personal Great Work, the individual art of blessing, lies in discovering how to gather these inner obstructions together and bring them into the unobstructed world. It's the work of freeing our internal energies that are stuck in habits and divisive perspectives. It's the work of personal reflection and honesty. It's the work of seeking out and learning from the examples of unobstructedness and flow, creativity and spirit, joy and spaciousness, in our world. And it's the work of giving unobstructedness and the spirit of blessing room to grow in our lives.

There are probably as many ways to do this as there are people. But one way is through our relationships with others. Although it sounds tautological, the way to discover blessing is to bless. For then we are stepping into the flow of a loving, spiritual presence that moves through the world. And when we do, it circulates through us as well, unblocking what is blocked, unsticking what is stuck, regenerating what has become stagnant.

To bless *is* a holy act. And learning the art of blessing is akin to learning to manifest holiness in our lives. As I said earlier, we must remember that holiness is not a state. It's not a crown that we wear but a spirit that emerges from an act of engagement. It radiates from any act in which we dissolve any barrier between us and another, any barrier between us and the sacred.

When, because of any action we take, another person feels his way has become less impeded, and the potentials of his soul more capable of being realized, then we've brought the spirit of the unobstructed world into his life. And we've brought it into our own life as well. It may not seem like a transcendent power zapping us from heaven, but it's a moment of grace, offered from one person to another. It's a blessing—a moment of holiness—that two people can create together.

The more mindful we are of this process, the more we add our blood and breath, the more our acts resonate with the power of blessing. And while a kindness may satisfy the heart and mind and create what might be thought of as a localized unobstructedness, a blessing—because we reach into our own souls to do it—touches the soul of another. There the effects can be long-lasting and far reaching in ways we may not realize or imagine. For the Great Work is more than an effort to change the outer conditions of humanity: It's also the work of inner transformation—an effort to change a quality of energy that, like a pollutant in the ocean, affects all of us who share this world. I might call this energy a *habit* of erecting obstructions, or a *will* to impede based on feelings of fear, hatred, and separation.

Anyone who works consistently with the non-physical dimensions of the world can recognize the existence of this habit and the energy or motivations it generates. It's like one discordant voice in the midst of a choir, throwing everyone off-key. The purpose of the Great Work is to restore that voice to harmony by sounding over and over again the proper notes it should be singing. These are notes of love, of compassion and caring, of an intelligent and wise relatedness that empowers and unobstructs. These are the notes of blessing.

When we bless, we connect ourselves, the sacred, and others in a spirit of spaciousness and unity, love and unobstructedness. When we bless we sound those notes. We release what we can certainly imagine as an energy into the world. And since the world of spirit doesn't operate with the same laws of scale as our physical world does, the impact of this energy can far outweigh the size of the event that generated it. For each blessing that we perform, great or small, private or public, the obstructing tendencies of the world are diminished and the melody of the Source can resound with greater clarity than before. With each blessing, the unobstructed world becomes more of a reality.

This is the promise of the art of blessing. In discovering how to bless, we add ourselves to the Great Work, which is, after all, simply the work of Life in pursuit of unfoldment, harmony, and the potentials of infinity.

PART II

THE ART OF BLESSING

A blessing is any event that enables us to experience in any degree the unobstructed world. To embody the spirit of this world such that others may experience it as well is what the art of blessing is all about.

Eleven

A TIME TO
BLESS

The first verse of chapter three of Ecclesiastes in the Old Testament declares, "To every thing there is a season and a time to every purpose under the heavens."

When is the time to bless?

Usually blessings take place at special times in our lives as ordained by custom or religious practice. Blessings are given and received as part of religious services and ceremonies. Blessings are invoked over meals. Blessings are asked for endeavors great and small: A chaplain asks for blessings on the proceedings of Congress, just as a coach asks for blessings on his team before a big game. Blessings are asked upon new marriages and new homes. We may ask for blessings upon our day when we arise and upon our sleep when we retire. When someone is ill or distressed, they ask for blessings. And when someone has died, loved ones ask for blessings on them as well for the ongoing journey of their soul.

Blessings are asked at beginnings and endings, and at many points in between. Indeed, any time we feel a situation or a person needs the benefit of divine providence, we ask for blessing. This is how we normally understand a blessing in our culture. It's an invocation of the presence and power of the sacred upon a person's life or upon the function of an object.

We normally don't bless in the middle of our work day at the office or on the factory floor, especially if the boss has just given us an extra assignment. We don't bless while sitting in a traffic gridlock. We don't bless while watching television or sitting in a movie theater. We don't ordinarily stop and invoke a blessing in the midst of our lovemaking (though the act itself may be a blessing), or while playing baseball, or cooking dinner, or mixing a martini. And when we're laughing in the sheer delight of a moment, we probably don't ask for a blessing then, either.

In short, in the midst of the boring times, the happy times, the angry times, and the routine times, performing a blessing may be the last thing on our minds. In the midst of the ordinary and the trivial, we tend not to think of the power of the sacred or the presence of the unobstructed world.

But like the orange juice that is not just for breakfast anymore, blessings need not only be for special occasions. A blessing can be anytime we wish to make a deeper connection with the life (and lives) around us. As much as it is an invocation, it's also an act of discovering the part of us that moves in harmony on the dance floor of creation. In fact, the art of blessing is not only about the act of blessing but about an attitude towards the world, a way of seeing things that goes beyond our ordinary perceptions. For instance, I usually think of the world around me as the visible manifestation of energy in motion, because that's what I see with my inner vision. The concept of subtle energy is not a theoretical or metaphorical one for me. Everything and everyone I see with inner sight is composed of energy that is highly interactive.

Imagine each of us as a heart through which the lifeblood of creation, which is spirit, circulates. Depending on how strongly we "beat" or how "clogged" we are, we can enhance or diminish this circulation. To bless is to beat strongly and clearly so the flow of spirit is increased. To practice blessing is to strengthen ourselves, to unclog our own inner arteries so we may participate in the circulation of spirit and life in less obstructing ways.

Think how strange it would be if our physical hearts only beat in those special moments when custom decreed it was time to bless. If that were the case, then we'd find reasons to be blessing all the time! But too often this is how we lead our spiritual lives. So, in a strong sense, the art of blessing is the art of perceiving the many opportunities in our everyday lives to be hearts that can beat strongly and send spirit circulating powerfully through our world. It's the cultivation of an attitude that does not relegate spirituality to special times, but sees it as a measure of how we're relating with all the times in our lives.

Custom is not the only issue that can affect us when we feel we can bless. Our inner moods and attitudes can challenge us. In one class, a woman asked me how she can bless if she is irritable, depressed, or just plain tired. Given that most of us do not feel joyous and energized twenty-four hours a day, every day, this is a good question. Is the power to bless conditioned by whatever mood we are in?

My answer is that our power to bless is not conditioned by our moods, but our choice or our desire to bless may well be. After a class exercise in which I had people exchange blessings, this same woman discovered she had answered her own question. In spite of feeling irritated with her partner, she was still able to enter into a state of blessing for him. This, she felt, was because of her intention. She desired and chose to bless another person in spite of her own feelings and mood at the time. Having made that choice, she discovered that a part of her responded with a sense of openness and expansion as she shifted her attention from how she was feeling to the well-being of the other person. She found her self lifted out of her mood. Her choice to bless set the flow of blessing in motion and carried her right along with it.

So, when do we bless? Anytime we want to. And how do we bless? Well, basically my answer is, as simply as possible. When we bless in a formal way, through a ritual or a ceremony, it's like aerobic exercise: Our heart beats faster and stronger because we're doing something that makes it do so. In a formal blessing, in which I may do a simple ritual that might involve a laying on of hands or an invocation, I am deliberately making myself as a spiritual heart beat more strongly. I am deliberately opening to a stronger circulation of spirit.

We don't spend our days in constant aerobic activity, of course, but our hearts never stop beating. The purpose of aerobics is to strengthen the heart so it beats more efficiently the rest of the time. Similarly, most of the time we're not in situations that demand or permit formal blessings, but that doesn't mean we're not still beating as spiritual hearts. If we simply maintain an awareness that we're always in the midst of a great circulatory system of spirit, then through that attitude we open channels through which spirit may flow more unobstructedly.

As I've said, there are times when I'm formally asked to bless someone or something. When that happens, I "beat" strongly and deliberately. I focus the flow of spirit in a particular way as the situation requires. But the rest of the time, I practice blessing largely by seeking to generally enhance the flow of energy and spirit around me in an unconditional manner. I give myself to this circulatory process. I add my blood and breath to it.

I'm not doing this every minute. My attention goes to other things, and my energy waxes and wanes naturally through the course of a day. But periodically, I stop for a "blessing break." I begin by simply looking at the things around me, and gathering them into my heart. I may just touch my computer, for example, thanking it for its loyal service and blessing it. I may bless the room in which I work, and the house around me. And in these blessings, there is a sense of partnership, for which I'm thankful. I realize how my house blesses me with shelter, with a space in which to be creative, and my computer is the blessing of a tool with which to write.

If I'm out and about instead, buying groceries, visiting my child's school, driving down the freeway, generally running all the little errands that make up family life, then I may mentally bless the people I see, the places I enter along the way. I don't project anything on them. I simply hold them unconditionally in my spiritual heart and in the circulation of spirit that embraces us both.

I don't do this all the time, nor do I feel a pressure to do so. Blessing is not a spiritual "should." It's an opportunity. For when I bless, I meet my own unobstructed self, which is a blessing for me. Blessing is its own reward, but it's not a requirement.

Sometimes, I can feel inwardly where the circulation in a place or in a person is blocked. I never try to deliberately remove that block, for no one has asked me to do so. No permission has been given. In all spiritual work, it's important not to impose our will or our perspective on a situation where we haven't been invited to help. I haven't met many store owners to whom I could say, "The energy in your store is clogged up. Would you like me to bless the place to try to clean it up?" But what I will do is put myself in a state of blessing, into what I call my "blessing place." As a metaphorical heart, I'll beat more strongly in that place and let the wisdom and intelligence of the circulating spirit take its natural course. Perhaps it will have an effect, perhaps not. It's not for me to decide. But it's an opportunity to offer a silent and unconditional blessing, allowing the sacred to determine what happens next.

This issue of permission is important, as I have said before. There is a difference between being in a state of mind and heart that enhances the flow and circulation of spirit in an unconditional way and deliberately projecting subtle energies at someone or into some situation with the intent of creating a specific effect. In the latter case, I may well be forcing myself and my perspectives onto another, while in the former I'm simply making certain energies available and allowing the outcome to emerge according to the will and choices of those who are involved and responsible. A blessing ceases to be a blessing when it is forced. A blessing has a liberating and opening effect quite at odds with any kind of coercion. If I want to take a more active and deliberate role in blessing someone or a situation, then I need to ask the permission of those who will be the recipients.

There are ways of seeing others and the world at large that, by virtue of their openness and supportive nature, enhance the possibilities for a relationship of blessing. They "beat the heart" more strongly. Such attitudes are familiar to us. We call them compassion, respect, the willingness to accept others as they are and not as we think they should be, the openness to listen, attentiveness, love. Such attitudes open our inner hearts to each other. They allow us, if only for a moment, to become one heart sharing the circulation of the unobstructed world. We may not think of them as blessings in the traditional sense, but they can be blessings nonetheless. If we can curse someone with a look, an unkind word, a mean and limiting thought, then we can bless someone by doing the opposite.

"To every thing there is a season . . ." And it's always blessing season. Implementing this perspective in our lives may mean reimagining just what we do when we bless or what a blessing looks like. That's why I like the image of a blessing as any act that to any degree gives us the experience of the unobstructed world—the world in which spirit, with all its love, creativity, and power, circulates freely. But how we define a blessing is less important than understanding in our bones—and our hearts—what we're doing when we bless. Then we truly feel the circulation of spirit about us and within us. Then, when Ecclesiastes goes on to say, ". . . and a time to every purpose under heaven," we'll know that for the purposes of blessing, under heaven any time is all right.

Twelve

LEARNING
BLESSING

I learned to swim literally by being repeatedly thrown into the deep end of a swimming pool by my swimming coach. Whatever you may think of the technique (and I certainly didn't think much of it at the time), it worked. I learned to swim and eventually found my way onto the school swimming team.

In a way, that's how I learned to bless as well. I began this book with the story of my first blessing. I was asked to do something I had never done before, for which I had few models of how to proceed, and around which I had feelings of performance anxiety and un-worthiness. The only thing I could do was to make a leap of faith. When I did, partly in response to the other person's faith in me, something lifted me above my self-concerns and enabled me to connect with her through a deeper sense of lovingness, allowing a spirit to flow between us. Whatever she received, I felt I was the one who was truly blessed.

Over the next few years, as I was asked to give blessings in a variety of situations—particularly during the three years I was a co-director of the spiritual community of the Findhorn Foundation in northern Scotland—I had to make that leap of faith many times. And I discovered that the best way to learn to bless was simply to do it and observe what happened, both within myself and for others. There was no secret to it, no ancient wisdom to unearth. I would just begin, opening my heart and mind unconditionally to the sacred and to my own humanity. From that openness, I would form a connection of love, respect, and celebration with whomever or whatever I was being asked to bless. Then I'd allow the blessing to emerge, shaping it to the uniqueness of the moment.

I discovered there was no single right way to do it, no technique (so you can skip reading the next few chapters if you want!). Each blessing was uniquely guided by the specific relationship between me, the sacred, and the situation itself. If there is a constant in the art of blessing, it's in this state of relatedness.

Consequently, when I teach a class on blessing, most of our time is spent practicing, doing exercises like the one I described in Chapter Two. Many of these exercises deal in some manner with relating. We actively bless each other, objects, places, and even situations in the world. We observe what happens within us and around us as we do so. We learn by doing. And each person learns his or her own way of doing, for the blood and breath in each of us is particular to who we are, and how we share it is unique.

I do present ideas, and we do spend time examining our various images of and thoughts about blessing, establishing a context for what we're doing much as I've done in the first part of this book. In learning the art of blessing, though, I see my role primarily as that of mentor rather than instructor.

This is difficult to replicate in a book, which by its very nature is linear and limited to the words that I've chosen to write. I don't have the luxury of having a dialog with you that can illumine your particular approach. And you don't have the richness of experience, of mutual reflection and assistance, that comes from participating in a group.

I will give you many examples of the exercises I've used in class so that you may try them out. But I emphasize that the art of blessing is not a mental process; it's not like following a recipe. It has an improvisational element, since every situation in which we might wish to give a blessing is unique. At the very least, this art requires us to be mindful. We need to pay attention to the situation at hand, and not to turn it into a rote occasion in which we act out of habit.

Having said that, for the convenience of teaching this art, there is still an order that I follow, which consists of four overlapping steps. The first step is identification. This simply is identifying yourself as a "blesser" and being comfortable with that identification. This is achieved by finding and gathering within yourself those inner forces and resources that give you a sense of spiritual power. It's the generation of an active psychological and spiritual energy that resonates with the spirit of blessing. It's the stage of attuning to your blood and breath.

The second step is opening, becoming receptive to that which you're seeking to bless. It's opening the circulation of your inner blood and breath to blend with the greater life of the world. It's aligning yourself with the greater wholeness so that you may act for the harmony of all involved. In this step, you open yourself to being part of a creative partnership with the blessee.

The third step is synthesis. Now you're combining the active and receptive orientations into an inner focus I call the "blessing place." It's this focus that carries the power and spirit of the blessing. In a sense, it's a new level of identification in which you go beyond being simply a blesser to inhabit the spirit of blessing itself. By standing in the place where blessings live, you become the blessing.

Finally, there is the step of actual blessing. This is performing the specific act of blessing itself, which completes the cycle.

I do want to point out that these steps are designed for a class or workshop, and a class by its nature is an artificial environment. In a class we're dealing with the art of blessing the way a scientist studies an animal under controlled conditions in a laboratory. This can yield important insights, but an animal lives as part of an ecology. To truly understand that animal, we must live in its ecology as well and observe it in its home.

A person may find himself quite naturally expressing a quality of blessing within the "ecology" of his everyday life. Yet, when that same person attempts to "perform a blessing" according to a four-step technique, the whole thing can seem contrived, for a blessing is an organic act, not a technological one! It lives in an environment of relationships, desires, feelings, thoughts, actions, and situations.

I deal with this in a class setting by assigning homework. I ask people to observe how they or others may spontaneously be giving or receiving blessings in the context of their family life or workplaces. I ask them to give blessings in these contexts in as natural and ordinary a way as they can, usually unobtrusively and always without trying to force a particular outcome, and observe what happens for themselves and others. I ask them to be aware of blessings as an integral part of life and not just as something injected into life in special circumstances.

In a class, on the other hand, the participants and I are working under the assumption that we're going to deliberately perform an act of blessing in a specific situation. We're intending to bless, and the four steps are a mental checklist for supporting and implementing that intention. Using these steps in a classroom situation, we are in effect slowing down a process—like using stop-motion photography—in order to get a sense of what's happening and what we're doing.

It's like teaching someone to drive: All their attention is initially on the mechanics of what they're doing, but in time these individual elements dissolve into a seamless blend of perception, action, and response. After nearly forty years of driving, I no longer have to ask myself, "Is this when I should slow down? Is this when I should check my rearview mirror? Is this when I should change lanes?" I simply do what I need to do to blend safely with the traffic around me and arrive at my destination.

Out in the ecologies of our everyday lives, away from the artificiality of classes and workshops, the act of blessing is a similarly flowing process. It's not an ordered sequence in which we say to ourselves, "All right, I'm going to do Step One. Right, got it! Now I'm going to do Step Two," and so on. It's a seamless action as the blood and breath of our spirit wells up and embraces another in creating a sacred moment. Indeed, as we practice infusing the spirit of blessing—the unobstructing spirit, the loving spirit, the connecting spirit—into our lives, then the art of blessing becomes increasingly effortless. We become a blessing, which is what we are in essence to begin with.

So in practicing the four steps, I ask my students—and you as well—to attune to the flowing, undivided spirit that is their essence. The steps are really, in Zen terms, four fingers pointing to something else. They can be useful, but they are not the reality itself. That reality lives within us, beyond naming, beyond images, in the spirit of wholeness and holiness at our core. As I said before, what I really teach in a class on blessing (or in any of my other classes, for that matter) is how to remember.

As my students practice the four steps and seek to step into the flowing spirit that they represent, I ask them to remember the following. . . .

First, blessing is not a technique we perform but a presence we embody. It's not an act we do to someone or something but a relationship we form with them that enables us all to be embraced in the presence of the unobstructed world. We don't learn the art of blessing as much as we enter into it as part of our lives. The only things we really need are a loving heart, a compassionate mind, and an open spirit.

Second, since each of us has a unique presence and relates in unique ways, each of us will discover his own way of blessing, not the right way of blessing.

Third, we are all innately worthy and capable of blessing. Blessing is not a special power reserved only for a few but a power inherent in each of us as a natural expression of life.

Fourth, a blessing can look like anything. It can take any shape, or none at all. It can be as simple as a glance, a choice of thoughts, a way of listening, a tone of voice. It can be a laying on of hands, an embrace. It can be a ritual. It can be something we say, a special mantra or just an everyday conversation. It can be an object we give or time and energy we offer. It can be obvious or it can be subtle. It can be a physical act or a spiritual one, a mental attitude or an emotional exchange. What makes something or some action a blessing is not what it looks like, nor its relative simplicity or elaborateness, nor the level of being at which we offer it. It's the whole-ness of the spirit that we bring to it, and the resonance of that spirit with the unobstructedness of the sacred.

Finally, blessings are not measured on any scale. Blessings can certainly vary in their effects, from being life-changing to simply making a particular task go a little more smoothly. But the blessing itself cannot be evaluated by its effects. Unobstructedness is un-obstructedness, whether in my office or in the world at large, whether lasting a moment or a lifetime. The sacred is the sacred, however simple or complex the experience that awakens me to its presence.

Thirteen

IDENTIFICATION

The first step in giving a blessing is believing that you can. I call this step identification because it involves identifying yourself as someone capable of giving a blessing and honoring the fact that you have the resources within yourself to do so. Being asked to bless can, as I've said, make us feel uncomfortable, unsure, or unworthy. We may wonder what right or authority we have to give a blessing. The answer is: If we can love, we can bless. All blessings arise from a source of love, whether that is the human heart or the heart of creation.

Our ancestors recognized that blessings could come both from the sacred and from themselves. In many older cultures, people regularly blessed each other, their work, their crafts, their homes, their animals and crops, as well as asked for blessings from whatever Source they regarded as transcendent or divine. They had a perspective on their spiritual identity and role in the universe that supported a sense of blessing as a human right and responsibility.

This perspective has taken a beating in the past two hundred years. Since the beginning of the industrial age, western thinking has been dominated by a rationalist, materialistic worldview that has cast doubt on the idea that we have a spiritual identity at all. Likewise, the twentieth century, with its wars, its attempts at genocide and ethnic cleansing, its assaults on the integrity and health of the biosphere, its totalitarianism and its terrorism, does not paint a particularly spiritual picture of humanity. The phrase *human nature* has often been used as an excuse for the most awful behavior, implying that we could not do otherwise. That we have virtue within us seems lost in the evil that human beings can do. We arrive at the beginning of a new millennium with doubts that we can do good in the world, much less be a source of blessing.

While the darker sides of human behavior cannot be denied or ignored, they should not overshadow our capabilities for love, caring, compassion, and the expression of spirit. As I have said, the fact that we can curse does not mean that we cannot also bless. And the first step towards blessing is to accept that this is so.

Accepting this is more than just agreeing to a nice idea. It is also coming to terms with the idea that you are someone capable of expressing spirit. The step of identification is identifying with the power of spirit within you: the spirit of yourself, the spirit of the larger world of which you are a part, and the spirit of the sacred.

Again, because of the overall dominance in the west of a materialist perspective, a natural recognition and acceptance of our spiritual nature and of the power of spirit within us does not always come easily. When we think of spirit, we may feel that we're on unfamiliar territory, away from the real world. We tend to treat spirit either as fantasy or as something otherworldly and therefore outside our practical concerns. Time enough to deal with spirit when we die, we may feel, but before then there are other matters to which we must attend, such as putting food on the table. As a consequence, we no longer have a ready sense of spirit or of blessing as a breathing of that spirit into the world.

Even when we accept the reality of spirit, we may still feel that it belongs not to our everyday personality but to a transcendent part of us, a transpersonal self. The personal side of us has long been treated in many spiritual traditions as an obstacle to the greater world of spirit, or as the part of us most mired in illusion and negativity. In fact, when I first arrived at the spiritual community of Findhorn in 1970, I discovered that practically the worst thing you could say about a person was that he was "acting out of his personality" or "caught at the personality level."

There is no question that we can all act in negative and obstructing ways. If we have an innate power to bless, the flip side is that we can curse as well. We can think, feel, and act in ways that cut us off not only from spirit but from our world and our fellow humans. We can act as if ours were the only reality that mattered in the world. This kind of behavior is all too common in our world. However, to say that our personal side or personality is exclusively composed of this kind of behavior while our transpersonal side is exclusively good is a dualistic oversimplification that's not born out in reality.

It is also an oversimplification of *spirit* to consider it as exclusively a transcendent phenomenon. Spirit is a primal, life-giving creative force that binds all the universe together. It is a manifestation of the ground of being from which everything emerges. Spirit isn't just in one part of creation and not in any other. By its nature it's present everywhere. Spirit is as much in the concrete world and in ourselves as physical individuals as in any subtle realm. It's important to acknowledge that spirit can emerge and radiate from our embodied personhood—from our everyday selves—as fully as from transpersonal states of consciousness.

In my classes on blessing, I begin by encouraging people to experience their personalized manifestation of spirit. I want each participant to experience him- or herself as a spiritual being whose presence includes a physical body with its accompanying biology and biography and not as a divided being split between a spiritual self and a human self, with the former wearing the latter as if it were a suit of clothes. I want participants to realize that they have a power to express a spirit that arises from the dynamics of their personal lives, rather than from a transpersonal source that has not taken part in the engagements and struggles of their personalities.

To aid in this process, I have coined a phrase to name the nourishing and transformative spiritual power that radiates from our ordinary, embodied personhood. I call it the *empersonal spirit* (not, please note, the "impersonal spirit"), which means the spirit that acts from within or arises from the personality. It is universal spirit manifesting in a unique, individualized form.

Like energy erupting from the big bang at the beginning of the universe, there is a spiritual energy that arises within each of us out of the act of taking incarnation. To me, whoever we are and whatever the circumstances of our births, each life begins at its core as an act of love. Each life is a unique gift from the sacred erupting from a creative moment of joy and love. And that love, that joy, that spirit, continues to radiate throughout our lives like the background radiation of our own personal universe. It may be obscured, dim, and hard to distinguish or it may be bright and evident, but it is always there. It is at the heart of our empersonal spirit.

The empersonal spirit also develops and emerges from the daily expression of love, wisdom, compassion, peace, courage, and other virtues as we experience them in our own individual lives—not as transcendent realities, but as virtues we have embodied in the midst of the circumstances that confront us. Each of us can look back in our lives and see things we wish we hadn't done. We all have our own particular complement of wounds, shames, angers, guilts, and regrets. But we can also look back and see those actions, thoughts, and feelings of which we can be proud. We can look back and see the wisdom we've gained, the insights we've accrued, the good works we've achieved. We can see the times when we have been tempted to think and act in hurtful, negative ways towards others or towards ourselves and we have resisted, instead transforming the situation in positive ways. From these experiences, we can draw a sense of personal accomplishment and power, which is also part of our empersonal spirit.

To my perception, the empersonal spirit's a true spiritual force, a real emanation of energy that surrounds individuals. In the alchemy of our everyday lives, we produce a spiritual quality that is expressed as a radiance born from the strength and power of our wholeness. It emerges from our personal effort to create unobstructedness and clarity within ourselves. It's the spiritual fruit of our personal histories and biographies. Its radiance may be weak or strong, but it's there in all of us.

The empersonal spirit is just as capable of empowering a blessing as that spiritual force that comes from the transcendent. So, in my classes, we begin by learning to identify with this "personal" power. I lead the class in a series of exercises (like those you will find later in this book) designed to encourage the participants to discover and honor in themselves qualities that are valuable and worthy. And I encourage them to discover the "background radiation" of their own personal big bang, the original calling of love and joy that brought them into incarnation and lies at the heart of their lives. For when they make these discoveries, they know they have the resources, simply as human individuals, that allow them to bless. Through this sense of their empersonal spirit, they can make the identification with being a blesser.

Interestingly, part of this process of identification includes coming to terms with being part of humanity. I've discovered over my years of teaching classes on spirituality that there are people who are ashamed of the human race. They seek spiritual attunement not as an act of wholeness or integration but as a way of getting away from their humanness. This, I feel, is a problem for the spiritual community as a whole, both in the mainstream churches and in alternative spiritualities. It manifests in a variety of ways: One particularly unsettling form is the anticipation that people seem to feel for apocalyptic prophecies that promise the decimation of humanity. I've had Christian fundamentalists and New Agers alike tell me that human beings are a "disease upon the earth" and should be wiped out.

There is no question that our species has a checkered and violent history. One need only contemplate the Holocaust or current ethnic cleansings, the rapid extinction of endangered species, and the degradation of the environment—and the truly apocalyptic conditions of disease, hunger, and fear in which so many live—to know that much of human activity creates curses rather than blessings. We have reason for shame and anger.

But humanity also has a track record of creativity and accomplishment, and imperfect as we are, we're still manifestations of the Source. As I mentioned in the chapter on the Great Work, what's needed is not condemnation or escapism but a willingness to be engaged with the world and to embody the gift of the unobstructing spirit.

Our personal lives are inextricably integrated with the life of our species. If we hate humanity but try to love ourselves, we encounter a dysfunctional split as if we were trying to grow a plant by keeping its roots out of the soil so they won't get dirty. Only you know how you feel about your own humanity. In my class, we do confront this issue and encourage each other to come to terms with our humanness. Ultimately, each of us must find our own way of doing so. But the important point is that our humanness is part of our empersonal spirit. If we wish that spirit to be wholly available, then we can't cripple it by cutting it off from the collective spirit of humanity in which it has roots.

The empersonal spirit, as might be supposed, expresses the power of blessing in personal, accessible ways. I can bless you because I'm one with you; we have the same breath, the same blood, and we have both known the joys and sorrows, the triumphs and burdens, of being human. It's not an emanation from a remote deity; it's the presence of the human smile, the human touch, the human understanding, that conveys a sense of shared challenge and shared empowerment. While I may not know how to transmit a transcendental energy to you, I certainly have a sense of how to share my heart.

When I do share my heart, however, I may also have a sense that I am becoming part of something larger, something that extends beyond my personal self into a larger world of connectedness and participation. If I explore this more fully, I find myself connecting with still deeper levels of awareness and spirit. I come to the threshold of a greater, more universal self. So once we have worked in class with the spirit that arises from our embodied individuality, we then look at its expanded counterpart arising from our transpersonal nature.

Although the term *transpersonal* almost always refers to a spiritual or non-physical side of ourselves, initially at least I want to use it in a different context. The word *transpersonal* means literally "beyond the personal." We can go beyond ourselves in the direction of the transcendent, or we can go beyond ourselves towards the vast, interconnected web of life that is nature. I want us to look away from the heavens for a moment and towards the earth. In many land-based indigenous spiritualities, the way into the heavens was actually through the earth, down towards what the ancient Celts called "the stars within the earth."

The issue of finding a balance between human growth and environmental integrity is an obviously pressing modern challenge. It's certainly important to question whether we can find personal and human blessing if we are cursing the planet on which we live— the very biosphere that sustains us—with our neglect and our pollution. Can we become one with the unobstructed world if we ourselves, like a river unleashed from its usual course, become a destructive flood? These questions are ones we each must answer. But what is germane to us is the role that nature plays in the art of blessing. It's a role with several parts.

At the very least, nature reminds us that we're part of a larger holism of life. We exist in ecologies of interdependence and interconnection. And if a blessing expresses a spirit of connectedness and wholeness, where better to find that spirit played out in tangible ways than in the natural world? Being out in the natural world leads us to think and feel beyond ourselves, to recognize that we are part of a community of living things. It helps us discover ourselves.

Like some ancient nature spirit, a part of our soul dwells in the natural processes of the world. We think our soul is safely tucked away within us, but in fact it peeks out from under berry bushes and from between the branches of towering pines. It burrows into the earth with worms and rabbits, and it soars with eagles. It howls gleefully with the wind, spirals with the dust devils on a desert plain, and crystallizes in flakes of snow on a winter's morning.

How can our souls not be of the world from which we draw our physical life and our nourishment? Souls thrive where there are blessings, and nature has always been a source of blessing. How can we deny our souls participation in the wholeness of life when they are fashioned from the essence of life itself? Souls are not bound by forms but dance in the circulation of spirit. They flow with the breath and blood of God, and that breath and blood have formed and informed things beyond just ourselves.

So part of who we are—part of our power, our grace and inspiration—lies in the natural world. And we must find it if we're to be whole. Learning to cherish the world, to engage with it, is an on-going process of soul retrieval. Or perhaps it's a process of soul expansion, for if the soul is like a dove within us, surely its wings are meant to take us further than the limits of our human sensibilities.

Using our human creativity, we can produce images and experiences that delight the senses and show us things we won't experience in nature. But they are are never more than the products of human imagination. In a way, we're always looking in a mirror at ourselves. What we see can be stimulating, but it's ultimately self-referencing. We do not learn how to see beyond ourselves. What we find in nature, though, is the continually evolving and often surprising and unexpected product of another imagination altogether. We find what is not ourselves and not human, and in doing so we find ourselves and our humanity in liberating and expanding ways.

The oldest known spiritualities, collectively embraced under the increasingly ubiquitous term *shamanism,* were all land-based. They recognized that the earth itself was alive, and that it emanated a spiritual power, which was a power of life. The fact that there were energies in the land with which one could align for the blessing of oneself and one's people was a central part of those spiritualities and the practices that evolved from them. Both in the modern material worldview and in the transcendent, heaven-oriented worldview of Christianity, this understanding of the land as a source of spirit has been lost, or at least misplaced.

But as we seek to identify sources of energy to bring to our acts of blessing—and to create a more holistic sense of identity within ourselves—I feel it is important to remember the power of the land and the natural world around us. We don't have to become shamans or return to the practice of an archaic religion, although some people do take that route quite successfully. We simply need to acknowledge the radiance of life from the non-human world and open ourselves to that flow. In seeking the unobstructed spirit, we cannot stop at the boundary of the human and refuse to embrace the energy and presence of the rest of life that can share that spirit with us.

There is one other role that the earth may play. Blessing is an embodied act. We may talk about the spiritual energies and visualize these energies passing between us, but we don't bless as disembodied spirits. We bless through our eyes in how we see each other; we bless through our ears in how we listen to each other; we bless through our flesh in how we touch each other. When I bless,

I feel something in my body: a flow of energy, an exhilaration of vitality, the pressure of a force seeking release. I share it with someone or something that I perceive with my senses, including the "senses of the soul." For blessing is an act of connection, and ultimately we connect through our senses.

Blessing is not an abstraction but something concrete and specific. When I bless, I bless a person or a place or an object or a situation, each of which is tangible and has dimension and substance. None of these things may be physically present to me, but they exist in a specifically physical way somewhere in the world. I can think about them in a concrete way. This is true even if I'm sending blessings to someone who has died. I still have a specific image of them that gives them dimension and substance. They may not be corporeal, but they are also not abstract.

There is so much in our human world these days that takes us out of our bodies, away from the immediacy of our senses. We work and play in cyberspace, for example, and those who are aficionados of surfing the Net speak disparagingly of the "meat world," the world we experience offline. In both the wired world and the spiritual one, we may speak approvingly of being "out of the body," implying a state of liberation and freedom, power and limitlessness. But true power and freedom are always embodied and specific. As I said earlier, the feeling of limitlessness is not the same as being unobstructed.

When we begin to think in abstract ways and give greater value to disembodied than embodied states—a fashion that can happen in spiritual circles as easily as in cybernetic ones—the danger is that we also begin to devalue what is specific and has substance. From there it's but a short step to devalue the specific, physical person, reducing him or her to numbers, statistics, or images on a screen.

We end up devaluing each other, and in that context, blessing is not possible.

The natural world, though, is nothing but embodiment. It initiates us back into a circle of life that's not abstract at all. It draws us into our senses, into our bodies. It restores our connections with substance and specificity. It takes us to our blessing place.

Blessing carries us into the swim of life as fully as we're willing and able to go. So what better way to empower our ability to bless than to go out where life is abundant, where life is different from us and thus "transpersonal"? Where better to go than where life can restore our sense of flesh and presence so that when we bless, it's not in some abstract, tepid, disembodied, "spiritual" way but with passion and presence, vitality and life, rich and grounded with a sensuousness that connects us through our blood and breath.

Blessing is an incarnational act. It plunges us more deeply into the world in order to find the unobstructed energies at its heart. It connects us, and thereby it gives us a deeper sense of embodiment. It pushes us towards wholeness, but wholeness has a constantly expanding edge. Where, after all, does my wholeness stop? With my flesh? With my family? With my town or nation? With the grass under my feet or the forest down the road? With my daughter's ferret or the bears in the nearby mountains or the whales that migrate along our shores? Or does it not stop until it reaches the farthest galaxy at the mysterious edge of the universe? And does it stop even then?

I think not. And this brings us back to the usual meaning of the transpersonal—that which exists as spirit beyond the confines of the earth. For wholeness certainly reaches in and through earth, around the circle of life, and then beyond it as well, into the energies of a non-physical reality.

Seeking this larger wholeness can be a challenge. Understanding and working with a spiritual or non-physical reality in our culture doesn't come easily. We must navigate a course between disbelief and glamor, between the Scylla of a materialistic view that denies any reality to a spiritual dimension, and the Charybdis of the opposing view that overly emphasizes spirit in an otherworldly way at the expense—and to the detriment—of material reality.

In addition, we must also chart our course past other potential obstacles: a view of spirituality as an ancient wisdom that must be reclaimed and lived out as if the past four hundred years of scientific and industrial revolutions had never happened; a restriction of spirituality to traditional institutional religious settings that denies it a place in other activities such as commerce or science; a peculiarly modern view of spirituality as a lifestyle choice, as if spirit were an accessory; and a rather mechanical perspective that sees spirit as simply a component of ourselves along with mind, emotions, and body, as if we were Lego people and spirituality were the process of acquiring and snapping in the spirit piece.

While I want the power of my empersonal spirit to give specificity, focus and personal groundedness to my acts of blessing, I also want these acts to resonate with something larger beyond myself. That is what contact with our transpersonal spirit can accomplish. I can discover the part of me that blends with the wholeness of life and seeks the well-being and blessing of everything that shares the cosmos with me.

Making this discovery is the function of a spiritual practice. Attuning to the transpersonal side of ourselves is not something we only do as an exercise in a weekend workshop or class; if so, we'll only scratch the surface. This process is something we do daily as part of a regular discipline. How we do it depends on what works for us. It could be through prayer, meditation, worship, ritual, service, inspirational reading, talking walks, exploring nature, or even engaging in play. The ways in which people reach for the sacred and explore their own spirituality are vast.

The step of identification is to experience power within ourselves: the power of our wisdom, love, and accomplishment (the empersonal spirit) and the power of our soul (our transpersonal spirit). The power of the former connects us to the world and to each other as specific personalities; the power of the latter connects us to the sacred and to each other as part of a unity. And it is their united power that we will share with another in an act of blessing.

In the modern science of cosmology, there's a concept called the "superstring," which is a theoretical image of the fundamental formative structure within the universe. Each superstring, which exists in multiple dimensions, vibrates, and these vibrations manifest as the elemental particles from which atoms are formed. As one physicist poetically put it, the universe is formed from the "music" of superstrings (a concept, by the way, echoed in some ancient spiritual and esoteric traditions that creation emerges from sound).

I can imagine each of us metaphorically as a superstring extending from the sacred and the numinous on the one hand to the personal and the embodied on the other. We tend to divide the string into pieces—the physical, the mental, the emotional, the spiritual, and so forth—but it's still really just one string. In the step of identification (whether performed as part of a blessing or not) we think of ourselves, and in time come to know ourselves, as this superstring itself, which is neither transpersonal nor empersonal but capable of vibrating as either and both. Its unifying presence is the power within a blessing. For in the domain of the "superstrings of spirit," we are all vibrating resonantly and harmoniously together to create the music of creation's dance floor, the rhythm of the unobstructed world.

The empersonal spirit is the presence of wholeness within ourselves, and we may have to go beyond our surface images of who we are in order to find it. We're looking at that part of us which has the courage, the wisdom, and the love to be unobstructing to the world at large. To find it is to find a treasure beyond estimation.

The transpersonal spirit is the presence of wholeness we experience in relationship with the world beyond ourselves, whether the physical world of nature or the non-physical worlds of spirit. Again, we may have to go beyond our images of who we are in order to find it, even beyond our assumptions about our spiritual nature. We're finding that part of ourselves that can open to the world, that can be inclusive and embracing, and—through the power of unconditional love—can feel the spirit of interconnectedness uniting us all. We're looking at that part of us that can let the world, in all its otherness, into the center of our compassionate heart and not be afraid. To find this is also to find a great treasure.

If all we did in a spiritual practice were to discover these wondrous aspects of ourselves, it would be magical. But these two spirits of wholeness and power are mirrors of each other, complements of each other, twins. When they merge within us, as they will do because they are one "string" and the spirit they represent is the same spirit whether discovered empersonally or transpersonally, we become a person whose wholeness and unobstructedness are his or her blood and breath. Then we stand in a place of transformative service.

Of course, this step of identification need not be relegated to a technique of blessing. It's a process we can engage in anytime simply for the sake of the inner knowledge and attunement it can bring. To do so enlarges us as a heart so that we beat more strongly not only when undertaking the exercise of a blessing but all the time. We increase the circulation of spirit around ourselves as a natural condition, not just as a special event. Then we truly become a blessing for our world.

Fourteen

OPENING

When I gave my first blessing, I fortunately did two things that allowed it to happen. The first was that I didn't back away, even though, as I've described, the thought of doing so was certainly in my mind. Instead, buoyed by the faith of the woman from my audience, I said to myself that I could do it. Just acknowledging that gave me a sense of energy and presence. It was my equivalent of the first step: identification.

However, at that point I still didn't know how to go about blessing. But I took the second step: I opened myself to her and to spirit. I opened myself to the situation with all its risk and potential. In effect, I surrendered to what wanted or needed to happen and didn't project my own will (or fears) upon the moment. Out of that openness came a clear sense of what to do. I became a partner with the woman and with the spirit that was flowing around us, within us and through us.

The blessing emerged from that partnership and from the openness that allowed it to form.

So opening is the second step. In some ways it's more important than the first one. Standing in the power of our spiritual identity, we might feel ready to leap in and do something on behalf of the situation. Being open, though, makes us pause. It's an acknowledgment that true power is grounded in humility. Instead of moving forward, we become receptive, ready to be informed or shaped by the situation itself. And it's from this openness that the quality of partnership arises.

Some people have no qualms at all about seeing themselves as sources of power, energy, or blessing for others. For them, the temptation to simply project their own will into a situation to control what is happening, and then call it a blessing, is always there. Even if we're not like the man who tried to "bless" me at the dinner party, we have such an ingrained perspective of being the subject who will act upon an object, that we can easily project without realizing it. Combine this with many people's natural desire to fix things for others, and you can appreciate the challenge of being caught up in the identity of a powerful source without being open to the spirit of the person we seek to serve, not to mention the spirit of the Source itself.

I speak from experience here, for I'm one of those people who wants to fix things. A phrase that has fallen from my lips enough times that a great pile of them lies heaped about my hips is "If only I had a magic wand . . ." You know the rest: I'd wave it and fix it, change it, make it better, and generally impose my sense of how things should be upon the world at large.

Fortunately, blessing is not a magic wand. It's something more akin to the old adage "If you give a man a fish, you feed him for a night, but if you teach him to fish, he can feed himself forever." A blessing may meet a particular need or solve a particular problem, but that's not its greatest function. The real power of a blessing is that it awakens us to the power of spirit. A blessing is an energizing of our sense of the sacred; the more we attune ourselves to that presence, particularly by practicing the art of blessing itself, the more we live in its midst. Spiritually, we learn to fish rather than just have God hand us a holy mackerel now and then.

To properly bless, I needed to rise above being Mr. Fixit. I could summon every bit of my inner power and feel confident that I was fully ready to give a blessing; my empersonal spirit could be flashing with empathy and earthly wisdom; and my transpersonal spirit could be dancing with numinousness and heavenly panache. But if I wasn't open to serve the situation, if I wasn't open to hearing what the situation had to tell me, if I wasn't open to a partnership, well, I could spiritually snap, crackle, and pop all day and nothing meaningful would happen. There would be no connection, no presence, no flow.

No blessing.

I realized I needed to be open, without conditions, in order to connect properly with the person, object, place, or situation that was the other half of the blessing equation, the "blessee" to my "blesser"—honoring and receiving their contribution to the blessing as well as my own. Inwardly, I had to bow in respect and love before that which provided the privilege of offering a blessing and thereby enabled me to participate in a mutual invocation of spirit. A circuit had to be completed for a flow to take place. And for this, I needed to be open to receiving as well as to giving. I could not just be the doer, the fixer, the one with the power.

Without that circulation between us, what happened would not to my mind have been a blessing, even if the recipient might feel it had been. At best it would be a kindness or a helpful transmission of energy; at worst, it would be a projection of my own images and needs, such as the need to be needed or the need to be a good fixer. So, having generated power in the first step, in the second we're asked to set it to one side and just listen and attune to the other. In this way, we create an open space in which our power, energy, presence (whatever we wish to name it), can be appropriately shaped by the situation and not by our own perceptions alone.

This openness to be guided and informed by more than just our own will is obviously important if we're intending to bless a living being with a will and perspectives of his or her own. Our objective in blessing is to serve, not to impose. But openness is also important if we're blessing something inanimate, for in the greater scheme of things, as all shamans and mystics have known throughout history, everything is alive in one way or another with the radiance of the divine. Everything, from the smallest pebble to the tallest tree, from the swiftest gazelle to the slowest turtle, and from the amoeba on the pond scum to the virus that makes us sneeze (so we can be blessed, of course), has an interiority in which the sacred dwells.

Blessing is always a link with that interiority, the sacred space within all beings, and we want to make that link with respect and honor as well as with love and consideration. I wouldn't dream of trampling with muddy spiked soccer shoes through a sanctuary you held to be holy; equally, I wouldn't wish to trample with opinionated feet and hobnailed projections through the sacred space that's the holiness within each creature and each thing.

The act of opening is one of giving yourself freely to the spirit in that interiority and to the highest good seeking to emerge from whomever or whatever you're blessing. It's cultivating an attitude of doing no harm. Having generated a sense of inner power, it's offering that power up to be part of an act of service, like someone who has earned great wealth and then placed it at the disposal of a worthy cause.

The act of opening is like becoming part of a team: You have your part to contribute, but however central or vital it may be, it's not the only part that's needed. So you must create a space for all the parts to be received, for all the voices to be heard. Whatever spirit of openness and awareness you would bring to a situation in order to do this, that's the spirit you need to bring to the art of blessing.

Opening is an act of being receptive: When we bring spirit into play for another, we also bring it into play for ourselves. Through our opening, we provide a portal for spirit to enter and bless our lives too. We cannot avoid being a participant—a receiver, too—if we're truly giving a blessing and not just projecting energy.

This wouldn't seem to be a problem. Just the opposite: Most of us would probably feel that the more blessings God or anyone else wants to bring into our lives, the better. Bring 'em on, we're ready!

But here we may be confusing a blessing with a kindness. A kindness gives us something, but a blessing urges us to be something, which for most of us means changing in some way. A blessing lets loose a spiritual presence that can promote and foster change, a power of rearrangement in our domain. It's as if we've opened the door to our house and a specialist in interior redecoration has moved in with us. Scary thought!

Being the receiver of an act of goodness and spiritual power isn't always the most comfortable place to be for other reasons too. As the person doing the blessing, I may have trouble receiving whatever "fringe benefits" may accrue as spirit enters my life more fully. Or, as the blessee, I may have trouble admitting I need help. My sense of self-reliance and independence may be challenged. I can feel obligated, in debt, disempowered—even though blessings are gifts, not transactions.

This was a big issue in my class on blessing. The exercises we did to put us in touch with our receptivity and openness were generally the most difficult, particularly for the men in whom they raised troubling feelings of vulnerability and loss of power. This is no surprise, really, for in our culture women have much more experience at being on the receiving end than do men.

To be blessed is to be drawn into the larger circulation of spirit: That, to my mind, is what makes the act or experience a blessing. But that means opening my boundaries to something larger than myself. It means surrendering to "go with the flow," and with that can come a feeling of loss of control. As long as the blessing is simply a kindness, like giving me money when I need it or helping me out in some way, that's easier to handle, but when the blessing comes from a deeper place, spirit is in my face. I feel myself touching the unobstructed world. If only for a moment, I'm in contact with a much larger self whose view of things is not constricted by or even concerned with the usual issues and perspectives, problems, and desires that so fill and shape my personality's point of view.

Any brush with spirit can change us in some way; by its very nature, it seeks to unite us with all our parts, to draw us from being just a segment to being the whole "superstring" of our being. It's precisely for this reason that we undertake a spiritual practice. But that doesn't mean it's easy, particularly when we're still most comfortable and familiar with leading the life of a fragment, enjoying and rewarding some parts of ourselves and tucking the other parts away where we don't have to deal with them (or so we think).

Asking for a blessing can take every bit as much courage as stepping forward to give one.

On the other hand, much of the difficulty and vulnerability a person may fear exists more in the anticipation than in the reality. For where spirit is concerned, we're empowered even as we become vulnerable. It's the paradox of spiritual practice that when we have most given ourselves away, that's when we truly find ourselves, and it's when we have made ourselves most open that we're filled with presence.

As the second step in the art of blessing, opening can confront us with as many challenges as does identification. But like the latter, this process is not restricted to being just part of a technique. It's a whole attitude towards life, and can be a continuous practice quite apart from blessing. As we work in various areas of our lives to explore openness and to create relationships, we're building the skills and wisdom we need to engage with others with a receptive and attentive heart. As we do that, no matter how powerful we may be, we learn to be harmless in the presence of others and to act from a shared connectedness for the highest good of all. Whether we're intending to perform a blessing or not, such actions are the seeds from which all blessings grow.

Fifteen

THE BLESSING
PLACE

There have been occasions when I've given a lecture on Sunday mornings at the Episcopal Cathedral of St. John the Divine in New York City. I did so as part of the high ritual of the worship service, so there was always pomp and ceremony involved. I would join the priests and other participants in a garbing room where we donned the robes appropriate to the roles we were to play in the morning's events. Then, with the choir singing and incense censers putting forth billowing clouds of fragrant smoke, we would walk in procession solemnly up an aisle, around behind the high altar, and out again on the other side to arrive at our respective places.

I'm usually a most informal speaker, disdaining lecterns and wanting to be as close to my audience as is practical. There certainly is no particular "uniform" that I wear. I'm lucky if my socks match! But I can understand the tradition of garbing in order to perform a particular spiritual role. For when I would pull the voluminous red and black scholar's robes over my head before processing into the cathedral, I could feel a perceptible shift in my sense of identity. I felt empowered to do what I was about to do, which was to speak to the congregation on matters spiritual and earthly. I was no longer only David. I was now the Scholar.

What I call the blessing place is like those robes. It's a state of mind that we can put on, and when we do, we feel empowered to bless. We're standing on the unobstructed dance floor; we're in the presence of the Source; we're attuned to the love, power, and connectedness of spirit; we're empersonally and transpersonally uplifted; we're open and receptive.

In short, we're garbed in our identity as a blesser.

We enter this inner blessing place as we synthesize the feelings of identity and power from the first step with the receptivity and openness of the second step. It's a state of familiarity with who we are and what we feel like when we're in the flow of giving a blessing.

This is a particular state of mind that will be unique to each of us and, in a way, unique to each blessing. I cannot describe just what this will feel like to you; you need to discover it through practice. In my class, I have participants pay attention to what happens as they complete the first two steps of identification and opening and as they synthesize them into a single, focused yet open state of mind. I ask them to identify and become familiar with that state of mind, the psychospiritual condition each of them creates in order to perform a blessing. For convenience, I call this their blessing place. Then, through practicing blessing over and over, I ask them to discern what remains constant in their experience of that state of mind and what changes as the situation in which they are giving a blessing changes.

After a short time, they no longer need to go through the first two steps, except perhaps as part of a larger spiritual process in which self-reflection, personal empowerment, and opening compassionately to others all play a role. I simply ask them to enter the state of mind in which they can give a blessing—to step into their internal blessing place and garb themselves in the robes of the Blesser.

The blessing place emerges as a particular experience of self-oriented towards a particular kind of engagement with the world, which is the act of blessing. What I call the steps of identification and opening support that emergence, but they are not the only ways to do so. A person can come to their blessing place through a variety of means; it may, in fact, simply arise very spontaneously from their own spiritual experiences. Likewise, this state of mind continues to evolve from experience. From every act of blessing we can learn more about who we are and what we're doing in practicing this art, and as we do, our blessing place changes and grows. It also becomes easier to slip into, a bit like having a Superman uniform on under our Clark Kent clothes.

There are other important ways to nourish this state of mind. Because it's fundamentally an expression of our spirituality and our humanness, anything we do that enhances either is going to enrich our blessing place as well. Whatever we do that develops our sense of accomplishment, our skills, our knowledge, our self-esteem, and generally our growth as individuals positively affects and deepens our blessing place. Whatever we do physically, mentally, or emotionally that heightens our vitality and benefits our health also energizes this state of mind. Likewise, whatever we do through prayer, meditation, worship, celebration, ritual, or other forms of spirituality makes our blessing place more accessible and powerful as well.

The point is to do things that allow us to experience blessings. I don't necessarily mean going to someone and asking to be blessed. I mean going to places and participating in activities that make us feel embraced by blessings.

The experiences that provide this will naturally vary from person to person. For some it may be through appreciating the creative human spirit present in architecture, art, literature, music, dance, and theater. Others may be uplifted by contemplating the scientific and technological achievements of humanity, enjoying what one writer, Samuel C. Florman, called the "existential pleasures of engineering." It might also mean participating in one's community and in the companionship and society of others. In particular, many people find themselves being blessed when they are taking part in services that bless others.

Still others, and this would probably include most people, find blessings through engaging with nature, in activities ranging from working in a garden to scaling Mt. Everest or trekking along the Appalachian Trail. I've already discussed how the natural world can put us in touch both with our transpersonal selves and with our embodiedness, essential parts of the art of blessing. But as far as the enrichment of our blessing place, what I have in mind is nothing more than just enjoying nature and marinating in its spaciousness and vitality.

What's most important is that I find ways to bless myself. It's harder to enter a blessing state of mind for another when I'm feeling deprived of blessings myself. Drawing on the strength of our empersonal spirit is one way of dealing with this, but it doesn't replace the sheer liberation of being loving and kind towards ourselves.

By blessing ourselves, I don't necessarily mean simply doing things that bring us pleasure and happiness. Happiness and pleasure are wonderful things, to be sure, and we should seek them out in appropriate ways. However, they don't necessarily take us into the unobstructed places of our being, nor do they necessarily foster in us a greater inner spaciousness or a sense of connectedness to a larger wholeness. Sometimes, in fact, the pursuit of purely personal pleasures takes us in the opposite direction.

By blessing, I mean giving ourselves those times and experiences in which we can feel truly spacious and through which we learn and grow, expanding our hearts and minds and developing confidence in ourselves through accomplishments. I mean encouraging unobstructedness by rooting out those attitudes, feelings, and images that impede us, whether through fear, intolerance, or some other inner state that comes between us and our potentials, between us and our world. I mean giving ourselves experiences that enlarge us, opening new connections between ourselves and others or giving us increased vitality and energy with which to engage the world. Some of these activities may not be pleasurable at first, like exercise or pushing through shyness to encounter others more fully. But they can all be blessings.

Mostly, I ask you to seek out joy. Joy is not the same thing as happiness. Happiness is so often dependent upon the externals in our lives, upon the actions of others and the events that befall us. But joy is not a product of anything else; it's a creative power and a vital energy in its own right. Indeed, I believe it lies at the heart of creativity, and it certainly is part of the spirit of blessing, for joy is the essence of the unobstructed world. It is itself a spaciousness, and it opens us up to the universe and its underlying Source as nothing else can.

You can't be on a serious spiritual path without discovering the joy of the sacred. It's like the pulse of all things. St. John wrote that in the beginning was the Word. But in experiencing the joy at the heart of life, I could equally say that in the beginning was the Laugh, and that all things were shaped not only from Light but from the Delight that erupted from that creative laughter. Even in my darkest moments, I can still feel that primal ecstasy and joy moving through my life as it does through the whole of creation. In this way, I remember what is at my core, alive in that primal act from which all things come.

A soldier takes on the duty of putting himself in harm's way to serve and protect his loved ones and his country. A person on a spiritual path—certainly a person on the path of blessing—similarly needs to put himself or herself in "joy's way." For we don't create joy the same way we create happiness; instead, we discover it by making ourselves available to it, by getting in its path. It exists within us as a natural part of the superstring we are, and we can imbibe it from our world as well. Happiness is a feeling, but joy is a spirit, and as such, it's transmitted through resonance. We find it by being where it is. We find it by opening up and letting it enter. We find it by drawing it out from within ourselves to give to others. For joy, like love, increases as we give it away.

Through joy, through learning and growing, through blessing ourselves, and through giving blessings in return, we nourish and strengthen our blessing place. In the process we discover that this state of mind isn't just one in which we feel ready and capable of blessing. It's one in which we feel blessed ourselves.

It could not be otherwise. What kind of blessing can we give another if we don't feel blessed ourselves? We give what we are, who we are. A blessing is not a package we receive, like a UPS person, and pass on to someone else. *We* are the package. Ultimately, we bless by inviting another into our blessing place, into the spirit and state of mind of being blessed that we've been cultivating ourselves. We bless by sharing a presence, and we are, in part at least, that presence.

As we realize this, we don't so much practice the art of blessing as we become it. Then all places become our blessing place.

Sixteen

THE ART OF
BLESSING

G ive me a blessing.

Yes, I will . . . but how?

In the movie *The Candidate,* Robert Redford plays a young lawyer who has just won a tough electoral campaign for national office. As his followers are jubilantly rejoicing in the auditorium where he gave a victory speech, his campaign manager—whose political savvy and techniques had been greatly responsible for the victory— finds the candidate sitting alone in a small storeroom near the stage. When he asks him what's wrong, Redford looks up with a stricken look on his face and says, "What do we do now?"

Like the candidate, once we're in our inner blessing place, whether we came to that state of mind through the route I've described or in another way, we, too, might look around and say, "What do we do now?"

What do we do physically, if anything? What do we do mentally or spiritually? How do we take the fourth step: performing the actual blessing?

Do we pray? Do we lay our hands upon the person or object to be blessed? Do we visualize energy streaming from us to them? Do we picture a field of blessing, like an aura of light, around ourselves, which we then enlarge to enfold the blessee? Do we do a ritual? Do we ask God to do it for us? Which of these is the right way?

I've known many spiritual healers over the years who are very effective at what they do. While they have things in common, each of them has his or her own way of working as well as of describing what they're doing and what's happening as they do it. But no two descriptions are exactly alike. It's what makes the whole field of inner work or energy work so frustrating for people who are used to a world in which things happen in a definite way upon which everyone can agree. In this sense, people who work with subtle energies are like the proverbial blind men groping an elephant: They all have their hands on the critter, but they're each describing a different part of it.

What's interesting, though, is that, generally speaking, no matter what part we have hold of, we can still get the elephant to cooperate with us. What seems most critical is not which part of the elephant we're imagining (I bless with an ear, you bless with a trunk) but our intent. The image is simply a way of communicating an intent, and intentionality itself is what moves the energies, fields, presences, or whatever in appropriate ways. In fact, intentionality may be the substance, or part of the substance, of the phenomena we usually call "energy."

In any case, I've used different methods, from laying on of hands to imagining a stream of spirit flowing from my heart to another, and from prayer to visualizing the presence of my blessing place enlarging and embracing the situation or the person I am blessing. They all work. Sometimes one method works better than another, depending on the situation. The only way to know that is by intuitively opening to the situation (that's part of the opening step) and seeing if any images or feelings arise that can guide you. Over time you'll begin to get a feel for the best way to approach a situation, a sensitivity that develops when you practice any craft or art.

Which brings me to a key point: Blessing really is an art, not a science. A scientist prizes detachment and objectivity (even though the full attainment of either is probably a myth), but for an artist, the subjective element is key. Blessing, like art, is a sensuous, subjective act arising from who we are; our inner nature, with its unique ways of seeing and relating to the world, cannot be divorced from the process.

Just as it is for any other art, imagination is an important part of blessing. In our culture, we tend to equate imagination with fantasy or unreality. But as a spiritual tool, it's better to think of it as the capacity to shape images in a way that focuses intentionality. So imagining an energy of blessing streaming from my hands or my heart to you may not be a scientific description of what's happening, but it tells a story that connects me to you in love and intentionality. And it's love and intentionality that do the work.

Using your imagination in this way can be challenging at first, for in our culture we're trained, implicitly or explicitly, to want to know the right way to do things and, if possible, to understand just what we're doing. But consider how many things in our lives we do use and depend on which we may not understand. I've only a rudimentary knowledge of how my computer works, but I'm more than happy to use it to write this book. For that matter, no one knows just what consciousness is or how it relates to the brain (no matter what a particular neuroscientist might say); yet, we go happily and consciously about our lives every day, doing what we need to do. We love, we hope, we imagine, we create, we envision and shape things that have never been known or seen before, and in the process, it doesn't matter at all that we don't know just how exactly we do these things. We just do them, and whole new worlds open up before us.

Later in this book, I offer some examples of how one might go about doing a particular kind of blessing. But the first principle underlying all blessings is that we engage our love, our sensitivity, and our imaginations from within our blessing place, from within the state of mind and being of being blessed. Love connects us, sensitivity gives us an awareness of how to proceed, and imagination gives us the images to focus our intentionality and to act.

Beyond any technique, blessing is akin to remembering. A good friend and colleague of mine, Dr. Michael Lipson, made this point during a discussion we had on this issue. He said that by opening to the mere possibility of blessing, we being to remember our involvement in the wider universe. We remember our connection to all that is seen and unseen. The spirit of this wider cosmos then comes nearer to us and flows into our interactions together as if invited by our act of trust and our willingness to pass on the gift of this remembrance.

It's good not to be set in how we imagine a blessing should be done. A blessing can be offered as part of an elaborate formal ritual, as in a marriage ceremony or as when my children were baptized in the Cathedral of St. John the Divine. But I've also seen people feel blessed by as little as a glance from another person or by a loving touch. I've seen people blessed in churches, and I've seen people blessed in concerts or even in movie theaters. Who can say just what event or setting will open a person up to experiencing the unobstructed world?

In fact, an act of blessing need not look like anything we might normally think of as a blessing. In the news recently, I watched a report on a factory in which the CEO of the company gave his workers freedom to completely change and redesign the factory floor itself, as well as how they did their work. He wanted his company to "evolve" like an organism "from the bottom up." He even stipulated that he didn't need to know specifically what they were doing or how they were doing it, as long as they got their job done. He gave them his complete trust.

Over the course of three years, the workers made more than four thousand changes, totally altering how they did their work and the environment in which they did it, making the whole process more human-oriented than machine-oriented. As a result, the workers felt more energy, more freedom, more creativity, and more joy in their work. Productivity more than doubled and the company's profits more than tripled. In effect, this CEO blessed his workers by liberating them, empowering them, and opening a space for them to create a factory that was several steps closer to embodying the spirit of the unobstructed world than it had been before. While there was no overtly spiritual element to this process, the end result was profoundly spiritual.

In my classes, I let people experiment with how to convey a blessing. They do it silently, with prayer, or with a laying on of hands, assuming the person they are blessing is comfortable with that. In my own case, I'm partly deaf, with practically no sense of smell and a consequently diminished sense of taste, so touch becomes an important sense that I use in connecting to my world. Therefore, if someone comes to me for a blessing, I like to lay my hands upon them or hold their hands, assuming, as I said above, that they are willing.

Another important way to bless is through how we see a person. By this I mean not only how we physically see them but how we interpretively see them, how we think of them in our minds and hearts. What expectations or images are we projecting upon them? As my two daughters grow older, I become increasingly aware—particularly in the case of Kaitlin, who is twelve—of the many limiting images they must navigate in order to be seen as who they are. Social and psychological studies have shown how often young women entering their teens lose their own powerful inner voices because of the projections and expectations that our society places on them.

The way we see people can also place obstructions in their way; the whole history of racial and religious intolerance is a testament to this. But the reverse is also true. When we see someone in unobstructed ways, we empower them. They can rise to fill the spaciousness of our perceptions. They've been blessed by how we see and think of them.

How we see the world is an important tool for blessing, particularly when we look from within our blessing place.

Many times, there's no overtly physical act that can transmit a blessing. The person or situation we're blessing may be far away. Or, as in the case I described of being in a store or place where I'd like to offer a blessing, perhaps to clarify some turbulent or stuck energies, unobtrusiveness can be important. At such times we should remember that we can touch our world inwardly through thought, attitude, perception, projection, and through the extension of our inner energies. As I said in a previous chapter, I don't have to do anything physically to beat more strongly as an inner heart and increase the circulation of love and spirit in an area. And if I'm standing in my blessing place, feeling blessed myself, then I can silently and naturally extend that presence out to all that I see. And when I do, it's my experience that there is a response that comes back, enhancing the power and blessing that I feel in a loop of mutual feedback and energy exchange. Blessing manifests in the relationship I feel with what is around me.

Besides, often the physical component of a blessing is only there to emphasize the contact, to support the imaginative action, or even just for showmanship. And when we think about it, in most cases what really transmits a spiritual or living energy between people are qualities such as love, respect, mindfulness, appreciation, goodwill, empathy, and a mentoring spirit.

As I've said in many ways, blessing is a relationship. To see blessing as an energy and ourselves as its source is to risk short-circuiting the process within our own projections—or because of the projections of others. Sometimes I've been asked to give blessings, and although I try my best, I feel no outward flow, no connection being made. The reason is that the others involved see themselves only as recipients or even worse, as an audience observing my "performance" as a blesser.

To offset this, I usually turn blessings into a group affair if possible. In the words I speak and the actions I take, I get everyone who is present involved, inviting them to offer their blessings and spirit as well, or to physically take part (sometimes simply by having everyone hold hands).

Sometimes people complain that this dissipates the energy of the blessing because it lacks a central celebrant or not everyone is fully participating, and sometimes this criticism is correct. But more often than not, what I and others experience is an increase in the presence and power of the blessing. By opening the act of blessing, making it co-creative rather than just an invocation or a projection from a single source, it becomes more an expression of that wholeness and connectedness that lies at the heart of a blessing's power. And even if some of the focus is lost, it often provides an opportunity for people who have never done so to give a blessing and to experience what that is like. And I always count that as a plus.

Which brings up an interesting question: Are all blessings equal? For that matter, are all blessers equal?

For me this is a trick question, the answer to which is yes . . . and no. Certainly, as in any art, a person who practices will develop a proficiency that won't be there for someone who does not. If I think of a blessing as a knock at a door, inviting us to open to the experience of a larger wholeness and the spirit of the unobstructed world, some knocks are louder than others and some push the door open a little more widely. People who have a clear spiritual practice and live more fully and consistently in the presence of the Source will inhabit a blessing place that can powerfully induct a sense of that presence. They can convey a blessing more easily and quickly than might someone who has little feeling for spiritual realities or has little contact with the presence of spirit either in themselves or in the world. (And we should remember here that just because a person seems to manifest a great deal of subtle energy, this says nothing about their spirituality or their capacity to bless. A person may have the inner energy with which to powerfully "zap" another, but not all zappings are blessings.)

I remember talking with one spiritual healer who said she'd done so many healings over the years—often several a day, with each one filling her with a healing energy—that now she was imbued with that energy and could manifest it anytime she needed. In effect, she'd marinated herself in the juices of spiritual healing until she was soaked through with their flavor. And I didn't doubt her, for there was indeed about her a rich sense of a healing force.

The art of blessing is like that too.

The more you practice the attitude and the act of blessing, the more you inhabit your blessing place as your natural place to be. Then blessings can happen around you without you necessarily having to set anything into motion, or even being aware of it. You become a node around which synchronicities manifest, a beating heart around which the circulation of spirit is quickened. This doesn't necessarily make you more enlightened, holy, or spiritual than anyone else, but it does give you more of a presence of blessing.

I've certainly known people like that, outwardly quite ordinary people not necessarily known to be spiritual teachers or leaders, but around whom blessings just seem to happen. Indeed, everyone at one time or another can spontaneously step into a blessing place of their own, if only for a short time, and when they do, blessings can manifest.

However, the sacred is not limited in any way by the state of our proficiency or by our practice at blessing or lack of it. The characteristics of the blesser are never constrictions upon the infinite. If love is there in any degree—if there's the slightest intentionality directed towards the well-being of another—then no matter how soft the knock or how tiny the crack between the door and the wall, the Source will respond. It will joyously fling wide the door and dance you out onto the infinite, unobstructed dance floor.

A person need not know anything about blessing. He or she certainly doesn't need to know anything about terms like *empersonal spirit, transpersonal spirit, unobstructed world, blessing place,* or the four steps I've described. Without knowing any of these things, he or she can still be a magnificent practitioner of this art. Happily, spirit transcends all techniques and simply flows wherever there is love, wherever there is a willingness to act on behalf of another so that person's life is eased and made more graceful, and their way made clear and more joyous before them.

GIVE ME A BLESSING.

Yes, I will . . . but how?

Any way you like. Any way you can. Just bless yourself and let the spirit that responds in your heart show you the way to go from there.

Seventeen

A RADIANCE
OF BLESSINGS

When my friend and colleague Dr. Brugh Joy signs a letter or autographs a book, he often does so with the phrase, "With a Radiance of Blessings!"

It's a lovely image. It suggests the multiplicity of ways in which blessings can manifest in our lives, the multiplicity of ways in which we can manifest them for others. And for me, it expresses the delight and joy in doing so.

So, with gratitude to you for engaging with me in this book, I offer the same thought in return.

In your life
and the lives of all about you,
may there always be
A Radiance of Blessings.

PART III

A BLESSING
WORKBOOK

Blessing is not a technique or a recipe to
follow but a creative and loving act of
standing in the blessing of your own life
and configuring yourself to the moment.

EXERCISES IN THE ART
OF BLESSING

EXAMPLES OF BLESSINGS

EXERCISES IN THE ART
OF BLESSING

INTRODUCTION

The following exercises offer an opportunity to engage in simple
processes of attunement and reflection, not unlike prayer or
meditation, in order to give you a concrete experience of the art of
blessing. They are not cast in stone, so you should feel free to adapt
them to your needs or even replace them if you come up with more
appropriate substitutes. Each is intended to give you an experience
of a state of mind or help you cultivate a particular perspective. If
you understand that objective, then you can also work on other
ways of bringing it about. In fact, I would encourage this!

One way to use these exercises is to record them on a tape
recorder and then play the tape back so you can follow along with-

out having to fuss with a book in your hand. Alternatively, you can have a friend read them to you. The key is to have quiet, uninterrupted time to concentrate on the attunement process.

Always have a notebook or journal handy to record what happened to you during the exercise. Keep two distinct sections. In one, write down whatever experiences, impressions, sensations, thoughts, feelings, or images arose as precisely and fully as you can. Then, in a separate section, write down your interpretations and evaluations of those experiences if you can or if you wish. I suggest keeping these sections separate because your interpretation and understanding of what happened may change or expand as you have time for further reflection or gain more experience.

These exercises are not intended to be therapeutic or to take the place either of a disciplined spiritual practice or of any therapy with which you may be engaged. Indeed, if you're studying with a teacher or working with a therapist, you may wish to show these exercises to him or her to ensure that they won't interfere with anything you're doing with them. I can't imagine that they would, but you never know.

At the least, it's good to be conscious that anytime a person seeks to know themselves in a fuller way—or to engage with the deeper forces of the psyche and the soul—thoughts, feelings, and experiences may arise that can be surprising, bewildering, or even challenging. The journey into oneself is never to be taken lightly.

I always recommend that a person embarking on such a journey do so with a friend who can be a source of empathetic, honest, and compassionate reflection upon the process. This person doesn't have to be a professional, but simply a buddy who can support you in your process. The buddy system is important when one goes hiking in wilderness back country, and it works equally well when venturing into what for many of us may be the wilderness—or at least the unfamiliar territory—of our own souls.

On the other hand, and I feel this is very important, we should never fear the journey into our selves. There are wonders and splendors, power and insights, to be found there; it is the route into the unobstructed world and into the presence of the sacred. It is the way into our own wholeness. But as with any journey, it's good to bring a sense of perspective and humor. And it's always nice to travel with another.

Most of these exercises evolved in a group context. Each person did the exercise individually and then, after writing down whatever he or she might have experienced, shared those experiences with two or three other people who could offer both their reflections and their own experiences in return. In particular the exercises that involve two people blessing each other, then exchanging feedback, are, as you might expect, difficult to do on your own. Split personalities are not encouraged! So you might like to gather a group together to study this text and do the exercises together, or, of course, you can always attend one of my classes on the Art of Blessing!

However, if you cannot find anyone with whom to share your experience, your journal can provide another kind of ongoing feedback and evolving reflection.

When doing any kind of spiritual work, you may run into inner resistance. The mind wanders, the body gets restless, your attention disperses, your intent becomes less clear. This is not at all unusual. Doing inner work almost always challenges the status quo. It offers the potential of opening us up to new perspectives, challenging us to change and even overthrow long-established habits and opinions. That can certainly create some reluctance to proceed. Inner work also exercises mental, emotional, and imaginative muscles you may not be used to using. It requires a particular kind of attentiveness and the gentle holding of a clear focus. It is real work, which takes energy. You may resist it in the same way you might resist starting a regimen of exercise after being idle for some time. The muscles protest at being used in new or strenuous ways.

Of course, over time and with practice and persistence, this will change. But just as I may have to push through resistance to getting up on a cold, dark, rainy winter morning in Seattle to take my daily walk, so I may have to push through resistance I encounter in doing my inner work.

There are many ways to do this. The ones that work best for me are the most gentle and non-coercive. In inner work, the phrase "No pain, no gain" is not true. You want to work with yourself, not against yourself. The key is not dictatorial control over your thoughts and feelings but engaging in a dance that may weave this way and that but still keeps in time with the inner music of your intent. For instance, in doing any of these exercises, keep clearly in mind just what the objective is and what you are seeking to accomplish. Then if your mind wanders or you get restless, don't fight it. Go with the restless energy but gently turn it back to your objective. Remember why you are doing what you are doing and draw your attention back to your intention.

On the other hand, there may be good reasons for any resistance you may feel. You may be too tired to do the work right then. You may need to rest and relax first, or you may need to eat something. Inner and outer work can both be stymied by low blood sugar. Sometimes you need to shift the mode of your work. There are times when I simply cannot sit and meditate. I physically need to move. So I meditate while taking a walk. Indeed, some of my best

inner work has been done while strolling briskly about the neighborhood or out in the woods.

And resistance can also be a warning, a signal to slow down or
stop your inner work for a time, perhaps because you are invoking
more energy and change than your life situation can integrate at the
moment. Most importantly, if at any time in working with these exercises on your own you feel distress or feel that you're engaging
more than you can handle at that moment, simply stop. Don't do
them anymore for awhile. Turn your attention to other parts of your
life that are refreshing, practical, and engaging. Your inner self won't
mind. The life of the soul is always there, ready to be explored and
integrated, but until we're ready, there's more than enough in our
outer lives to learn from, to challenge us, and to enrich and bless us
as well.

Just what a feeling of resistance may mean for you is for you to
determine. Indeed, learning how to discern the kind of resistance
you are experiencing—from simple inertia and unfamiliarity to an
outright warning to stop until you are more developed and ready—
and whether or not to push through it or accept it and stop, is itself
an important part of spiritual work. Use common sense, just as you
would if you were dealing with physical exercise. Some tasks are
within your capability, others require some preparation but are still
possible, and some are beyond you until you build up your muscles
and stamina. It's basically up to you to know yourself honestly and
well enough to discern which is which.

All of these exercises, however, are fairly simple. I have used
them successfully many times in workshops and classes with people of widely differing familiarity and skill at doing inner work. They
are designed to be gentle and as much as possible to incorporate a

sense of naturalness and integration with your everyday life. This is in keeping with the idea that blessing itself is not a Herculean spiritual task but a natural expression of our capacity to connect with another and to share the love and compassion that is in our hearts.

Preceding each of the following exercises, I offer a brief commentary to put the exercise in context or to provide some specific information that I felt didn't fit in the main text of the book. Hopefully, this will enable you to do the exercise more mindfully and with greater understanding of what you wish to achieve. Then if you feel you'd like to change the exercise in some way, you can do so knowing where the exercise is intended to take you and what its effect should be.

In doing these exercises, find yourself a place and time in which you won't be interrupted. I suggest sitting comfortably in a chair. If you do the exercises lying down, you'll have to be careful not to fall asleep. Each exercise should take no more than thirty minutes. I have indicated places where you should pause to take some time to reflect and pay attention to whatever is happening at that moment. How long you pause is up to you, though in my classes we average about three minutes, depending on the nature of the exercise itself. Some moments of reflection should last longer or need to last longer than others. However long you take, it should be long enough to let you honestly reflect on what's happening, but not so long that you lose the thread of what you're doing. Experience will help you here.

Although you can obviously move at your own pace, to begin with I recommend doing no more than two exercises in one day, and preferably only one unless you're familiar and practiced with this kind of inner work. This is to allow time for you to assimilate what you've done. Think of it as eating a meal: You want to have some digestion time afterwards. Rushing through the exercises one after the other simply to finish them does not allow the process to deepen. Your experience may remain superficial. And, like rushing through a meal, indigestion and confusion may result.

Feel free to do each exercise as many times as you wish or feel is necessary. Likewise, there's no reason why you cannot go back and repeat something you've done before while working on a later exercise. In fact, some of them require it and it will be so stated in the instructions. The order of the exercises is deliberate. In some cases, earlier exercises provide a foundation for later ones; in other cases, I've presented the exercises to correspond with the order in which their associated concepts are presented in the main text.

If you wish to begin each exercise with a prayer or an invocation of the sacred or of those spiritual forces with whom you feel aligned, please feel free to do so. I have not provided any particular invocations because people have different beliefs and practices in this regard; in general, you want to consecrate or dedicate the time and space in which you do these exercises to your highest good and to the highest good of any and all who may also be present or who may be affected through their connections with you. Otherwise, beyond suggesting you have a quiet and uninterrupted space, I leave it to you to create whatever environment best suits you or feels most comfortable.

You should always do whatever helps you to feel safe, including not doing the exercises if you're feeling anxious. There's nothing in these exercises that's dangerous, but popular fiction and movies have populated the inner worlds with all kinds of nasty critters, leaving many people with a sense of unease when it comes to working with the subtler side of life. Do whatever you wish through prayer or any other means to counteract this unease. From years of experience, I can say that if you lead a life of good moral character, with a heart and mind inclined to foster the well-being of others, you've nothing to worry about. The rule of thumb is that the subtle world around us reflects the subtle world of thought and feeling within us.

As with any spiritual practice, you will have greater benefits and accomplish more if your mind and emotions are clear and stable and you can consequently more accurately register the subtle energies you may encounter. Drugs and alcohol can interfere with this process. If you are on regular medication, follow all your doctor's prescriptions and advice but be mindful of your medication's effects on your inner sensitivity and powers of concentration. Always work within the boundaries of what is safe and balanced for you.

If after doing an exercise you feel any aftereffects such as restlessness, a slight disorientation, light-headedness, or an energy "buzz," the best thing is to have a hot drink like tea or coffee (though my preference is for hot chocolate), to eat something, or to get some exercise. Turning your attention to something entirely different is also useful. These things all ground your energy and provide time for your experiences to be assimilated and integrated.

One final thought: You'll find there are roughly two types of exercises. Exercises 1 through 7 are introductions to ideas that can be part of any spiritual practice or art, not just that of giving blessings. They're especially intended for people who may have little or no experience with doing inner work. And as I said earlier, they're foundational for the other exercises that follow them. Those exercises, from numbers 8 to 18, are directly related to material in the main text of this book.

Whether you wish to do the exercises or not, I do encourage you to read the commentaries and even read through the exercises as illustrations of ideas in the text. The commentaries expand on some ideas basic to a spiritual practice and, as I mentioned, also on some of the ideas in the text itself.

Good luck! And many blessings!

———— *Commentary* ————

I start with this exercise because an important tool for any kind of inner work, not just the art of blessing, is the capacity to imagine or, as it's sometimes called, to visualize. Research has amply shown that the primitive emotional and physiological centers of the brain don't distinguish clearly between an experience that's happening "out there" in the physical world and one that's happening "in here" in our mental world. Imagining meeting a tiger (or an income-tax auditor) can make our heart pound and our palms sweaty as much as meeting one in reality. This fact lies behind the power of drama and storytelling to deeply affect us. It's at the heart of the power of positive (and negative) thinking, the phenomena of psychosomatic medicine and psychoneuroimmunology, and the enhancement of performance in sports and business through visualization.

The word *visualization* is often used to describe this process, but it can be misleading if it suggests that we must see inner pictures. When I speak of an "image" in my classes, I mean something that can draw on all the senses; so, if I ask a person to imagine holding a rose and they smell it but cannot see it in their minds, it's still a successful imaging. The most important thing in most cases is not the image itself but the sensation, impressions, and effects that it creates within the body-mind. The "image" may actually be a feeling or a presence without shape or form.

For example, if you can experience the essence of an orange whether or not you see it, taste it, smell it, or feel it in your mind, then you've succeeded. This is using the imagination and its images as a route inward to deeper levels of consciousness and into the creative domain of the soul. There, I've experienced, the sense of perception is neither visual nor aural nor anything quite akin to one of the physical senses, although it comes closest to touch. In fact, I think of this kind of imaginal or soul perception as being "clairtactile" instead of clairvoyant.

In the context of a spiritual workshop, I've often had people tell me, "I can't visualize." But in their everyday lives, they can plan ahead, worry about paying the bills next month (as well as conjure up vivid images of what will happen if they don't), imagine lying on a beach in Hawaii, formulate a vision for a business, picture what they're going to make for dinner, have their mouth water just thinking about the taste of chocolate cake, or simply sit back and daydream. Almost everyone has fantasies, and not just sexual ones, although they may be the most fun!

All these activities are forms of visualization that we take for granted. It's not that we don't or cannot visualize as a matter of everyday experience. We just don't call it that. I think of it as going into imaginal space, just as with our computers we can go into cyberspace (which itself is a product of our imaginations). Neither one is tangible in the same way my desk is, but both are real nonetheless and have powerful effects in our lives. So I tell the participants in my classes that they are not going to visualize in the sense of using their eyes or having a visual experience (although there can be a visual side to whatever they experience), but they are going to imagine. In so doing, they are going to open up a natural form of inner perception, which I think of as imaginal space. And to enter their imaginal space, they should go to that familiar place within themselves where they go when they daydream or fantasize. I call this our "inner theater of the heart and mind."

<hr>

Exercise

Please get comfortable and close your eyes. Later, with practice, you may discover that you do your inner work more effectively with your eyes open. But for now, I want you to focus your attention inward in your own inner world.

Allow yourself to summon the power you feel when you daydream and fantasize, your power to create images and stories for yourself.

When you've a sense of that power, use it to remember when you last went to the theater or simply picture what it's like being in a theater. Imagine sitting alone in the audience, looking at the stage or the screen before the show has started. The stage is empty. There are no props, no images or sounds. It's an empty, open space waiting for something to happen.

Feel the creative power of that empty stage. Feel the sense of anticipation that you've experienced before the show starts. Who knows what adventures may unfold? Anything can happen. Any story might be told. Any image might manifest. The whole scene is alive and pregnant with possibility and potential. Feel into that evocative emptiness, into the presence of potential. Feel the excitement and wonder of the empty stage. It's akin to what a child feels on Christmas morning, lying in bed in the dark, wondering if Santa came, wondering what's under the tree, wondering what's in the packages.

Nothing has taken shape yet. Everything is possible.

Now get up and go onto the stage itself. There is no one in the audience. You are all alone on the stage. Standing there, you become part of the creative spirit that this stage represents. Feel yourself immersed in that spirit. Breathe that spirit into yourself. Let it become an open, anticipatory space within you, a place where images, impressions, and sensations may arise. It's an inner place of intuition and discovery.

It's imaginal space, the inner theater of your heart and mind.

Take however long you wish to experience what this space feels like to you. What is its state of mind like for you? Remember, you're not trying to see any images; you're not putting anything on the stage. You're simply paying attention to the evocative emptiness of the space itself.

When you're ready, open your eyes and look around, but remain in your inner theater.

When I look at the world around me from my imaginal space, everything I see becomes charged with imaginative possibilities. It's as if things exist both in the physical world and in imaginal space as well, sharing the empty stage with me and adding to its potentials for new insights, revelation, and creative discovery.

What's it like for you?

When you're finished, close your eyes again for a moment and see yourself stepping down off the stage and leaving the theater. Consciously reenter your everyday world, grounded and balanced, with a feeling of being refreshed, regenerated, and in harmony. Feel free to take as much of the spirit of your imaginal space with you as you feel you can integrate into your everyday life.

The first few times you do this exercise, note in a journal any impressions, sensations, ideas, images, and so forth that may have arisen for you while entering and leaving your imaginal space.

This is a key exercise that you should practice until you become comfortable and familiar with it. In most of the exercises that follow, I will ask you to begin by entering your inner theater. Then, at the end, I will ask you to return to a normal state of consciousness by imagining yourself returning to this theater and stepping down off the stage. This is simply a code to indicate entering and leaving the open and expectant state of mind that attunes you to your imaginal space.

Once you know what this state of mind is like, you don't need to use any metaphors to enter it. When I ask you to enter your imaginal space, the inner theater of your heart and mind, you'll know what to do. You'll go immediately into this state of mind, anticipating whatever story may emerge, whatever images may appear.

EXERCISE 2: STILLNESS

Commentary

In my daughter's preschool, just before it's time to go home, the children all sit in a circle and have a time of quiet. Up till then they have been busy playing, their energy running at full tilt. But in this circle they're gathering themselves together, settling their energies down, and becoming still. To do this, the teacher has them hold their hands above their heads and breathe deeply. As they breathe, they slowly bring their hands down into their laps, pushing the scattered energies within themselves and around them down into the earth, which itself is still and deep and peaceful. They become calm and centered, ready to make the shift from being in school to being at home. They discover stillness.

Every spiritual tradition and practice of which I'm aware highly values and has techniques for achieving a state of inner stillness. Often these techniques utilize some form of breath, and the simplest one of all is to breathe deeply until we feel calm. Some form of focusing the mind may also be used. One technique with which we're all familiar is counting to ten in a moment of stress. The calm that breathing deeply and counting to ten can induce is generally superficial, but it still mirrors and resonates with the deeper inner stillness that is usually one of the objectives of a spiritual practice. A quiet pool, though shallow, can reflect the light of the moon every bit as well as a calm ocean.

This stillness might be called the point of balance, inner poise, undistractedness, or even silence. But it's not a passive state at all. It's constantly integrating the byplay of all the forces around us so we are not pulled in this direction or forced to move in that one. But at the same time, stillness feels effortless.

Stillness is not an emotion, like tranquillity or serenity, although the latter can certainly contribute to it. It's not necessarily a state of quiet or one in which nothing is happening either. It's a mindfulness, a tensionless gathering of one's forces into the moment. It's a state that can arise when our attentiveness is wholly focused.

Just like a quiet pool, inner stillness is a state in which images can arise undistorted by the ripples of our emotions or thoughts. This is obviously important for inner work, in which you're trying to attune yourself to subtle forces in the world around you. The voice of the sacred is known as a "still, small voice"; what better way to hear it than to be still yourself?

I also don't think of stillness as a state of detachment or withdrawal. If anything, it's a peaceful presence so deep that it can embrace and contain all the noise and static, movement and mayhem, chaos and activity, in our lives and not be dispersed by it. Instead, it begins to impose its own rhythm of order and calm on our activities, much as a consistent drumbeat organizes the melodies that dance above and around it. Stillness participates and is engaged.

With respect to the Art of Blessing, there are two reasons for cultivating stillness. The first is to be able to attune oneself clearly to a person or situation, to see what may be needed or how a blessing should proceed. This is part of the opening step. The second is to preserve the integrity and focus of whatever energy or presence we use in the blessing. If one is inwardly still, like a martial artist before engaging in action, then one is not being pulled this way or that by emotions or thoughts (their own or someone else's). A person can act cleanly from the center of his or her being.

The cultivation of stillness can be a lifetime engagement. It's a depth that has no bottom. Certainly it involves more than can be encapsulated in one or two simple exercises. But these exercises are designed to get a person started, with the understanding that in pursuing the Art of Blessing—or any other spiritual art—they'll also pursue their own still center of being and ways of achieving and maintaining it in the midst of everyday life.

Exercise

Please make yourself comfortable and close your eyes. In whatever way you choose, go into the inner theater of your heart and mind, into the place where you daydream and fantasize, into the space of your imagination.

Remember a time when you stood outside in nature. Perhaps it was on a beach, perhaps in a forest, perhaps on the slopes of a mountain. Wherever it was, put yourself imaginatively back into that place and feel what it was like. Feel the earth under your feet, the sky above you, the world around you. Make this feeling as concrete and specific as possible by remembering your physical sensations as clearly as you can: what you felt against your skin, what you smelled, what you heard, what you saw, and even, perhaps, what you tasted.

You may have a visual picture of yourself in this situation or you may simply have a feeling, a remembrance, of what it was like: the essence of the experience. Either one will work.

Now imagine that streaming into you from the earth beneath your feet, from the sky overhead, from the world all around you, are streams of energy. These bring vitality into you, but they also stabilize you. You feel centered in their power. Nothing can move you unless you wish to be moved, for you are connected to and rooted in all the world around you. To move you, the world itself would have to move. But if you choose to move, the world will dance with you wherever you wish to go.

In this way, you are held in balance and safety. Take a moment to explore, to make as concrete as you can, just what this feels like to your body, to your emotions, and to your mind.

[Pause]

When you have an embodied sense of being held and protected (and you may wish to stand up to feel the full effect), take some deep breaths. As you do so, feel your breath drawing you down into your body's center of gravity, in the hips, below the solar plexus. Shake your arms and legs, wiggle your torso, feel relaxed and flowing as you breathe tension out of yourself and center yourself in your center of gravity.

From your center of gravity you're balanced and poised, able to initiate by an act of will movement in any direction. You're light on your feet. You feel yourself in the middle of a dynamic stillness.

Take a moment to experience this state. What is it like? What impressions, feelings, or sensations arise for you, physically, emotionally, and mentally?

[Pause]

When you feel familiar with this balanced, supported, and poised state, turn your attention to everything going on around you or to your inner emotional and intellectual world. Open your eyes if you wish. Let the distracting thoughts and feelings of your busy day surround you, like paparazzi flashing lightbulbs in your eyes, calling your name, demanding your attention. Take a moment to observe whatever it may be, either in this moment or regularly during your day, that takes you out of stillness and away from your center. Don't become engaged with those thoughts or feelings; simply observe them and acknowledge their presence in your life.

Close your eyes again. Now, from your center, feel a surge of peaceful power radiating in all directions, as if your own center of gravity is expanding. All the demands and distractions that had been clustering around you are still there, but they have been pushed back. It's as if you stand at the calm center of a hurricane. Around you but unable to touch you are the swirling winds and tumultuous waters. The sea around you, though, is placid, able to reflect any subtle or deeper forces that may be present in yourself or in the world around you.

The whirling winds cannot reach you, but you're not disconnected from them. You haven't retreated into a higher world. You're in this world, where your body is, where your everyday life is. You're aware of the winds and what they represent. You don't resist them. You're not in conflict with them. You acknowledge their presence and incorporate them into the stillness, into the balance of your life. Then you can respond to them if you wish. When you do, it's your choice. And you respond from your center through the power of your will and your love. They cannot make you move.

Enjoy the sensation of being in this place of stillness, choice, and power. Feel yourself connected to the world around you, drawing on the calmness that comes from its ancient, slow rhythms. You're standing in the axis of the world; everything is revolving around you, but you're still and unmoved unless you choose to engage. Feel the balance at your center. Be aware of any sensations, impressions, or images that may arise for you to help you make this state of mind more real and present.

[Pause]

Once you have felt a sense in your body and in your heart and mind of what this centered stillness is like, touch some spot on your body as a point of remembrance or choose an image in your mind that resonates both mentally and emotionally. Or you can do both. Either way, the touch or the image will remind you of this state and aid you in entering it at any time you choose.

Having done this, see yourself back on the stage in your inner theater of the heart and mind. See yourself stepping down off the stage and leaving the theater, consciously reentering your everyday world, grounded and balanced, with a feeling of being refreshed, regenerated, and in harmony. Feel free to take with you as much of the spirit of your imaginal space and of this stillness as you feel you can integrate into your everyday life.

As you go about your day, call yourself back into stillness as often as you wish. Once you've a sense of what it feels like, you needn't repeat this exercise. Simply go to the stillness itself. It transcends any exercise.

There are many other ways of entering that still space. Seek out places, activities, music, movements, and attitudes that draw you into it. Pay attention to anything you do naturally or automatically in order to enter it. Practice being still in the midst of engagement. Practice when everything around you is quiet. There's no time when stillness cannot be a blessing—or the foundation of one. Then when the paparazzi of your inner—and outer—life invade your space, you won't be discomfited. You can embrace them in that stillness that's your center. Then the clamor will subside. There will be just you and your world, the love and compassion that connects you, and the will to choose how you'll act to fulfill that love.

EXERCISE 3: SHIFTING

—— *Commentary* ——

We experience shifts in consciousness every day. The most obvious is the shift from waking to sleeping. Another is from daydreaming to attentiveness to our surroundings. When we pray or meditate, we're also shifting to a consciousness of greater attunement.

The ability to shift from one state of consciousness to another is an important skill in spiritual work. Think of the ability to shift into an imaginal state or the state of stillness that we have already explored, something that can come through practice.

Of particular use is learning to shift into a mode of consciousness in which you are more sensitive to the subtle energies that move throughout your world. This would include sensitivity to the atmosphere and mood in places, around people, around objects, and around yourself, and could extend into more developed forms of psychic sensitivity. Although you certainly need not be psychic to practice the Art of Blessing, the ability to turn on and off your sensitivity to the subtler aspects of your environment can be helpful. At the very least, I'm talking about a shift from an active state of mind to one that's more receptive, alert, and attuned, qualities that are very important in the opening step.

The following is a very simple exercise, designed not to "tune you in" to anything in particular but to make you familiar with the experience of shifting into a state of attunement. It's akin to what we do when we pause to listen closely to a faint sound in the distance. There should be no strain involved at all. If there's a feeling of effort or tension, it's not attunement.

This exercise is about opening a portal into the subtle worlds of spirit and energy, or, if you prefer, about opening your inner senses. Its essence is the practice of mindfulness and awareness. I first observed this exercise being used by R. J. Stewart. He's the author of many books on the spiritual path, an outstanding teacher of attunement and of working with the subtler, supersensible side of reality, and, I'm privileged to say, a good friend. It's a traditional exercise that he learned from his teacher (who, presumably, learned it from his). I've modified it and use it to good effect with participants in my own classes.

For this exercise, you'll need matches, a candle and candleholder, and a table to put them on. The important thing is that the candle and candleholder are stable and won't be in a position to be knocked over. You'll be lighting the candle and blowing it out several times, and you don't want any accidents to happen.

There are three parts to this exercise. The first involves using the physical candle. The second takes you into your imaginal space, where you'll use an imaginary candle. The third (also, please, in the imaginal space!) turns you into the candle. You can do each of these three parts at a different time, but there will be a deeper process of learning for you if you do them all at once. However you choose to space them, please do them in the order given.

Please note that the purpose of this exercise is *not* to make contact with any unseen force or to receive information psychically or mystically. The purpose is to feel the shifting consciousness within yourself from one mode of awareness to another. It's like paying attention to what happens when you go from being inside your house, surrounded by four walls, to being outside your house in the open air, under the vast blue sky, aware of a much larger landscape. In this exercise, it does not matter what that landscape may look like or what it may contain. It's the opening of the door and the crossing of the threshold—the shift itself—that's the object of your attention. When we shift from one mode of awareness to another, we do cross a boundary. As you do the exercise, pay attention to the experience of the boundary itself and to being on that boundary. What's that like for you?

A final note: This boundary between levels of attunement is very permeable. In truth, we go through our days often with one foot on one side and one foot on the other. And we often cross over automatically without being aware that we've done so, going from a state of relative inattention to one of mindfulness of all that's going on around us. Practicing this shift more deliberately gives us greater control of the process, and that's the ultimate object of this exercise.

———————————— *Exercise (Part 1)* ————————————

To begin with, light your candle as if you needed the light. Pretend the power has gone out in your house, or pretend you're lighting a candle on a birthday cake. This is a very matter-of-fact, down-to-earth procedure that we have all done from time to time, and usually without thinking much about it. Allow yourself to experience the physical action of lighting a candle and to appreciate it for what it is, with no subtle, metaphorical, or spiritual overtones. However, I do wish you to pay attention to the act itself and to how it feels physically and even mentally or emotionally when you light the candle.

Let the candle burn for a moment or two, enjoying its light and warmth and the overall aesthetics of a lit candle. Then blow it out.

Please repeat this candlelighting two or three times, enough to be familiar with and appreciative of the physical act itself.

Now think of the candle not just as a source of light but as a source of inspiration and as a symbol of spiritual light. Candles have been used for millennia in religious and magical ceremonies. Their flames have symbolized life, spirit, the soul, and the presence of the sacred. Lighting a candle is an act of invoking spirit or invoking the sacred that's known throughout the world. It's the opening of a portal. It's the shifting of one's consciousness into a mode of attunement.

Imagine that the table on which your candle is resting is now an altar. You're going to light the candle that invokes the sacred, turning the space around you from ordinary space into sacred space and shifting your focus from everyday concerns to a state of interior awareness. Now you're not just lighting a candle for light; you're lighting it as a deliberate spiritual act.

Once this intent is clear in your mind, light the candle as an act of spiritual invocation. As you do, you can invoke the sacred in whatever way is appropriate for you and your beliefs. What does it feel like to do this? What do you feel like? What images, impressions, sensations, thoughts, or feelings arise?

How is this experience of lighting the candle different from when you lit the candle earlier as a simple physical act of creating a flame?

[Pause]

When you've had time to reflect on these questions, blow the candle out, giving thanks as you do so for the spiritual presence that you invoked and releasing it back into a larger, inclusive world.

Now light the candle again, but this time imagine that in so doing you're shifting into a deeper state of attunement. You might try imagining that when you light the candle, you're turning a key and opening a door; or you're passing through a gate in a hedge into a new landscape; or you're turning on your computer and entering the Internet's World Wide Web.

Whatever images you may use, the key is to notice the sense of shifting into a different mode of awareness. This shift is a subtle "tuning" or "repatterning" of your inner state. Some people experience it as a soundless click within themselves; others as becoming more expansive or as becoming still within. But in each case there's a feeling of deeper perception, as if an unseen world has drawn closer or as if inner senses have awakened and are now on the alert for whatever they can detect.

With that in mind, reflect on any sensations, images, impressions, thoughts, or feelings you may have. Then blow out your candle and notice the shift again. This time you're moving in reverse, deliberately see yourself closing the door, crossing the gate back into this world, or turning off the computer. You are reengaging with your everyday awareness.

Now relax, take a deep breath, and re-light the candle, again doing it deliberately, as an act of invocation and of shifting into a deeper mode of awareness that's attuned to the spirit within yourself and within your world. Pay attention to what you feel as you do so. What happens to you? What happens to your awareness?

Then blow the candle out again, once more reversing whatever images you may have used to facilitate the process. If you imagined yourself entering a room, exit it now, closing the door behind you. If you imagined yourself expanding, consolidate back into your everyday consciousness, grounding yourself in your normal physical awareness. Again, pay attention to this process.

Practice lighting and blowing out the candle a couple more times, each time focusing on the experience of shifting from one mode of awareness to another and back again. It may be you'll feel nothing at all; not everyone feels the shift in this manner. If not, don't despair. Other exercises may help you experience the same thing. At the very least, think of the shift as going into a focused mode of quietly and deeply listening, in contrast to the usual hectic activity in our minds as one thought chases another and our attention wanders and jumps throughout our day.

Take a moment to pause and relax before we begin the second step.

Before we proceed, please note that in the exercise you just did, you facilitated it by using the physical act of lighting a candle and the imaginative act of seeing the candle as a symbol. The lighting of the candle represents a boundary between two states, between darkness and illumination, for example, or between everyday awareness and a more subtle attunement. We used a candle because of its traditional spiritual associations, which resonate with the intent of this exercise. However, we could've used any number of other physical acts to practice the same thing. For example, you could do the same exercise by physically stepping across the threshold of a door, moving from inside to outside or from one room to another. You could do the same thing by putting on or taking off a special piece of clothing or jewelry. When I lived in Morocco, I observed that many of my friends who were Muslim had prayer rugs, which they only unrolled and used when making the customary prayers to Mecca five times a day. Stepping onto that rug automatically induced a shift in consciousness from their everyday mind to a mind prayerfully attuned to Allah.

To repeat: It's not the new state of consciousness that's the object of this exercise but awareness of the shift itself—what it feels like and how you can initiate it at will, so that any time, any place, of your choosing, you can move safely and swiftly into a deeper state of connectedness with a larger spiritual world around you.

———————————— *Exercise (Part 2)* ————————————

Here we're going to do our work in our imaginal space. You can't always carry a candle around to light whenever you want to shift into a more attuned mode of awareness. You must learn to do it as an inner act based on your memory and understanding of what the shift feels like for you and how to induce it.

Please make yourself comfortable and close your eyes. In whatever way you choose, go into the state of mind I call the inner theater of your heart and mind, into the place where you daydream and fantasize, into the world of your imagination, into your imaginal space.

Imagine there's a candle before you. Repeat the exercise of lighting and blowing out this candle, of shifting from one mode of awareness to another, doing it entirely imaginally. As you do so, pay attention to what it feels like crossing that boundary, just as you did before. Also pay attention to any differences there may be for you in doing this act in your imagination instead of doing it physically. Is it easier? Is it harder? Does it make any difference at all? Is the sense of shifting any different?

[Pause]

When you are finished, see yourself back on the stage in your inner theater. See yourself stepping down off the stage and leaving the theater, consciously reentering your everyday life grounded and balanced, with a feeling of being refreshed, regenerated, and in harmony. Open your eyes. This would be a good time to stand up and stretch.

Do this exercise three times.

Pause for a moment and relax. Take some time to write down in your journal any impressions or thoughts, sensations or images, insights, or feelings you may have had while doing this part of the exercise.

———————————— *Exercise (Part 3)* ————————————

Now perform the same shift of awareness that you have been doing without using any candle, real or imaginal, to help you. Or, if you wish, imagine yourself as the candle and you are lighting yourself by shifting into a state of heightened awareness. Then, as you shift back into your ordinary state, imagine your flame integrating within you, becoming a place of stillness and balance at your center. As much as you can, though, try to experience this shift of consciousness as a simple act of will and refocusing of your attention without needing props to assist you.

Pay attention to what this feels like for you. Is it easier or harder than when doing the shift by lighting and unlighting a candle?

Record any impressions or sensations, thoughts or feelings, images or insights, you may have had from the totality of this exercise as well as from this part into your journal. Most importantly, you want to remember what making the shift of awareness felt like so you can learn to do it at will, like shifting from being concerned only with your own affairs and needs to being aware of and concerned for the needs and affairs of others. For once we've learned how to do it, we make this shift in order to serve, not simply to explore a different state of consciousness or as an experience for its own sake.

Final Commentary

I've cast this exercise in the context of learning to shift levels of attunement, from being aware only of the physical world to being aware of the more subtle world of thoughts, feelings, and spirit.

However, the capacity to shift has other uses beyond enhancing our receptivity that are just as important and in some cases much more so. The ability to shift moods, for example, is vital to the Art of Blessing. You simply cannot bless anything if you are stuck in a bad or negative mood yourself. You need to shift your perspective and your awareness. You must shift your attention out of your own mood (although you may still be aware of your own feelings) and your own needs and troubles, and open your heart to the requirements of the person or situation you wish to bless. Otherwise you run the risk of bombarding your environment and others with your negativity. If you've ever felt as if someone has punched you in the solar plexus when you were in the presence of a person who was very angry (even if they didn't direct their anger towards you) or found yourself becoming depressed in the company of someone who was depressed (even if no words pass between you), then you've experienced this phenomenon.

Anyone who sets out on a spiritual path assumes increasing responsibility for his or her energies, field, presence, or however you wish to describe the subtle influence we have on one another—the influence beyond the level of direct physical, emotional, or intellectual interaction. This doesn't mean you can never feel any negativity, but that you learn to contain it, transmute it, and, when there's a possibility you can inflict it upon others—or when you're attempting to do inner work like blessing—to shift it. The ability to shift moods and energies is thus an important skill and directly related to the exercise you've just done.

So, for example, when you "light yourself," you can see this as a shifting into a good mood, into a flow of benign and benevolent energy, or into a radiance of compassion and nourishment for others. And when you want to practice the Art of Blessing, you can use your ability to shift modes of consciousness and states of mind and emotion in order to ground yourself, relax, and enter a mood rich in positive imagery and energy. It's from there that you will open into a state of spiritual attunement and unobstructedness from which the blessing may proceed.

—— *Commentary* ——

Open space is my term for a certain quality of inner spaciousness and expansiveness of mind and heart. In its openness, it creates a place for growth and unfoldment.

The feeling of the empty stage that was the focus of Exercise 1 is an aspect of open space. The primary difference is that the empty-stage image focuses upon creativity and imaginative evocation, whereas the open space simply embodies the sensation of openness itself. It has the quality of "allowing," creating space for something to happen that otherwise would be too constricted. This can mean allowing a person to be him- or herself, freed from social or attitudinal restrictions. It can mean allowing an idea room to grow rather than being squelched at the outset for being too radical. Thus, open space is at the heart of creative brainstorming.

Open space is an attitude, even a form of perception, that provides an opportunity for people and objects, events and situations to "speak" to us, to tell us who they are before we obscure them with our own projections and expectations. Open space is thus also at the heart of perceptive and active listening. It gives our intuition room to operate. It allows the time and the attitude necessary for the interiority of a person or situation to reveal itself.

For example, there's a young woman at a school where I sometimes teach who is creative, imaginative, and interesting. But to engage with these qualities—to engage with *her*—one must acknowledge, accept, and pass through the boundary of her somewhat startling gothic appearance, for she dresses like Morticia from *The Addams Family,* all in black with a black wig, black lipstick and eye shadow, and her face a ghostly white.

A quality of open space is one that embraces all of this young lady—all of each of us—not picking and choosing parts to accept and parts to reject. Open space is inclusive. It's an expression of unconditional love.

Open space is nonjudgmental but not undiscerning; it's embracing but not passive. It calls forth the inclusiveness, the forgiveness, the openness, the lovingness, the spaciousness, the expansiveness, within all that it embraces. And this, as you might expect, can have a transformative effect. I often hear people say things like "Her actions opened my heart," or "He inspired me to be a better person." This is the impact of open space when it's conceived and experienced, not just as a passive receptacle into which anything may be poured, but as an alchemical alembic that distills and transforms whatever it contains.

In my cosmology, then, open space is a quality of spirit, and to hold and to extend open space is a spiritual act. In effect, open space is a radiation and extension of love. It's also an extension of a person's attunement to that universal spirit that compassionately (and passionately) desires nothing more than the well-being and the perfect unfoldment and fulfillment of each unique member of creation. Open space is a spirit of hospitality, but for those who accept it and enter into it, it's also the challenge to be hospitable themselves.

I see open space as expanding out of a sense of joy. It's difficult to extend openness when we're feeling constricted by fear or unhappiness ourselves, although I can testify that it can be done. As I said in the main text, joy is not the same as happiness; it's independent of any outer cause and arises in us as we choose to attune ourselves to the sacred. However, thinking of something that brings us happiness can be an opening to the spirit and energy of joy. Like Peter Pan, we can fly when we add our happy thoughts!

Open space is, for me, at the heart of a blessing. It creates an openness in which unobstructedness may occur or be experienced. When I embrace a person in a spirit of blessing, I'm inwardly seeing him in a spacious place that allows stuck energies to become unstuck, cramped muscles of mind and heart to stretch and relax, and stagnant forces to flow again. I see his inner "heart," the pulsing core of his life, having room to beat strongly, cleanly, and clearly, coming into rhythm and alignment with a universal pulse that beats for his highest good. I don't attempt to project how that person's energy and life should go, in what direction it should flow, or what shape the blessing should take. I simply visualize his life opening into a spaciousness and freedom that allows it to go where it needs to under the direction of his own inner intelligence and spirit.

As with all the other exercises, the full benefit of this one comes with practice as you develop a sensitivity to the subtle feelings and awarenesses involved.

Exercise

Please make yourself comfortable and close your eyes. In whatever way you choose, go into the inner theater of your heart and mind, into the place where you daydream and fantasize, into your imaginal space.

Once you're comfortable, imagine yourself standing in a room that's familiar. It could be a room in your home, a room where you work, the room you're in as you do this exercise. The only stipulation is that it have a window through which you can see the world.

[Pause]

Look out this window and see something that brings you happiness. It could be a person, an object, a place, a situation. It's personal to you. As you look through the window, feel the impact of that happiness within yourself. Feel your heart expand and glow. Feel your body relaxing within this warm glow. Feel yourself growing lighter as the warm pleasure of feeling this happiness flows through your body.

Feel this happiness flowing in your legs, giving you a sense of stability and energy.

Feel this happiness filling up your abdomen, and take a deep breath as it does so. Relax into your center of gravity, letting tensions and strains flow out, down your legs, through your feet, and into the great, loving heart of the earth.

Feel this happiness collecting and overflowing in your heart, opening you to the circulation of love and joy within creation.

Feel this happiness filling your mind, bringing calm and a poised alertness to your thoughts. Feel it aligning you with an inner joy that transcends earthly causes and pressures: a joy of life, a joy of being, a joy of blood and breath, a joy that's the presence of the sacred.

If attuning to this joy is difficult and you need help in shifting from a feeling of happiness to one of joy, you may find it useful to remember any experience you've had of the sacred. Or, try thinking of images of the sacred that are meaningful to you, or thinking of the awe that contemplation of the miracles, beauty, and vastness of creation can inspire.

As you feel this joy coming alive within you, it exerts a pressure that pushes against and then dissolves the walls around you, removing anything that stands between you and that image of happiness you saw through the window. Empowered by the warm glow of this joy, your being expands like a sun coming out from behind an eclipsing moon to embrace that image, incorporating it into your being. You go beyond the image to the core of happiness itself, and from there to the spirit of joy that can open and nourish your heart whatever your circumstances upon the earth.

Take time to be with this sensation, this sense of joy. Take note of any impressions, feelings, thoughts, sensations, and the like that occur to you and see which of them can act as a trigger to bring you back into this state.

[Pause]

Now feel this joy expanding, and as it does, creating an open space all around you. You can be open because in your joy and your attunement to the Source, you can be unafraid, you can be loving, you can be allowing.

Picture any images that might represent this open space to you. It could be the wide ocean, the flatlands of the prairies, or the vastness of outer space; it's a feeling of open vistas, unimpeded sight, roads stretching into the distance until they disappear. Choose an image that represents this open space to you so that when you think of it, you can invoke the sensation of open space into your mind and heart. Remember, as an image, it does not have to be a visual picture; it can also be a sensation, a feeling, or a sense of presence.

When you picture this image, also feel that it carries with it the power of its openness. Just as gazing upon the rolling sand dunes of an immense desert or the infinite distances of outer space makes us feel expanded and open, so this presence of spaciousness evokes an openness from others and from within situations. It's not just an image, not just a passive receptacle. It is a power.

Draw this image into your body, into your heart or your center of gravity, wherever it feels most comfortable. You are drawing this spaciousness and its power into yourself so that you embrace it, embody it, encompass it, as if in your body you contained the wholeness of the universe. You're spaciousness that has become flesh. Take a moment to observe what that feels like and note any impressions, thoughts, images, and the like that may come to you.

[Pause]

Now open your eyes. Extend this sense of open space to whatever you see about you. See it enveloped in spaciousness. What does it feel like to do that? Remember, you're not projecting a power at anything. Rather, you're enveloping it in a liberating, inviting, open space that is itself powerful.

Close your eyes again and imagine a friend. Envelop this friend in the same spaciousness. Remember, you're not doing anything to him or her. You're only seeing them in a spaciousness in which they can relax, stretch, and expand under the wisdom and guidance of their own inner intelligence and spirit.

Now imagine someone you don't like. Your inner spaciousness is large enough, fearless enough, liberated enough, to embrace that person as well. Surround him or her with spaciousness. Remember, you're not doing anything to him or her. You're not trying to heal them, change them, make them less negative, or make them like you. You're only seeing them embraced in a loving, hospitable open space that itself offers room to expand, transform, and feel liberated, guided by their own inner intelligence and spirit. Often when we're negative towards a person, it's a projection of our own feelings of constriction and fear. So in seeing them embraced in spaciousness, you may well provide them with an opportunity to shift and to alter their response to the world and to yourself.

Finally, embrace yourself in the spaciousness. Step fully into your own open space. Feel its impact upon you. Feel the places where you begin to unwind, unstick, stretch, expand, and flow again. Feel the pull to become this openness, to embody spaciousness more and more in your daily life.

Take a moment to reflect on this entire exercise, recalling any impressions or sensations, feelings or thoughts, images or insights, you may have had.

[Pause]

When you're finished, open your eyes and step out of your imaginal space and back into your everyday world. If you wish, see yourself back on the stage in your inner theater. See yourself stepping down off the stage and leaving the theater. Feel yourself deliberately reentering your everyday life, grounded and balanced, with a feeling of being refreshed, regenerated, and in harmony.

Should there be anything you wish to record from the totality of this exercise, do so in your journal.

———— *Commentary* ————

The idea of subtle energies is an area that needs considerably more scientific investigation. In the end, it may be apparent that the paradigm of "energies" is not the best way to describe or understand the phenomena involved or that it only covers a small percentage of these phenomena.

On the other hand, in the area of practical application, the use of "energy" as an imaginal description of subtle and spiritual interactions between people and the world is undoubtedly useful. From my own experience, I would agree that nearly everything in the world is enveloped in and radiates a field of influence that has decidedly wave-like or energy-like characteristics.

However, my own mode of inner perception usually experiences these phenomena not as energies—like rays or beams of light or currents of electricity—but as presences or fields of information and interaction. Consequently, believing that one should operate from one's strengths, I do very little of what usually passes for "energy work" or "energy perception" in my classes. We do equivalent kinds of things, though, using the images of fields and presences and using the principle of touch rather than sight for developing inner perception.

There are those who do teach these things professionally and have much more experience doing so than I. I usually recommend

Dr. William Bloom and Dr. Brugh Joy, both of whom I know. They are excellent teachers and writers of high integrity and experience, working with an extraordinary depth of spiritual compassion and knowledge. I've also been impressed with the work of Rosalyn Bruyere and Barbara Brennan, two healers who have each written and taught extensively in the area of energy medicine. Dr. Caroline Myss, another friend of mine, has also written excellent books in this area and is a pioneer in the field of medical intuition and energy diagnosis. Likewise, there is extensive material about energy work in literature on oriental spirituality and healing as well as the martial arts. A good introductory book in this area, for example, is *Chi Gong* by Paul Dong and Aristide H. Esser. I leave it to the reader who wishes to pursue a deeper understanding of subtle energies to do so by utilizing these other resources.

Having said that, this workbook would not be complete, nor would I have laid a proper foundation for working with "fields" and "presence" and the other aspects of the Art of Blessing, if I did not include something dealing with subtle energies.

The following exercise, which is divided into different parts, requires that we accept the notion of subtle energies radiating around all things and flowing between things. This flow can be enhanced by intentionality, imaginal or mental direction, and emotional feeling. Whatever these emanations may truly be, we can make them easier both to detect and to direct if we think of them simply as energies in motion.

Some people find it easier to visualize these emanations as rays or beams of energy streaming to and from themselves, as well as from everything around them. I prefer to think in terms of fields. To have a sense of "fields," think of the force fields from science fiction such as *Star Trek* or *Star Wars*. Or think of a cell wall or even of your own skin. A field, as I use the term, is simply a boundary that surrounds us like a bubble or an egg and differentiates that which is inside from that which is outside.

Using imaginative direction, we can expand this field or contract it. When we do expand it, it carries our presence, our energy, out into the space around us, touching the equivalent fields of people and objects around us. Where they touch, energy can be sensed and exchanged. Blessing can take place.

I like the image of the field around me because this image carries more of a sense of my presence and of the involvement of my whole being in an act of blessing than does the image of emanating rays and beams. This is as much a matter of personal style as it is an actual description of what is happening. My sensitivity to inner energy takes the form of touch and sensation. I feel the emanations of people and objects as they play against me, much like the sense of sunlight or wind upon my skin. I am not so much clairvoyant as I am "clairtactile." This kind of perception extends 360 degrees around me, rather than only in front of me like my sight. It is as if I am surrounded by an inner skin that acts as a sensing organ for my soul, much as my outer skin does for my body.

Furthermore, I like the image of a field rather than a ray or beam because the field seems to me an extension of all that I am. It draws upon and represents the synthesis of all my qualities of heart, mind, body, and soul. It is not the emanation of a particular energy center or chakra within my body but is itself a master chakra, surrounding me and synthesizing all the component elements and energies that make me up.

What's important to remember here, though, is that the images of fields, beams, and energies are imaginal tools for the most part. What these images describe is a state of connectedness and engagement. So when we work with energies, we are basically working with connection and with the quality of our engagement and interaction with the world around us. I could, for instance, say that I am sending you beams of loving energy or embracing you in a field of loving energy, but the essence of what I am doing, however I describe it, is that I am connecting with you mentally, emotionally, and spiritually in a loving and caring way. It's important to keep mindful of the actual nature of what we are doing and not become too caught up in the imaginal descriptions of how we are doing it.

In doing the following exercise, one thing to keep in mind is that it's difficult to just sit in a room alone and detect these energies. They emerge from relationship and from dynamic interaction. Sometimes I find it helpful to imagine ourselves not as being immersed in subtle energies, like fish swimming in an ocean of water, but rather as live wires. When we get close enough to another live wire—which might be a person, a place, or an object—a spark of electricity jumps between us, momentarily connecting us. I think of subtle energies as actively connecting us rather than simply existing as a glow around us and between us. In my experience, this participatory element is important.

The corollary to this (and it's one that has been borne out for me both in my personal life and in my classes) is that if I wish to detect subtle energies, I cannot be passive. I must be energetic myself. I can be receptively energetic, but I must engage. I cannot just sit back and tune in, so to speak. To detect what's in motion, I must be in motion myself, just as I cannot stand still and hope to catch a moving train.

This does not mean I have to be physically active, although usually I can sense subtle energies in my environment most clearly when I'm walking about. Nor does it mean that my mind and my emotions need be busy, although in maintaining the dynamic, poised alertness that characterizes the open space from our previous exercise, they're certainly active and participating in the process.

What it does mean is that I need to energetically match myself to the energies that I wish to perceive. In metaphysical-speak, I need to raise my "vibrations" in order to detect energies that are "vibrating" more swiftly than I am (which is one of the ways the subtle, inner world is defined: as a hierarchy of dimensions of progressively higher vibrations). If I think of myself as a radio, I'd at least have to turn myself on before I could tune myself in. The equivalent here is a process of heightening our inner energy, becoming more aware and alert in the moment. That is the focus of the first part of this exercise.

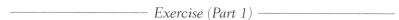

—————————— *Exercise (Part 1)* ——————————

Please make yourself comfortable and close your eyes. In whatever way you choose, go into the inner theater of your heart and mind, into the world of your imagination, into your imaginal space.

We're going to go through a series of images, each suggesting in some way an increase in your energy on one level or another. Allow yourself to focus on the sense of raising or heightening your energy. The images themselves are immaterial; they're only little narratives to help you capture the felt sense of increasing your energy.

First, imagine yourself as water in a pot on a stove. As the heat increases, feel yourself beginning to boil. At first the molecules within you are sluggish and slow-moving, but as they absorb more heat energy they begin to move faster and faster. They dance within you, creating swirls and bubbles. Feel their energy increasing. Feel your energy increasing.

[Pause]

Imagine yourself standing in a crowd at a rock concert. Everyone around you is swaying with anticipation. The band, which is one of your favorites, begins to play. You feel the primal rhythm of the drumbeat as if it were the heartbeat of the earth itself rising up through your feet, up your legs, into your hips. As the the music builds, the melodies and rhythms swirling around you and within you, you begin to sway, to dance, to move. You feel the energy of the crowd around you, the music, the yelling, the cheering. It flows into you and through you. Your feel your energy rising.

[Pause]

Now imagine yourself in an airport, waiting to meet the person you love most in all the world. You've not seen each other for a while, and you've been missing each other intensely. As you wait, you feel the energy of anticipation rising within you. You're excited that you'll be together again. You've made wonderful plans for the evening, for the days ahead, and you know it will be a happy, joyous time like no other you have known. Now the plane has landed and people are beginning to walk down the jetway. Your heart is beating faster. At any moment you'll see your loved one coming out and heading towards you. Then your loved one is there, coming towards you, smiling, excited. You feel your energy rising.

[Pause]

Imagine yourself in an auditorium. Someone you love—a child, a spouse, a close friend—is about to be honored with the Nobel Prize for service to humanity. The room is abuzz with excitement. You're excited as well, joyous for what this person has accomplished and for this honor they will receive. Your heart swells with an unselfish pride. Suddenly someone comes to the podium and announces the award. The audience is on its feet, clapping. You're on your feet as well, clapping enthusiastically. The person for whom you feel such pride and love stands up and walks to the stage. The applause increases. You feel your energy rising.

[Pause]

Imagine yourself in a seminar room. One of the most brilliant minds you've ever known is laying out, with intellectual clarity and with practical wisdom, a teaching that you know will empower you and change your life. It possesses an elegant logic and a grace of understanding that will cast your profession into a whole new light. As you listen, you become more and more excited. Your mind seems to have come alive in a new way, as one insight, one revelation, one "'Aha!" after another cascades through your thinking. And as the speaker approaches the climax of the presentation, you can hardly wait. Everything is falling into place. Your mind has never felt so enriched and engaged. The speaker pauses before the final resolution. In anticipation, you feel your energy rising.

[Pause]

Imagine yourself in a calm and beautiful place outdoors. You're about to meet a person whom you and many others consider one of the holiest people alive today, a person radiant with love and compassion, with a robust intellect and an open heart, and a vibrant body that radiates health. Although this person's experience and knowledge of the spiritual world and the spiritual life seems unequaled, you've never sensed the slightest bit of arrogance in this person. An honest humility, an easy humanity, and a ready wit make this person wholly accessible. You've read about this person for a long time; you've even attended some lectures this person has given. Your heart has been lifted, your soul inspired, your life transformed. And now you're about to meet this person, who is equally interested in meeting you. Even now, you hear footsteps approaching, and you can feel a growing radiance in the atmosphere around you, as if every stone, every plant, every animal, in your vicinity is rejoicing in this person's arrival. A subtle feeling of joy vibrates in the air. Then this person appears and strides forward, taking your hand, smiling at you. You feel your heart opening, your soul expanding. You feel your energy rising.

[Pause]

You feel your energy rising. In each of these stories, you felt your energy rising. Was it the same energy? Was it different each time? What did it feel like? If it differed in each situation, how did it differ? Most importantly, could you experience inwardly what it felt like when energy rises? Could you replicate that experience at will? Could you raise your energy when you need to or want to? Take some time to consider these questions and to reflect on any impressions, sensations, thoughts, feelings, images, or insights that may have come to you during these imaginal narratives.

[Pause]

Now, go into stillness and to your open space. Recover this feeling of your energy rising physically, emotionally, mentally, lovingly, compassionately, spiritually. Shift into sacred space; say a prayer to that which you consider holy. Invoke its presence. See or feel yourself begin to glow. Open your heart as if it were a source of fire and light and allow its compassionate, unconditional love to flow. Energized by this glowing power, you'll experience the world around you in a heightened way. You become a being of pure energy, pure light, pure flame. What kind of world do you now inhabit? What do you feel around you? What do you feel within yourself? What energies are moving around you, within you, from you, towards you? The whole universe is energy, and you're part of it. You see with eyes attuned to energy, hear with ears attuned to energy, touch with hands attuned to energy. Your heart is the energy of love, and you beat on behalf of all creation. Take time to reflect on what it means to be energy.

[Pause]

Now feel yourself rematerializing, but remember what it's like to perceive the world as energy because you're energy yourself. As you condense, you transform back into form, into matter. You become yourself, back in your physicality, your heightened energy integrating with grace and balance into your body, with any surplus flowing into the world to go where it's most needed as a blessing.

When you're finished, open your eyes and step out from your imaginal space back into your everyday world. If you wish, see yourself back on the stage in your inner theater of the heart and mind. See yourself stepping down off the stage and leaving the theater, consciously reentering your everyday life, grounded and balanced, with a feeling of being refreshed, regenerated, and in harmony.

—————————————— *Exercise (Part 2)* ——————————————

In this part of the exercise we are going to experiment with the image of the field of energy around you. This energy is not separate from you but it *is* you, the emanation of your being. In advanced work, a person may discover that this field is really composed of several layers, each representing the quality and vibration of a different aspect of ourselves, such as our mental energy, our emotional energy, our physical vitality, our spiritual presence, and so forth. But for our purposes here, we are going to keep this very simple.

Please make yourself comfortable and close your eyes. In whatever way you choose, go into the inner theater of your heart and mind, into the place where you daydream and fantasize, into the world of your imagination, into your imaginal space.

Imagine that you are within an egg-shaped transparent container. Turn your attention to your general state of mind. Don't focus upon any particular thought or train of thoughts but rather get a felt sense of the quality of your thinking. How do you generally experience yourself as a thinking person? What is the general quality of your thoughts? What is the nature of your mental presence in the world? Once you have a sense of this, imagine this presence dissolving into a light that begins to fill the transparent container around you.

Turn your attention to your general state of emotion and feeling.

Again, don't focus upon any particular emotion but rather get a felt sense of the quality of your emotional life. How do you generally experience your emotional life and yourself as an emotional person? What is the general quality of your emotions? What is the nature of your emotional presence in the world? Once you have a sense of this, imagine this presence dissolving into a light that blends with the light that is already in the transparent container around you.

Turn your attention to your spiritual life. Don't focus upon a specific spiritual image but, rather, get a felt sense of the quality of spirit that you experience. How do you generally experience your spiritual life and yourself as a spiritual person? What is the nature of your spiritual presence in the world? Once you have a sense of this, imagine this presence dissolving into a light that blends with the light that is already in the transparent container around you.

Finally, turn your attention to your body. What is the quality of your physical vitality and state of being? How do you generally experience yourself physically? What is the nature of your physical presence in the world? Once you have a sense of this, imagine this presence dissolving into a light that blends with the light that is already in the transparent container around you.

You are now surrounded by a light that represents the distilled and blended qualities of how you experience yourself. You are immersed in the light of your presence, at least as you currently experience it. This light and presence is the field of energy that surrounds you. What does it feel like to you? Take note of any impressions or images that may arise for you.

You can imagine yourself standing inside this field, much as you are within your skin. But when you heighten yourself, when you light yourself as a candle, you can *become* the field.

Bring yourself to a heightened state centered at your core of stillness and attunement to the sacred, and extend your awareness into the field that surrounds you. Let your heart center pour its compassion and love into the field. Now, project your field outward as if your eyes and ears, heart, and hands were at the edge of it. You're an expanding field of love, compassion, and perception. What does this feel like? How far can you go? Do you have a sense of touching or encountering anything? Take note of any impressions or insights, thoughts or feelings, sensations or images, that may arise for you.

[Pause]

Draw yourself as a field back to your embodied self. Withdraw your awareness from your field, and center yourself in your place of stillness, balance, and wholeness. When you are finished, open your eyes and step out from your imaginal space back into your everyday world. If you wish, see yourself back on the stage in your inner theater of the heart and mind. See yourself stepping down off the stage and leaving the theater, consciously reentering your everyday life, grounded and balanced, with a feeling of being refreshed, regenerated, and in harmony.

Take time to record in your journal anything that you wish to remember.

——————————— *Exercise (Part 3)* ———————————

Please make yourself comfortable and close your eyes. In whatever way you choose, go into the inner theater of your heart and mind, into your imaginal space.

Now, drawing on your experience of the first part of this exercise, raise and heighten your energy. Light yourself as a candle; shift yourself into a more perceptive state. Enter stillness; see with the eyes and heart of that open space. Be in your world not only as a particle but as a wave as well.

When you feel this sense of heightened energy, open your eyes and look around you. Remember that every object in your room, everything you can see, is also vibrating and radiating. Like you, it is made up of energy. Pick one of these objects, any object, and give it your attention. Think about what it is, what it does, what it means to you, why it's here in your room, and anything else that engages you with it.

Now close your eyes and picture this object. Drawing from the radiating energy that fills and surrounds you, send some energy to this object. You can do this either by visualizing a beam of energy going from you to it or by becoming your field and imagining that the bubble of energy and presence around you expands to include and embrace that object. Then pause and become actively receptive. See if you can feel an energy coming back in return.

Open your eyes, pick another object, and repeat this exercise.

Altogether, try this exercise with four separate objects and see what difference, if any, you detect in their energies, in their response to your energy, or in your energy in relationship to them. As always, also note any impressions, thoughts, images, feelings, insights, and sensations that may arise. In particular, if you worked with both natural objects, like stones, and artificial objects like a carving or a toaster, what differences did you detect, if any?

[Pause]

When you've finished with the fourth object, try this exercise with a living plant. If you have more than one plant in your room, or if you're doing this exercise outdoors, you can do the exercise with up to four plants, observing any differences you may feel in their response to your energy or in your energy in relationship to them, as well as any impressions, thoughts, etc., that may arise. In particular, what differences did you detect, if any, between working with the energy of an object versus working with the energy of a plant?

When you're finished, open your eyes and step out from your imaginal space into your everyday world. If you wish, see yourself back on the stage in your inner theater of the heart and mind. See yourself stepping down off the stage and leaving the theater, consciously reentering your everyday life, grounded and balanced, with a feeling of being refreshed, regenerated, and in harmony.

——————————— *Exercise (Part 4)* ———————————

This exercise is one that Dr. William Bloom uses in some of his energy workshops. It will require the help of another person. In this exercise and in the one that follows, pay attention to the experience and quality of connectedness you feel with your partner. Remember, connectedness and engagement is what this use of energies is all about.

Either outdoors or in a large room, begin by standing twenty feet apart from your partner. Both of you should look carefully to be sure you know where the other person is standing. Make sure the space between you is free of obstructions, since you'll be walking towards each other with your eyes closed (though some peeking is allowed!).

Each of you should go into your inner stillness, into your open space, and shift into a state of heightened energy. Then hold your hands, palms open, towards each other. Close your eyes. Imagine beams of energy flowing between your open hands, connecting them like threads of light. What does it feel like?

Keeping your eyes closed so that you can concentrate on the feeling of the energy (a bit like flying a plane on instruments alone), begin to walk towards each other. If necessary, open your eyes and peek now and again to make sure you're not diverging in some other direction. As you move closer together, feel any changes in your hands or in the feeling of the threads between you. Keep going until you're about two feet away from each other. Was there any point in this journey when the energy felt stronger? Any point where it seemed to diminish?

Open your eyes. With your eyes open but your palms still extended, walk backward, remaining in the heightened state and still beaming energy to each other through your hands. When you're back to about where you started from, drop your hands.

Now close your eyes and feel the beam of energy and light flowing from your heart to the other person's heart. Repeat the exercise of walking towards each other. Does this energy feel different from the energy that flowed from your hands? Again, does it seem to be stronger at certain points along the way and weaker at others?

When you're about two feet apart, open your eyes and back up as before until you're back where you started.

Do this exercise two more times, once with energy flowing from the center of your forehead and once with an energy flowing from your solar plexus, each time connecting with a similar flow from your partner. Again, pay attention to whether the energy differs when flowing from the head or the solar plexus, the hands or the heart.

When you've completed these four exercises, both you and your partner will now stand in silence, eyes closed. Feel your heightened energy integrating into your body, and any excess draining into the earth or radiating out into the world to be used wherever it may be needed. When you're finished, open your eyes and re-enter your everyday world, grounded and balanced, with a feeling of being refreshed, regenerated, and in harmony.

―――――――――――――― *Exercise (Part 5)* ――――――――――――――

This is the same as the previous exercise but uses the image of the field rather than that of beams of energy. As before, you and your partner should stand in front of each other. This time, however, see yourself immersed in your field of light and presence. Becoming your field, extend yourself as this field towards your partner as if you were moving towards him or her, asking him or her to do the same. Imagine the two fields touching and interpenetrating as you embrace your partner with your energy. What does that feel like? Is it different from when you imagined yourself beaming energy to each other?

Walk towards each other until you are able to comfortably touch each other's hands, then back up until you are where you started. Did you notice any difference in the quality or intensity of how you experienced your own field or the field of your partner as you physically moved closer to or away from each other?

Pull back from being your field and see it surrounding you as a bubble of light and presence. Now imagine the energy emanating from the center of your heart, the center of your forehead, and the center of your solar plexus. These different energies converge and blend within your field, allowing your field to become a master chakra or energy center embracing, integrating, and synthesizing all other energy centers within your subtle body. Extend this field from you to your partner as if you were stretching forth your hands, asking him or her to do the same. Imagine these fields touching and interpenetrating. What does that feel like? Is it different from when you were the field itself?

As before, walk towards your partner until you are able to comfortably touch each other's hands, then back up until you are where you started. Did you notice any difference in the quality or intensity of how you experienced your own field or the field of your partner as you physically moved closer to or away from each other?

When you've completed these exercises, both you and your partner will now stand in silence, eyes closed. Feel your heightened energy integrating into your body, and any excess draining into the earth or radiating out into the world to be used wherever it may be needed. When you're finished, open your eyes and re-enter your everyday world, grounded and balanced, with a feeling of being refreshed, regenerated, and in harmony.

Take time to record in your journal any impression, thoughts, feelings, ideas, images, sensations, or insights that may have come to you while doing any or all of the parts of this exercise.

EXERCISE 6: CONNECTEDNESS

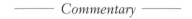

Commentary

Connectedness is more than just an idea of interrelatedness and interdependency. It is, for me, also an experience of being at home in the universe. It's the sense of being part of the cosmic family, kin to stars and starfish, comets and cockatiels, planets and periwinkles. It's an experience of belonging.

In this day and age when *ecology* has become a household word, it's important that we understand just how thoroughly our destiny and well-being is woven into the fabric of all life on this planet and how interdependent we are with the integrity of that life. But when we bless or are blessed, what may awaken in us is not so much an environmental sense of interrelatedness as a sense of community—of being connected to a support system that has our well-being firmly in its heart, even of being cared for and loved as one of the family.

As someone desiring to give blessings, the more you can experience this sense of belonging and communion, the sense of connectedness within yourself and with the whole of creation, the more you can communicate it subtly to another. It becomes part of your energy field, an element in your open space, part of that deeper, higher, more attuned consciousness to which you shift when you "light" yourself from within. And as such, it becomes part of the relationship you share with another in the act (and energy) of blessing.

I often use the word *presence* to suggest the wholeness, integration, and power that we share with another in the act of blessing. This presence is itself a manifestation of our connectedness and our sense of belonging and participation. It's an expression of the coherence we have inside ourselves and with our world that allows spirit to flow within and from us in unobstructed ways. It is an expression of how relaxed and at home I am within the community of my own body, thoughts, and feelings, as well as within the community of the cosmos. The more I feel that I belong, that I am at home, that I am connected to and at one with a universal community of life, the more coherence there is for me. Then the greater the presence that I can bring to focus upon the moment.

We may think of presence as charisma or force of personality, but it is more than these. Charisma can attract us to another, but it can be separating as well. I can see myself as a satellite orbiting a charismatic sun within another person. I can be dominated by another's force of personality. Presence, though, does not dominate; it embraces. It includes others. It gathers them up into communion and community. It manifests its power through connectedness and belonging. In the instant of blessing, as presence passes between us, we belong to each other. We are in community together. We are connected.

As with so many of the other concepts and exercises I've presented, weaving this sense of connectedness into your life is a long-term project. It's not something that can be accomplished through a few psychospiritual exercises. What's important is that you continue to deepen the realization of your connectedness as you go through life. Doing a spiritual practice is not like earning a degree; there's no point at which you can say, "Well, that's it. I've completed the course and now I'm enlightened!" One enlightenment only leads to another.

So we must find ways in our lives to emphasize and to experience our sense of connectedness and belonging, and one vital way to do this is to extend that sense to others. The more we help others experience acceptance and connection, the more we will experience it ourselves. It's the paradox of all spiritual work: to gain something, we must first give it away; to learn it, we must do it. And when we do extend ourselves lovingly and empathetically to connect with another, that is when energy flows and fields expand.

Exercise

Please make yourself comfortable and close your eyes. In whatever way you choose, go into the inner theater of your heart and mind, into the place where you daydream and fantasize, into the world of your imagination, into your imaginal space.

Imagine yourself in a vast hall. You are a disembodied point of view. You've no body, no presence, no power, no spirit, no potential. You're no thing at all.

Around you in a circle are figures, robed and cloaked. You have no idea who or what they are.

One of the figures comes forward. The cloak falls away, and you are looking at No Thing, at pure void, at the darkness and lightness of a Mystery you cannot begin to comprehend. You hear a voice that says, "I am Source. All that is, is what I am. I give you potential."

As the voice speaks, you feel the tiniest stirring within the nothingness that you are and you become . . . Something.

A second figure steps forward, and its cloak falls away. It also is No Thing, but yet there is some thing there, a movement, a vibration, a seed. It's still a Mystery you cannot comprehend. You hear a voice that says, "I am Being. All that is is what I am. I give you spirit and existence."

As the voice speaks, you feel another stirring, and you become a presence.

A third figure steps forward. Its cloak falls away. It's pure Light, a vibrating, shining presence that's finally Something but still a Mystery you don't comprehend. You hear a voice that says, "I am Light. All that is is what I am. I am the Lord of the Strings. I give you music and dancing. I give you energy and movement."

As the voice speaks, you find yourself vibrating and glowing, filling the void around you with activity.

A fourth figure steps forward. Its cloak falls away. This being is also a shining figure of Light, but it pulses in rhythmic ways, and within its glowing depths you catch a glimpse of many colors intertwining, weaving a Mystery that warms and attracts you. You hear a voice that says, "I am Logos. I am Love. All that is is what I am. My right hand is chaos and my left hand is order. From their joining, I give you life."

As the voice speaks, you find yourself pulsing with light, feeling within yourself an irresistible urge to unfold, to grow, to explode into form and substance.

A fifth figure steps forward. Its cloak falls away. This being is shaped like a spiral galaxy spinning in space. You feel a kinship with it; like you, it is also Life. You hear a voice that says, "I am Cosmos. All that is is what I am. I give you pattern and coherence."

As the voice speaks, you feel yourself gathering into a spiral, taking on a pattern, an organization, a form.

A sixth figure steps forward. Its cloak falls away. This being is a star that shines brightly upon you and then explodes in a shower of particles. You hear a voice that says, "In my heart, elements are formed. I am the womb of the universe, and from me worlds are born. I give you substance."

As the voice speaks, you feel your form becoming tangible, built from atoms forged in the heart of stars and released into the universe as that heart erupts outward in a nova-blast of sacrifice and giving.

A seventh figure steps forward. Its cloak falls away. This being is the Earth, shining in space, brilliant in blue and white, brown and green. You hear a voice: "I gather the elements and give them a place to meet and join, a place where life can take form and substance and begin to grow. I give you a place where your life can be and can become."

As the voice speaks, you find your form gathered by the earth into a primal cell, the ancestor of all organisms. And in your depths you feel all that will one day emerge, from redwoods and roosters to swordfish and nightingales.

An eighth figure steps forward, and its cloak falls away. You see a person wrapped in light, a person who seems neither man nor woman, young nor old. You hear a voice that says, "I am Humanity. I invite you into my destiny and give you shape and form to be part of my becoming."

As the voice speaks, now you become a person, with body and head, arms and legs, hands and feet. You have substance and presence, and all that you've been, all the infinity from which you've come, inhabits this form and empowers it.

A ninth figure steps forward, and its cloak falls away. You see two figures, a man and a woman. Behind them and around them are many other figures, indistinct but nonetheless present and part of the two who step forward. They say, "We are your parents. Around us gather our ancestors and all who share humanity with us and with you. We give you a particular body, a particular life, through which the spirit, the world, and your own humanity may emerge. We call you to this Earth. We give you specificity."

Now you are yourself, the identity you have come to know all the years of your life, the identity that's still unfolding in all the years to come. You are part of a vast family, from the Source to the Cosmos to the Planet to your Personhood. You are formed from spirit, birthed from stars, wrapped in the green juiciness of life, and gathered into Humanity. You are home.

There is one figure left. It comes forward. Its cloak falls away. You see it's not a figure at all, but many figures—some human, some not—and many worlds stretching all the way into the cosmos and into the spirit, the Light, the Source beyond. You hear a voice. "We are all that come into being because of you. Descendants, creations, possibilities, potentials, we will take form because you've taken form; we live because you live. We are the future you will shape, in part through your will, in part through your deeds, and in part simply through the fact of your existence. We are part of your belonging. We give you the gift of Future."

The figures all step forward and one by one fade into your heart, into your body, into your soul. Now all are in you, and you in them. You're at home. There's noplace else you could be.

Take time to reflect on this exercise, taking note of any impressions, ideas, thoughts, feelings, images, intuitions, or sensations that may have come to you. Feel what it's like to belong to creation and to belong to yourself. Feel what it's like to be connected.

When you're finished, open your eyes and step out from your

imaginal space back into your everyday world. If you wish, see yourself back on the stage in your inner theater of the heart and mind. See yourself stepping down off the stage and leaving the theater, consciously reentering your everyday life, grounded and balanced, with a feeling of being refreshed, regenerated, and in harmony.

EXERCISE 7: THE INNER HEART

——— *Commentary* ———

There are different ways of imaging connectedness, and one is to see ourselves as all part of the body of a great organism. Depending on how expansive we wish to be in our thinking, we can imagine this organism variously as our family, our ethnic group, our nation, all of humanity, the whole planet, the solar system, the universe, or even as the sacred. For the purposes of this exercise, it doesn't matter. What does matter is that we see ourselves as part of larger systems, larger wholenesses, just as we're made up of smaller systems and wholes, right down to our cells and the proteins and molecules that make them up.

Within this greater organism, whether conceived as stretching from the infinitely small to the infinitely large or only encompassing the range and dynamics of a relationship between myself and one other person, "something" circulates. We may call this "something" Life, Love, Spirit, Energy, Joy, or anything. But the something we are naming is the flow of nourishment, support, activity, connectedness, and organization that enables the whole to exist, to grow, and to unfold. It's the circulation that creates order, form, and life.

As I mentioned in the main text, one of the images I like to work with in the Art of Blessing is myself as a heart, pumping within this greater circulation and flow of love and life, spirit and energy. This "beating" and the circulation that moves around and within me as a consequence happens automatically, just like the beating of my own physical heart. But I can engage with it consciously and deliberately. I can "beat" myself more powerfully, enhancing the flow within the system.

What drives this "beating" is really our mindfulness, our attentiveness, our empathy, our compassion, and our love, all expressed in vital, active ways. The more I love, the more I care, the more I seek your well-being and happiness, the more my heart circulates life and love, spirit and energy into the world.

A blessing is an expression of this heartbeat. It's an embodiment of the flow and circulation that nourishes and empowers us all.

———————————— *Exercise* ————————————

Please make yourself comfortable and close your eyes. In whatever way you choose, go into the inner theater of your heart and mind, into the place where you daydream and fantasize, into the world of your imagination, into your imaginal space.

Imagine that you and everything around you, everything in the world, is immersed in a great fluid. This fluid bathes you, nourishes you, gives you life and energy; its substance is love. I will call this fluid *spirit*.

Imagine yourself as a heart within this fluid. You're beating with a steady rhythm, and spirit's moving around, through, and within you. You're part of a flow of circulation.

Holding on to this image, open your eyes and look around. Notice the things around you. Now close your eyes and reach out to those things in a loving way. Feel your presence extending itself to these things, making connections, opening pathways for the circulation of spirit. As you do, imagine yourself beating more strongly, your heart powered by the compassion, the interest, the mindfulness, you feel towards what's around you. See yourself as a heart pulling spirit in and pumping spirit out. Feel the fluid around you flowing more freely in response to your beating. It swirls around you and out from you in widening waves. You can direct and channel it through the focus of your presence and your intent, or you can simply let it flow from you in all directions, enlivening the circulation of spirit in the world around you. Either way, as you do so, you become aware of other hearts like yourself picking up this beat and extending it further.

Now, as this spirit circulates powerfully through you and around you, you become aware of one other heart in particular. It's a deeper, more powerful heart, the pulse of its rhythm supporting everything else like a drumbeat underneath a melody. You realize that the fluid around you is coming from this deeper heart, that it's the source of the spirit and its circulation.

With no strain at all, effortlessly and happily, you align your beat with this deeper rhythm. You let this greater heart beat through you, supporting and empowering your own beating as a heart of compassion and love. As you enter into this alignment, you feel the circulation within and around yourself becoming even stronger, its flow more powerful, its embrace widening. This places no effort upon you whatsoever; instead, you feel filled with strength and vitality.

Experience what this feels like. See in your mind's eye the circulation of spirit sweeping away obstructions and obstacles within you and around you, enlivening stuck or stagnant energies, bathing all within its enriching, vitalizing, transformative flow. Just rest in this rhythm and let yourself beat in time with the great Heart, supported by its power. Just beat. Beat. Beat. Beat. Beat. . . .

[Pause]

When you're ready, let your beating settle into a rhythm that feels natural and comfortable for you as you prepare to leave your inner theater of the heart and mind. When you've done this, open your eyes and move out from your imaginal space into your everyday world. If you wish, see yourself back on the stage in your inner theater of the heart and mind. See yourself stepping down off the stage and leaving the theater, consciously reentering your everyday life, grounded and balanced, with a feeling of being refreshed, regenerated, and in harmony.

As you do, remember: You are a heart.

——— *Commentary* ———

With this exercise and the eleven that follow, we'll be dealing with concepts and issues that I've already discussed in the main text, usually as part of the four steps I described in Chapter 12. With two or three exceptions, little additional commentary should be needed.

As with connectedness, the way to develop a spirit of unobstructedness in one's own life is to be unobstructing in one's dealings with others. (Remember, I differentiate between an obstruction, which simply halts and blocks a flow, and a limit, which directs or defines it.) At the least, I can avoid placing obstructions in the way of others through mindlessness or ill will, and at best, I can be alert to opportunities to remove them.

Of course, what may lead me to be obstructive are my own attitudes and the feelings that can arise from fear and other negative emotions. So whatever I do to unobstruct my own inner life will be important.

But unobstructedness is more than just removing (or not creating) impediments. It's also an active engagement with others in a way that promotes a more graceful flow between us in mutually enhancing ways. Likewise, ways in which I can love and appreciate myself and develop self-confidence and a sense of accomplishment will enhance my own inner flow and gracefulness.

One note: Part of this exercise asks you to look at negative elements in your life that affect or obstruct you and others. And it's important that you do so nonjudgementally, without blame or remorse. The purpose of the exercise is to learn how you may become unobstructed and unobstructing by understanding some of the reasons you create obstructions in the first place. It's an exercise of self-reflection, which will work best the more honest you are with yourself; it's not an exercise designed to be therapeutic. Doing this exercise won't necessarily remove those negative elements; that's something only you can do within the active context of your life through your choices and behaviors. To handle persistent issues of self-sabotage or the sabotaging of others may require professional help, or at least friendly and empathetic counseling, in whatever way that would be appropriate for you.

Exercise

Please make yourself comfortable and close your eyes. In whatever way you choose, go into the inner theater of your heart and mind, into the place where you daydream and fantasize, into the world of your imagination, into your imaginal space.

Enter your still center, and from there shift into your open space. In this space there's no judgment, but there can be discernment. With loving but discerning eyes, I want you to reflect upon yourself. What attitudes, qualities, habits, thoughts, or feelings within you manifest in ways that can obstruct others? Remember that preventing the negative behavior of a person towards yourself or towards another is exercising a boundary, not being obstructive. When you're obstructing, you're setting obstacles in the way of another, unwittingly or deliberately, with no greater intent than to make their way more difficult or to make your way easier at their expense. So, in your open, loving space, I want you to reflect on anything in you that would indulge itself in such behavior, driven by fear, self-doubt, spite, or some other emotion.

As you reflect, name as specifically as you can just what these elements are. Do this as if you were describing an obstacle course in order to determine the way through it. You're not assigning blame; you're simply looking for a clear path to follow by identifying the obstructing elements.

Once you've named at least one of these elements within yourself, think of a specific example of when you expressed this attitude, feeling, or image in an obstructing way towards another. What did you do, either unwittingly or deliberately, to obstruct the energy, the efforts, the work, or the life of another? Remember, thoughts and feelings about another can also be obstructing in subtle ways.

As you remember this specific situation, see the other person begin to transform into an obstacle within your world. This doesn't mean they become vindictive or angry; it only demonstrates that you cannot obstruct without creating an obstruction. When a flow is blocked, it becomes a block for everyone involved, including you. Blocked energies create their own repercussions, and not one of us is immune to the consequences.

Finally, picture this person actually turning into a large concrete block that obstructs your way and your view.

Now remember another time when you were obstructing. Be as specific as you can in your memory and take responsibility for your thoughts, feelings, and actions in the situation. See this second person you obstructed also turning into a large concrete block.

Now, in your mind's eye, look out on the landscape of your days: the landscape of your work and workplace, the landscape of your family and home life, the landscape of your friendships and relationships, and any other important parts of your life. How many large concrete blocks are there? In what way do they make the flow and grace of your life (not to mention the lives of those around you) more difficult or less direct and clear? In what way are they obstacles for you?

Take a moment to reflect.

[Pause]

Now, with equal honesty, look at your inner landscape. What large concrete blocks have you created through attitudes that may diminish or obstruct your own sense of self, spirit, power, or well-being? Where do these blocks exist in your life? What have you done to create them in the first place? As clearly and specifically as you can, name the attitudes, thoughts, or emotions that you identify as being inwardly obstructive. Remember a recent time when you expressed such an attitude, thought, or emotion and brought another concrete block into being. Be clear about what was happening and its effect upon you.

[Pause]

Shift back into your still place if you've left it. Be open to your presence. Drawing on the experience of the last exercise, allow yourself to become a heart beating with the circulation of love and spirit, energy and life. Just take time to attune to this "heart space," and to the larger Heart that beats within all creation. Feel yourself supported, empowered, and enriched by the circulation of spirit around, within, and through you. Allow yourself to gradually beat more powerfully in time with the greater Heart.

[Pause]

Now see your inner landscape with all the concrete blocks that obstruct the flow of love within yourself and towards yourself. See these blocks immersed in the fluid of spirit. As you beat as a heart, spirit circulates with ever greater strength around the blocks. You don't have to do anything to them; you simply have to see them immersed in the circulation of spirit and love, and see yourself as a heart beating in time with the heart of the sacred to heighten the flow and power of that circulation.

Like water around a rock, spirit flows and swirls around these concrete blocks, eroding them, weakening them, and, as you beat and watch, washing them away. As each block crumbles and dissolves into spirit, project your presence into the place where the block was. The block represented the effect of an attitude, a thought, an image, or a feeling that you've already identified and named. Now name its opposite and deliberately insert that positive feeling, attitude, image, or thought in the place where the block was, into the inner situation that gave it birth. If the block arose out of fear, for example, then now say, "In this place, in this situation, I honor my courage and my strength. I love myself for my ability in this moment to rise above my fear, to put it into perspective, and to invoke faith and courage in its place." Of course, you should choose your own words appropriate to your own unique situation.

Do this with each block as it dissolves, so that you've a memory of actively addressing the situation that created the block with an alternative set of responses—responses that remove obstructions, that empower you, and that align with the beating of the great Heart and with the circulation of spirit and life, love and energy. If you come back to this process whenever you feel yourself creating inner obstructions, you'll begin to build an approach that opens you to flow and spirit, an approach that allows you to be less obstructing towards yourself so you can in turn be unobstructing towards others.

Take time to feel what this dissolving and re-creating process is like. Take note of any impressions, sensations, thoughts, feelings, images, or insights that may arise.

[Pause]

Now look at the landscape of your life, your work, and your relationships. See the concrete blocks there that you previously identified and remembered, the obstacles you created for yourself when you created them for others.

See these blocks immersed in the fluid of spirit. As you beat as a heart, spirit circulates with ever greater strength around them. You don't have to do anything to them; you simply have to see them immersed in the circulation of spirit and love, and see yourself as a heart beating in time with the heart of the sacred to heighten the power of that circulation.

Spirit flows and swirls around these concrete blocks, eroding them, weakening them, and, as you beat and watch, washing them away. As each block crumbles and dissolves into spirit, project your presence to the place where the block was. The block represented the effect of an action, an attitude, a thought, an image, or a feeling that you've already identified and named. Name an alternative action or attitude, thought or feeling, that would have helped the other person or the situation, that would have been empowering, supporting, unobstructing. Think of yourself as a bridge that helps the other individual or the situation get to where it needs to go for fulfillment or accomplishment; think of what you can do to ease the way. Take note of what it feels like to think and respond in that way. Be aware of what it would take or what you need to do to be such a bridge, to be unobstructing, to be a heart beating on someone else's behalf as well as your own. Above all, be aware of the power you have to do these things and to be these things, in alignment with the great Heart that embraces and beats for us all. Observe any impressions, thoughts, feelings, images, ideas, sensations, or insights that may arise as you reflect on this.

[Pause]

Go into your still place. See yourself embraced by the circulation of spirit. Acknowledge any pain or remorse, or any other emotions, arising from this exercise in self-reflection. Commit to doing what you must in order to have no obstructions between your everyday self, your self as a powerful heart, and the Heart of the Source. The deep truth of spirit is that when you don't obstruct, you enter the world of the unobstructed.

When you're finished with your reflection, open your eyes and step out from your imaginal space back into your everyday world. If you wish, see yourself back on the stage in your inner theater of the heart and mind. See yourself stepping down off the stage and leaving the theater, consciously reentering your everyday life, grounded and balanced, with a feeling of being refreshed, regenerated, and in harmony.

To fully complete this exercise, you may need to take some concrete actions in your everyday life to resolve or remove obstacles you may have created for others. It's one thing to see these blocks be washed away by spirit in your imaginal world; it's something else again to apologize, make amends, or otherwise correct a situation in order to unblock its potentials for everyone involved. Not that the imaginal work is "only fantasy"; I can testify from my own experience that this is not so. Work done carefully and mindfully in imaginal space does communicate its intents into the realm of spirit that we all share, from where it can have an effect, sometimes a dramatic or miraculous one, upon our outer conditions.

Nevertheless, imaginal work is only one half of the coin for us who are embodied beings. It often needs to be grounded in action. A loving thought is wonderful, but so is an apology, a gracious touch, a handshake, or an overt honoring of the reality of the other person.

And if no action is possible, then look upon the situation as a learning experience and resolve to act the next time in a way that honors your power as one who practices the art of blessing, and in a way that opens for everyone involved the doorways into the unobstructed world.

——— *Final Commentary* ———

This exercise focused on our responsibilities for creating blocks and thereby obscuring the door to the unobstructed world. I chose this deliberately, since when we acknowledge responsibility, we also invoke the power necessary to fulfill that responsibility. To deny that I can be obstructive to myself or others is only to perpetuate a potential that can create and maintain obstructions from which I, as well as others, suffer; but just as important, it denies me the power and engagement I need to correct and transform the situation.

However, there obviously are times when we're the recipients of another's obstructing actions, thoughts, and feelings through no fault of our own. One response to this may be anger on our part, perhaps a desire to get even, or feelings of victimization, all of which can lead us into obstructing behavior ourselves.

An alternative way to do this exercise is to enter imaginal space and inwardly see the blocks that we believe others have created in our way. Then, rather than reacting to them directly or to the people who have been obstructive, go into your presence and into the state of being a heart and do that part of the exercise in which you beat more strongly, stirring spirit into greater activity and circulation, and seeing those blocks eroding, crumbling, and dissolving. You're then free to look for alternative ways to proceed. You're saying in effect that your inner heart, your open space, is large enough that it can envelop blocks and go beyond them. A block may be there, but you don't feel obstructed by it. Having read enough exercises by now, you're familiar with the process and can create a personal exercise that will help you achieve this state of mind of not feeling obstructed by obstructions! You can do it! I encourage you. Just remember to have a proper beginning and ending in which you move into imaginal space and out again mindfully and with grace.

As I said at the end of the exercise above, it may well be that in order to properly deal with someone who is deliberately or unwittingly creating obstructions for you and others, you'll need to combine working in imaginal space with some form of activity or dialog in the physical world. Just remember who you are as a practitioner of the Art of Blessing, with courage, strength, and a power that comes from love and a clear desire to enhance the life of another if at all possible and appropriate. If after your sincere attempts at resolving or correcting a situation you are unsuccessful, just leave that person to his or her own landscape of concrete blocks, and get on with the spirit of unobstruction and creativity in your own life.

——— *Commentary* ———

One of the ways I've observed in which people may feel obstructed in their lives is through their anger at humanity and shame at being part of the human race. Their own personal power becomes diminished or distorted because of these feelings. Such feelings can be compounded by religious images that only view humanity as being in a fallen state and that portray human nature in the most negative, debased, or restrictive of ways.

Heaven knows, there are plenty of good reasons to be angry at our kind and our impact upon the world and upon each other. But there are plenty of reasons to be proud as well. One can start in the usual places, such as galleries, museums, and libraries, that preserve for us a record of human achievement in the arts, in culture, and in science. But eventually one should look around one's own community or town, where in a multitude of ways, usually unnoticed or unannounced, one can see people performing acts of compassion, blessing, and just plain everyday goodness—not for any special reason but as a matter of course, because that's what being human is all about. For those who feel human nature is intrinsically bad, I also recommend a lovely book called *The Brighter Side of Human Nature: Altruism and Empathy in Everyday Life* by Alfie Kohn.

In any event, proud or ashamed, angry or delighted, we're all stuck with being human. We may as well make the best of it, or better still, *be* the best of it. After all, it's through each of us and what we do that humanity becomes defined.

―――――――――――――― *Exercise* ―――――――――――

Please make yourself comfortable and close your eyes. In whatever way you choose, go into the inner theater of your heart and mind, into the place where you daydream and fantasize, into the world of your imagination, and into your imaginal space.

As you stand on this empty stage, everything shifts around you, until you find yourself in front of a large building shaped like an H. The entrance is in the middle of the building that connects the two wings. Enter the building.

Now you're in a hall. In front of you is a door, but it's locked. You see that it has two keyholes. To your right down the hall is another door, which is open, and to your left down the hall is another open door. Go towards whichever one you wish.

The door takes you into one of the sides of the H, a long hallway with displays along both walls. There are no windows or other doors in this hall, but at the far end you see a table. As you walk down the hall towards the table, you take time to see the displays, presented like living dioramas in a museum. What you see is up to you, but the scenes will either be those of humanity's accomplishments, reflecting its positive, creative attributes, or those of its failures and deeds of destruction, reflecting its negative, hurtful, fearful attributes. Before you leave the building you'll see scenes from both sides, but it's up to you which you see first.

You cannot run down the hall to avoid seeing the scenes, for as you pass each one, it envelops you. You step into it as if it were a hologram and experience it as if you were present in it.

What you see is up to you. How long the hallway is and thus how much you see is up to you, though you will see more than one. The purpose here is to see what impressions, feelings, thoughts, or images arise in you as you contemplate either the positive or negative aspects of humanity. You're confronting your own humanness, your human legacy. You shouldn't push yourself beyond what you feel is appropriate; this isn't an exercise in self-flagellation or self-congratulation. However, do give yourself an honest opportunity to explore your feelings about your humanity and the impact that humankind's positive and negative legacies may have upon you and your self-image.

Walk down the hall, exploring each scene that arises before you, whatever it may be. Eventually, you come to the table at the end of the hall. On it lies a key. Pick it up and put it in your pocket. When you do, turn and go back to the door that led into this hallway. On the way back, however, the displays are gone. The walls of the hallway are blank.

When you reach the center hallway, go through it to the door at the other end. This will take you into a hall identical to the one you just left except that all the scenes will be different. If the hall you've already visited showed you the horrors that humanity has inflicted upon itself or upon the earth, this hall will show you the beauty and grace, the insights and accomplishments, that humanity has produced, and vice versa.

Once again, you cannot run down the hall to avoid seeing the scenes, for as you pass each one, it envelops you. You step into it as if it were a hologram, and you experience it as if you were present in it.

And again, what you see is up to you. How long the hallway is and thus how many scenes you see is up to you. The purpose here is to see what impressions, feelings, thoughts, images, or sensations arise as you contemplate either the positive or negative aspects and history of the humanity of which you are a part. You're confronting your own humanness, your human legacy. You should not push yourself beyond what you feel is appropriate; again, this is not an exercise in self-flagellation or self-congratulation. However, as in the previous hallway, do give yourself an honest opportunity to explore your feelings about your humanity and the impact that humankind's positive and negative legacies may have upon you and your own self-image.

Walk down the hall, exploring each scene that arises before you, whatever it may be. Eventually, you reach the table at the end of the hall. On it lies a key. Pick it up and put it in your pocket. When you do, turn and go back to the door that led into this hallway. On the way back, however, the displays are gone as before. The walls of the hallway are blank.

Once again you're in the central, connecting hallway. This time, go to the door opposite the main entrance, the door with the two keyholes. To open this door, an understanding of both humanity's positive and negative sides—and your reactions to each of them— is important.

You put the keys in the door and it opens. You step into a small, circular, domed chamber. It has no other doors or windows. The walls are unadorned, but in the middle of the room is a circular pedestal with three steps leading up to it.

You go into the room, climb up the steps, and stand on the pedestal. Immediately, you're surrounded by a beam of light, and all the walls begin to flash with scenes of possible destinies and futures for humanity. Ahead of you, the wall dissolves, and you're looking into infinity, however that may appear to you.

As you stand there, you hear a voice that says, "Whatever humanity has been, whatever humanity has done, what humanity will become rests in you. If you despair, the future will be despairing; if you're angry, the future will be molded by that anger; if you're ashamed, shame will shape your destiny. But if your pride in all humanity has done makes you arrogant, you may miss your step and fall into a future you would not wish. Be mindful, be patient, be persistent, be loving. Be imaginative and see beyond the hallways of the past, the images of triumph and of failure. The past can stop in this room with you. The future will be born in this room—from you."

The lights go out in this chamber and you find yourself back in the theater of your heart and mind. Take note of any feelings, sensations, images, impressions, insights, thoughts, or ideas that come to you from your imaginal experience.

[Pause]

Then when you're finished, open your eyes and step out from your imaginal space back into your everyday world. If you wish, see yourself back on the stage in your inner theater of the heart and mind. See yourself stepping down off the stage and leaving the theater, consciously reentering your everyday life, grounded and balanced, with a feeling of being refreshed, regenerated, and in harmony.

——— *Commentary* ———

In Exercise 11, I write about the role of the earth in the Art of Blessing. In developing our attunement to the empersonal spirit, one of the elements we draw upon is the intelligent power inherent in our bodies. This intelligence, or body wisdom if you wish, in turn emerges from a biological history that's ancient indeed, extending back beyond the human form to the first cells in the first oceans. The blood that flows in us is a remnant of those ancient oceans, and the life our cells lead is not much different from that of their ancient ancestors. In some respects, we've internalized and miniaturized that primeval world and now call it the body.

For many people, there's a spiritual strength that comes from nature and their connection to the land on which they live, and this strength and spirit would form a vital element of their power to bless. In our highly mobile and urbanized culture, we may lose track of this connection and thus that particular source of spiritual energy as well. There are a number of spiritual practices, both ancient and modern, that can reconnect us to the earth in positive ways. And of course, the ecological sciences continue to increase our insights into the interdependence that exists among us, the world in which we live, and the creatures that share this world with us. These provide numerous avenues for exploration for anyone wishing to add a sense of natural spirituality to how they practice the Art of Blessing.

But in invoking the empersonal spirit, it's not only the environment to which we turn: It is also to the inherent power and wisdom of our bodies themselves and to the biology from which they're formed and to the lineage of organic life from which they emerge.

Exercise

Please make yourself comfortable and close your eyes. In whatever way you choose, go into the world of your imagination, into your imaginal space.

As you sit with eyes closed, be aware of your body. Run your hands over your legs and arms and torso, and feel your love and appreciation flowing into the billions of cells that make you up. You are a communal being—and your life is supported by and mutually dependent upon the lives of these ever-renewing creatures whose ancestors once swam freely in the steamy oceans of the primeval earth. Simply appreciate the fact that you exist as an organic entity because of the lives and activities of countless billions of cells, each of which is a highly complex and, in its own way, intelligent being with its own connection to life, to spirit, and to the Source.

With your eyes closed, explore your organic interiority. Feel the inner space occupied by your organs and tissues. Feel the organic insideness of you. Not your inner thoughts or feelings or spirit, but the inner bodiness—the inner embodiedness—of you.

Feel into your organs: your heart, your lungs, your stomach, as many as you can imagine or sense. Feel into your bones: They seem so hard and strong, but they're far from static; they're living tissue from the interior of which your blood is born. Feel into your blood as it streams through your body, reaching into the tiniest inner corner of yourself to nourish the most distant cell and to spread information and messages throughout the body's nation.

Feel your bodiness with love and appreciation.

As you do, imagine yourself shrinking and falling into the interiority of your body, descending into the realm of the cells. Pick a part of your body and imagine yourself journeying to it like a fantastic voyager afloat on a single cell. You're in the company of a complex creature with a history far more ancient than your own, its lineage going back to the dawn of life on earth.

Place your hands lovingly upon the cell wall and feel yourself blending with the intelligence, the consciousness, the spirit, of this cell. Let your spirit and that of the cell intertwine and speak deeply to each other in a language of pattern and shape and ancient memory.

As you do, you find yourself traveling back in time, back to the first cell, the ancestor of all life on earth. What does this feel like? What intelligence or wisdom do you sense in this First One. It's much, much simpler than the cell with whom you're communing, but it's still infused with life, the first life. It has in itself the power of origination. It's the pioneer, the one who crossed the threshold from simple proteins interacting into something dynamic enough, complex enough, stable enough, that something entirely new could emerge: life.

Feel the power of this ancient entity that lies in this crossing of the boundary from inorganic to organic. Feel the power of this moment when life emerges with qualities and capabilities never before seen on earth. In this moment, a new world is born, a new future is created. In this moment, the spirit of the earth erupts in joy for the threshold that has been crossed.

In this place of the First One, the first cell, you can feel the roots of life going back even further. You can feel deep into the chemistry of the earth and the spirit of the world, deep into the "mineral-ness" of our beginnings, into proteins and molecules, elements and atoms, and all their myriad interactions. If you wish, you can even feel the roots of life descending into the quantum flux, the realm of probabilities and fields where space and time as we know them cease to exist and all is enfolded into the creative music of the spheres, and from there deeper into the Mystery of the Source.

From those roots, you return to the presence of the First One, the first cell, and from there you can feel yourself rushing forward along the paths of life. It's as if you're the first cell now, and your own impulse of life is a widening web from which emerge all manner of beings, from bacteria to budgies, dinosaurs to dachshunds, and ferns to flounders, from the scaled to the smooth-skinned and the furred to the feathered. In all these creatures, you can feel your life flowing. You're in trees and plants, fish and fowl, animals and insects. You are in all of humanity.

You have become Gaia, the biosphere of the earth, regulating the planet for its survival and its growth. From you as first cell a world has grown, and all the variety and wonder of that world emerged from the potential that's in you. Feel what that's like, feel your deep kinship with the earth. Feel your roots in the planet and your roots in life. Along these roots flows a spirit, a wisdom, a power, that can act as an ally in your embodiedness. Take note of any impressions, sensations, ideas, images, thoughts, feelings, or insights that may emerge as you reflect on the web of life and your connection to it.

[Pause]

Now, as first cell, resting at the center of a planetary web of life, you feel your awareness rushing along one particular strand and you find yourself back in the presence of the body cell with whom you first made contact. In it this vast web of life, the life of the world, is internalized in a unique way. In each of your cells, this web exists, the earth exists.

Offer your appreciation to this cell for its presence and work on your behalf and for the work and support of all its kin throughout your body. Far from being alone, you coexist with billions of allies who share the organic identity of "you."

Feel yourself expanding as you return to your full human awareness. Sit with your eyes closed, taking a moment to appreciate the wonder and power of what's organically within you. You're host to uncounted miracles of life each day, each hour, each moment. You're host to a world. In you that breakthrough moment when life emerged still exists, just as it exists in every blade of grass and leaf of tree, every animal and bird, every fish and insect, every form of life there is in the world around you. And because of it, you have the power of breakthrough as well, the power of emergence, the power of life to give birth to what the world has never seen before. Take a moment to reflect on this.

——— *Commentary* ———

The purpose of this exercise is to illustrate one possible way of attuning to the Empersonal Spirit, the spiritual energy and presence that you possess within your personal self as an incarnate individual. In it, we will draw upon the work done in the previous two exercises: attunement to our humanity and attunement to our connections with the earth.

——————— *Exercise* ———————

Please make yourself comfortable and close your eyes. In whatever way you choose, go into the inner theater of your heart and mind, into the place where you daydream and fantasize, into the world of your imagination, into your imaginal space.

See yourself in a favorite room in your house. All is familiar except that in the room is an altar with a single box lying upon it, and on the floor near the altar is a chest. At this time, don't touch or open this box. Instead, you go over and open the chest. In it are seven other boxes, which you take out one at a time.

The first box is labeled "Ancestors." Don't open it yet. When you do open it, you'll find an object that represents whatever strengths and wisdom you've gained from your parents or grandparents or that has come down through the family lineage and history. How has your life been shaped and enriched by your genetic and family heritage? Certainly they have given you a specific biological identity, and the opportunity to be part of this world. If your family history is an unpleasant or abusive one, you'll have gained the strength of a survivor and perhaps insights on how to avoid such dysfunctionality yourself. If you can think of nothing you've gained that's positive and empowering from your ancestors, then the box may be empty. But don't anticipate this. Something unexpected may be there that could throw a new light on your family experiences and what they have given you that has been positive.

Now open the box and see what's inside. It may be familiar. It may be mysterious. Its meaning may be obvious, or obscure and unexpected. Whatever it is, place it on the altar. It is your ancestors' contribution to your empersonal spirit.

The second box is labeled "Humanity." Don't open it yet. When you do open it, you'll find an object that represents whatever strengths and wisdom arise from your humanness and from being part of humanity's lineage and history, its accomplishments and its catastrophes. What do you feel about your humanness? What power, wisdom, or spirit comes into your life because you are a human being, heir to the human heritage? Think back to the exercise you did on attuning to your humanity. If you can think of nothing you've gained that's positive and empowering from your humanness, then the box may be empty. But don't anticipate this. Something unexpected may be there that casts a new light on what your humanness offers you.

Now open the box and see what's inside. It may be familiar. It may be mysterious. Its meaning may be obvious, or obscure and unexpected. Whatever it is, place it on the altar. It is your humanity's contribution to your empersonal spirit.

The third box is labeled "Earth." Don't open it yet. When you do, you'll find an object that represents whatever strengths and power you've gained from nature and the earth itself. How has your life been shaped and enriched by your natural heritage and your sense of the interconnectedness of all life? Like your human ancestors, nature gives you life, a specific biological identity, and the opportunity to be part of this world. Think back on the exercise you did attuning to the earth and to the web of life unfolding from the first cell. If you have little affinity for nature and you can think of nothing you've gained from the natural world that's positive and empowering, then the box may be empty. But don't anticipate this. Something unexpected may be there that puts your connection to the earth and what it offers you into a new perspective.

Now open the box and see what's inside. It may be familiar. It may be mysterious. Its meaning may be obvious, or obscure and unexpected. Whatever it is, place it on the altar. It is the earth's contribution to your empersonal spirit.

The fourth box is labeled "Body." Don't open it yet. When you do, you'll find an object that represents whatever strengths, power, and wisdom you've gained from your body and its biological intelligence. What gifts does your body offer you? If your body's history is an unpleasant one, if it's been abused or ill, it can still offer you wisdom and insights into how to avoid such dysfunctionality in the future. And it has a remarkable power to heal. At the very least, your body gives you location in the here and now and provides a place for the integration of spirit and a physical presence from which to interact with the world. If you can think of nothing you've gained from your body that's positive and empowering, then the box may be empty. But don't anticipate this. Something unexpected may be there that changes the way you think about your physical experiences and the positive things they've given you.

Now open the box and see what's inside. It may be familiar. It may be mysterious. Its meaning may be obvious, or obscure and unexpected. Whatever it is, place it on the altar. It is your body's contribution to your empersonal spirit.

The fifth box is labeled "Experience." Don't open it yet. When you do, you'll find an object that represents whatever strengths, insights, power, and wisdom you've gained from your unique life experience. How have you been shaped and enriched by life? What has your life given you that would be empowering or enhancing for others? Think of specific experiences that have benefited you or from which you've learned. What can you distill from those experiences into a spirit of wisdom and support that you can offer to others? If you can think of nothing positive and empowering, then the box may be empty. But don't anticipate this. Something unexpected may be there.

Now open the box and see what's inside. It may be familiar. It may be mysterious. Its meaning may be obvious, or obscure and unexpected. Whatever it is, place it on the altar. It is your life experiences' contribution to your empersonal spirit.

The sixth box is labeled "Accomplishments." Don't open it yet. When you do, you'll find an object that represents whatever strengths, insights, power, and wisdom you've gained from your positive accomplishments, from projects finished, from things well done about which you're proud. How has your life been shaped and enriched by your accomplishments? Think of specific instances. What have you gained from these achievements that you could use to support or mentor another? What richness of mind and feeling, body and soul, has developed in you that could be shared with others, in essence if not in detail? If you can think of nothing you've accomplished that's positive and empowering, then the box may be empty. But don't anticipate this. Something unexpected may be there that casts a new light on your efforts and their gifts.

Now open the box and see what's inside. It may be familiar. It may be mysterious. Its meaning may be obvious, or obscure and unexpected. Whatever it is, place it on the altar. It is your accomplishments' contribution to your empersonal spirit.

The seventh and final box is labeled "Vision." Don't open it yet. When you do, you'll find an object that represents your future vision of yourself. It's your sense of potential, your vision of what you wish to become or could become. It's the vision that urges you to grow and evolve, giving you hope. The power to have that vision and to see yourself capable of changing is one of your greatest strengths. It frees you from the dominance of habit and the tyranny of the familiar. It's the threshold within you from which a new world may emerge. What power do you feel when you contemplate this ability to change and grow? What energy or vitality arises from your vision and from the power to envision? How might you share this with another? Your sense of who you can become is as important a part of you as your memory of who you've been. It's part of your power, part of your spirit, and whatever is in the box will reflect this back to you. If you cannot think of any vision for your future, then the box may be empty. But don't anticipate this. Something unexpected may be there that renews your faith in your potentialities and possibilities, as well as your capacity to change and grow.

Now open the box and see what's inside. It may be familiar. It may be mysterious. Its meaning may be obvious, or obscure and unexpected. Whatever it is, place it on the altar. It is your vision's contribution to your empersonal spirit.

Look once more into the chest. Are there any more boxes? If so, take them out one by one, read their labels, and reflect on what object may be in that box for you. Use the seven boxes you've already opened as examples of how to proceed. When there are no more boxes, you may close the chest.

When all the objects which you've found are on the altar (and if there are fewer or more than seven, that's all right), open the box that was already on the altar when you first began. This box is labeled "Will." It contains something that represents both the sacred will, the will of the Source that brought you into being in the first place, and the will of your soul that specifically initiated and crafted this specific incarnation. This box contains the spirit of intentionality that generated your life and continues to guide its development. It's the spirit that fashioned all the other boxes that you've found.

Now open this box. When you do, you may see something specific in it, and if so, take note of what it looks like. But what you also see is light overflowing this box, embracing and connecting all the other objects on the altar. As it does so, these objects begin to glow themselves and begin to merge into each other, blending their strengths, their insights, their wisdom, their power. When this has taken place, a single glowing light is left upon this altar, a spiritual presence emerging from the different aspects of your embodied personhood, its history, its lineage, its connections to the earth, its experiences and accomplishments, and more. This light, this presence, is your empersonal spirit.

Now step forward and place your hands into this light. Feel the

presence that's there flow into you. Feel the power of your empersonal spirit flow into your body, into all your cells. See it flow into
the space around you and become an aura that radiates from you
with the power, the wisdom and the spirit of your embodied personhood, your earthiness and earthliness, your humanness, your
uniqueness.

Take a moment simply to be with this presence. Feel the meaning and nature of your empersonal spirit, what it is and what it can
offer. Take note of any impressions, insights, thoughts, feelings,
sensations, or images that may arise.

[Pause]

When you're finished, open your eyes and step out from your
imaginal space back into your everyday world, carrying with you
the sense of your empersonal spirit for as long as you wish or are
able. If you wish, see yourself back on the stage in your inner theater of the heart and mind. See yourself stepping down off the stage
and leaving the theater, consciously reentering your everyday life,
grounded and balanced, with a feeling of being refreshed, regenerated, and in harmony.

———— *Commentary* ————

If the empersonal spirit represents a state of mind in which we feel the focused power and presence of the richness and goodness of our personalities, then the transpersonal spirit represents that state of mind in which it's natural for us to feel an unselfish and unconditional love, a sense of unity with others, a sense of connectedness with the world, and an attunement to the sacred.

Obviously, it's the intent of all spiritual practices to bring us to such a state of mind, to bring us into the realm of the numinous from which we may draw spiritual insights and energies to bring into our personalities and the activities of our everyday lives. No single exercise is going to accomplish this. This is where the Art of Blessing both complements and in turn depends upon whatever other spiritual practice and attunement you have in your life, whether it's simply a routine of daily prayer, a regular discipline of meditation, the deeper practice of yoga, the performance of spiritually oriented ritual and worship, or any other practice that connects you with the spirit of the sacred on a daily basis.

To suggest such a practice is beyond what I wish to do in this book and is, in any event, a highly individual choice that you should make in freedom and personal attunement to your own vision of the Highest. However, people who are serious about mastering the Art of Blessing do need some activity in their lives that aligns them with the transpersonal side of their beings and with the presence of the Source by whatever name or image they choose to identify it.

I should note that in the following exercise, I make use of certain traditional imaginal conventions, such as rising up to find the transpersonal, as if this state were above us. However, the transpersonal does not exist in any one direction but is all around us. If you should prefer to go down into the earth to find the star in the exercise or go sideways or not move in any direction at all, that is quite all right. You can stand still and let the star come to you right where you are. The imagery is not as important as the sense of being drawn into a place and a presence beyond your ordinary personality.

--------------------------- *Exercise* ---------------------------

Please make yourself comfortable and close your eyes. In whatever way you choose, go into the inner theater of your heart and mind, into the place where you daydream and fantasize, into the world of your imagination, into your imaginal space.

Whether drawing upon memory or imagination, see yourself in a place that's holy to you. However you name it or envision it, in this place you either have had or imagine you can have an encounter with the sacred and with the presence of the spiritual worlds. To prepare for such an encounter, go into your inner stillness. "Light" yourself as a candle, shifting into a state of mind that's open to the source of all beingness. When you feel this openness, feel yourself transforming from "candle" into "heart," beating the power of unconditional love out into the world and feeling as you do the rhythm of a greater Heart beating alongside and within you.

[Pause]

As you stand in this place, become aware of a brilliant light above you in the form of a star. As you deepen your attunement to an environment of unconditional love, with every beat of yourself as a heart in the vast circulation of spirit, this star comes closer and closer until eventually it envelops you. As it does, you feel very light and joyful. You begin to rise. If your holy place is inside a building, then you simply pass effortlessly through the ceiling and up into the sky.

As you rise, you're treated to a vast vista as the world spreads out around you. You have no fear whatsoever. You feel as safe, as loved, as embraced, as you've ever felt before. You know you cannot fall.

You continue to rise, the earth unfolding before your vision until you see the curvature of the planet itself. Then, before you know it, you're rising so quickly that you've gone outside the atmosphere and are looking back on the earth from space. Although you're in vacuum and in the cold of space, you have no trouble breathing. You're perfectly comfortable within the light of this spiritual star.

Suddenly, everything shifts, and now you're looking from a perspective in which it seems you can see the entire cosmos. Galaxies wheel around you in all their splendor. Uncounted stars blaze in glory. You gaze upon the universe and it seems wholly alive, filled with the presence of the Source.

As you watch, all the colors and lights of the galaxies and stars seem to brighten and brighten and begin to run together into one great Light, until all you can see is this Light all around you. It's welcoming, and you will yourself to enter it. But your will and intent alone is insufficient. You discover that you can enter this Light, but to be fully present to it and one with it, you must also allow it to enter you.

So open yourself to the Light. Make your own invitation to the sacred to fully enter and infuse your life, which, after all, is *its* life as well. Feel each cell in your body opening to Light. Feel each organ opening. Feel your mind and emotions opening to the unconditional love and wisdom of the Source. Feel yourself merging into Light.

[Pause]

Filled with Light, one with Light, you see before you all the elements of your life. You see your parents and the lineage of your ancestors stretching back through time. You see your own life stretching from when you were a baby to the present moment and even on into a field of multiple possibilities that represents the future you have yet to create. You see the people you've known and those you currently know. You see your loved ones, your friends, your co-workers; you see those whom you don't like, even those you fear or hate. You see where you live and the work you do. You see the way you play and the hobbies you enjoy.

In short, you see your entire life. As you watch, each part of it, past, present, and potential, is filled with the Light in which you're immersed.

As you see this, you become aware of a presence standing next to you. Looking at it, you see that it's yourself blazing with Light, filled with unconditional love, filled with grace, filled with wisdom. It's the part of you that encompasses but also transcends your personality with all its needs and desires, fears and hopes. It's the part of you that's at home in this Light, at home in wholeness. It's your transpersonal spirit.

It has no fear of the dark or of the flesh; it rejoices in the whole of life. It's not the "good" you, the "positive" you, separate from what you perceive as the "bad" or "negative" you; it's not the "light" you as opposed to your shadow self. It's the you that exists as one-ness, able to enter into, embrace, and transform any shadow, any unclaimed or disaffected part of you; it's the you that heals and in-tegrates, enabling you to be whole.

Feel what this part of you, this transpersonal spirit, is like. Take note of any impressions, thoughts, images, sensations, or insights that may arise. What does it feel like to be this transpersonal self? Who are you as your transpersonal spirit?

[Pause]

As you watch, this spiritual self of yours begins to dissolve into liquid Light. Most of it flows into you and around you, but part of it sprays out over the display of your life, a drop falling on each part of it, even on those whom you fear or dislike. As it does, you hear these words:

I am in all parts of your life. Look for me in the others you meet and the places you go, for I will be there. Honor them, for they carry a part of your highest self—your whole self—even as you carry a part of theirs. And in so doing, recover me each day from where I live in the midst of others. Remember me and remem-ber others.

The Light fills every corner of your life, and for a moment, Light is all you see. Then this Light parts again and beneath you; the earth comes back into view, gleaming brilliantly, beautifully, in space. It glows not only with the reflected light of the sun but with its own inner Light, and it seems to you the most wonderful and beautiful place. With a surge of joy, filled with the Light and presence of your transpersonal self, you plunge back to earth, eager to reenter your world and your life, eager to begin the adventure of discovering that drop of your own inner light in the hearts and lives of others and offering from your life the drop of their highest self back to them.

Then, with grace and ease, you're back in your body, back in your everyday self. But you remain filled with a sense of your transpersonal spirit, that part of you that is one with the world around you, even as it's one with the sacred. Appreciate this part of you for as long as you wish. Then when you are finished, open your eyes and move out from your imaginal space back into your everyday world. See yourself consciously reentering your everyday life, grounded and balanced, with a feeling of being refreshed, regenerated, and in harmony.

EXERCISE 13: SUPERSTRING

 *Commentary*

Attuning to your empersonal and transpersonal spirits is part of the step of Identification, which I discuss in the main text. However, these are only images of two parts of your own wholeness, like two sides of a coin. The key to Identification in the Art of Blessing is to be the you that's the integrated blend of both. In effect, if you are metaphorically a "superstring" stretching in consciousness from the most universal and holistic spirit on the one hand to the most specific and personal on the other, then the empersonal spirit manifests when you pluck the string in one place and the transpersonal spirit manifests when you pluck the string in another, like two notes from the same guitar string.

But what you are in essence is neither one note nor the other but the string capable of producing the many notes. And it's in your "stringness" that the true power of blessing, which is the power of wholeness, resides. You can discover the string by listening to the various notes it can make. Indeed, this is how some philosophies describe the meaning of life and the evolution of the soul: that over many lifetimes we identify with and experience a wide range of notes, at times believing that a particular note or chord is all there is, until eventually we come to discover the "superstring" that's actually producing the notes. We then begin to identify with it, shifting our perspective and power from the awareness of a single note to being the whole string.

—————————— *Exercise* ——————————

Please make yourself comfortable and close your eyes. In whatever way you choose, go into the inner theater of your heart and mind, into the place where you daydream and fantasize, into the world of your imagination, into your imaginal space.

You're standing in the midst of your open space. You're all alone. Then you feel a trembling in the space and atmosphere beside you. You realize that something is attempting to materialize there, and as you attune to it, you realize it is your empersonal spirit.

Remember when you discovered and invoked this spirit in a previous exercise. Remember what it felt like. Draw on that memory to help this presence manifest beside you. As you do, your empersonal spirit takes shape next to you.

Now you feel a trembling in the space and atmosphere on the other side of you. Again, you realize that something is attempting to materialize, and as you attune to it, you realize it is your transpersonal spirit.

Remember when you discovered and invoked this spirit in a previous exercise. Remember what it felt like. Draw on that memory to help this presence manifest beside you. As you do, your transpersonal spirit takes shape next to you.

Now you're standing between these two aspects of yourself, both of which pulse with power and creativity. You feel attracted first to one and then to the other. One embodies the essence and gifts of your earthly (and earthy) self, the other the essence and gifts of your spiritual self. Which one should you be? Which one should you choose?

But you don't have to choose one or the other. You choose to be both, to allow them to blend and integrate within you. For you are neither one nor the other. You *are* both.

Holding out a hand to each of these presences, you grasp them and draw them into yourself. As you do, you begin to transform into a long string of light. You become a creative superstring, and from your wholeness worlds can be born. You stretch from spirit to earth, from universality to particularity; yet, you are neither one nor the other. You are that which encompasses and embraces both. You can play the note of the personal self, you can play the note of the transpersonal self, and you can play all the notes in between and beyond.

Feel what it's like to be this presence of wholeness and power, this superstring of life and beingness. Note any images, sensations, impressions, insights, thoughts, or feelings that may arise as you do so. It's this fused presence of the earthly and the spiritual, the personal and the transpersonal, the particle and the wave, the specific and the universal, that you wish to be when you bless, for then you bring to bear the best of all worlds. On the superstring of your life, you can play the melodies that will resonate with the moment and sing the blessing into being.

When you are finished, consolidate the feeling of this merger of empersonal and transpersonal spirits within you. Then open your eyes and step out from your imaginal space back into your everyday world. If you wish, see yourself back on the stage in your inner theater of the heart and mind. See yourself stepping down off the stage and leaving the theater, consciously reentering your everyday life, grounded and balanced, with a feeling of being refreshed, regenerated, and in harmony.

——— *Commentary* ———

There are many ways of actually opening to a situation or person: listening, observing, paying attention and extending your awareness to become part of the other. The idea is to halt the projection of our own wishes, opinions, thoughts, and will into a situation and to become unconditional in our approach, allowing that which needs to happen for the highest good of all of us to happen. It's an exercise in receptivity that can give coherence and attunement to our power and presence, for we respond to what is, not to what we think ought to be.

The key to this receptivity, though, is often nothing more exotic than willingness. It's our willingness to open that does the trick. But this willingness may come only as we confront our own fears, our need to be in control, our need to be safe, our need to preserve the status quo of our lives.

It's one thing to see oneself as the powerful spiritual or magical adept who beams out rays of blessing from a mountaintop above the fray. But it's something else again to see each situation as a chemical interaction needing to be charged into activity, and yourself as an enzyme that will catalyze that activity but at the risk of being transformed by the process. It's the openness to one's own change that makes the Art of Blessing both powerful and risky. Remember, blessing is an act of relationship; by entering into it, we become part of the action, not a detached operator or observer.

I include two exercises here. One is designed to be done solo by the reader. The other invites you to explore receptivity in a more interactive way.

———————————— *Exercise One* ————————————

Please make yourself comfortable and close your eyes. In whatever way you choose, go into the inner theater of your heart and mind, into the place where you daydream and fantasize, into the world of your imagination, into your imaginal space.

Imagine that you're standing outside a building that has one very narrow door and narrow, opaque windows. There's a light around this building that suggests a spiritual force is at work, or at least potentially present within it, but you have no sense of its purpose. You do sense that something inside the building would benefit from your presence. However, you can see only vaguely through the windows to see what's happening inside. To truly know, you must open the door and enter, willing to encounter and engage with whatever you find.

You are prepared for this. At your feet is a toolbox containing any number of tools that may be helpful. You also have a briefcase carrying any number of plans for how such a building may be decorated or restructured. Some of these tools and plans you like very much and some reflect the artistry and craftsmanship of some of the finest teachers and philosophers in the land.

As you look down at yourself, you realize you're wearing a bulky environmental suit like the ones workers wear when they're cleaning up toxic spills. Inside this suit, you know you're fully protected. Garbed in this suit, armed with your toolbox and briefcase, you're ready for anything, and there's no situation you feel you cannot enter and transform in perfect safety.

Take a moment to feel and appreciate this sense of power and safety. Take note of any impressions, sensations, ideas, feelings, or insights that may arise for you.

[Pause]

As you look at this building, prepared to enter and fix whatever is wrong, you realize that the door is so narrow that if you open it, there's only room for you to squeeze inside if you take off your suit and leave behind your toolbox and briefcase.

Looking through the window, you see shapes and movement, some of which appear potentially threatening, some of which seem friendly, and some of which are obscure and mysterious. If you want to know more, if you want to be able to help, you must enter the building, but to do that, you must leave behind your garb and tools of power. You must go in the building naked and unprotected, simply open to what is there, depending on the light itself to guide and help you. You must have faith in the protection of that light and in your ability to attune to it.

What does it feel like to be in this situation?

What do you do?

You realize that, using your suit and tools and plans, you have the power to act on this building and whatever situation is taking place in it from the outside. Based on what little you can see, you can push and pull the building, try to shift it into a shape that seems more in keeping with what the plans you carry suggest as its ideal configuration. It may even stay in that new shape for a while, and you can hope that will resolve the situation. But if it doesn't, then the activity that you could not see will more likely than not cause the building to revert to the shape it's in now.

You know you can act *on* the building; the question is, can you act from *within* it to achieve a deeper, more attuned and long-lasting result?

To do that, you must take off your suit, leave behind your tool-box and briefcase, open the door, and step into whatever awaits you, naked and receptive.

Are you willing?

There is a risk. You could be changed yourself. You probably will be. You'll enter as a catalyst, not as a protected, separated agent.

What do you do?

If you choose to walk away, there's no shame in that. Indeed, that might be the best course. Doing nothing, especially when we're not sure what to do, is often the right thing. There can be as much blessing in not acting as in acting. We often encounter situations in life that either are not ours to help or that we fear, and that's all right. None of us is the Mr. Fixit of creation.

If you choose to walk away, then you direct a helpful charge of energy from your suit to the light that surrounds the building. Ask that an intelligence greater than yours that does understand the needs of the interior take this gift of spirit and use it in whatever way it sees fit for the highest good of all. Then move away. As you do so, a door appears before you, amply wide for you, your suit, your briefcase, and your toolbox. Going through that door, you find your-self on the stage of your inner theater of the heart and mind. There you are, back in your everyday garb as your everyday self. See your-self stepping down off the stage and leaving the theater, consciously reentering your everyday life, grounded and balanced, with a feeling of being refreshed, regenerated, and in harmony.

IF YOU CHOOSE to enter the building, then take off your suit and open the door. It's very narrow, but you can squeeze through.

Feel what this is like. Feel what it's like to be open and receptive, not defending yourself, not isolating yourself, not trying to be all-powerful or in control. Feel what it's like to squeeze through this narrow opening into vulnerability.

[Pause]

Now you're inside the building. You're open to whatever is happening there. You enter your inner stillness, and from there you shift into your open space. In that openness, that spirit of allowing, you listen, you observe, you attune. The light around the building and within it flows into you, and you feel safe and protected even without your suit. You attune to its voice, you listen to what it seeks to do, you attune to the blueprints it offers, if any, or it may invite you to use one which you've brought.

As you attune and listen and observe, you find the walls of the building expanding until now they include your suit and the briefcase and tools you left behind. You've lost nothing. All is available to you, but now you can use your tools in harmony with what's happening in the interior of the building. You can use them in harmony with the light. You can use them, but you don't have to use them. In the power of your open presence, you now have many options, and you can engage with the light as the "superstring" that you are. From the relationship between your knowledge and power and your openness and receptivity, insight will flower and blessing will emerge.

Feel what this is like. Take note of any impressions, insights, thoughts, feelings, sensations, or images that arise for you.

When you're finished, open your eyes and step out from your imaginal space back into your everyday world. If you wish, see yourself back on the stage in your inner theater of the heart and mind. See yourself stepping down off the stage and leaving the theater, consciously reentering your everyday life, grounded and balanced, with a feeling of being refreshed, regenerated, and in harmony.

——————————— *Exercise Two* ———————————

In order to experience receptivity and openness in a different way, I offer the following suggestions:

First, using whatever procedure or ritual is comfortable for you within your spiritual tradition or practice, ask the sacred for a blessing and consciously open yourself up to receive it. You're asking unconditionally, not specifying how, when, or where this blessing should take place, what it should look like, or what its effects should be. You're leaving this to the will and wisdom of the sacred—or, if you wish, the will and wisdom of your own higher spiritual principles. In so doing, you're relinquishing control and putting yourself in the hands of spirit.

What does it feel like to do this? Does it feel scary? Uncomfortable? Pleasant? Some of us have a hard time letting go and being fully receptive to the sacred. Are you such a person? If so, don't berate yourself but take this need for control into account. Recognize it is a factor in your life and that at times it can interfere with a deeper spiritual process. It may also be that there are conditions in which you feel quite capable of letting go and situations when you cannot, which may be perfectly appropriate. There are many situations in which we should be observant and aware but not vulnerable and open. Learn to distinguish these, and work creatively with your own boundaries.

But often a desire for control stems from fear and from not feeling safe. So do what you can in gentle and appropriate ways to deal with this, to find out what you fear. Do things that help you develop trust in yourself and in others. Do things that give you a sense of accomplishment. There's a rich tradition and network now of psychological and spiritual techniques, teachers, workshops, and methodologies designed to help us deal with issues of fear, control, vulnerability, and the proper use of boundaries. Don't hesitate to make use of these resources in whatever way seems appropriate.

My second suggestion for experiencing openness is that you find a person whom you can ask to bless you. Obviously, be sensitive and appropriate in making your choice. If you're doing these exercises with a buddy or in a group, then you already have someone who can do this for you. If not, you may need to search around a bit, but one obvious place to look is in whatever religious or spiritual tradition is part of your life. Most such traditions have official representatives—priests, ministers, rabbis, mullahs, priestesses, gurus, and the like—who will be willing to give you a blessing according to their training and insights.

The purpose of doing this is to make the receptive condition very real and specific for you. You're opening to, becoming receptive to, and giving over control in this matter to a tangible, flesh-and-blood human being, not to an image in the privacy of your imaginal space. This is a whole other experience, and one that can be very instructive as well as potentially empowering. It has the side benefit of enabling you to receive a specific blessing from another person, and in this day and age, we can use all the blessings we can get!

Commentary

The "blessing place," as I've said in the main text, is a state of mind that is the synthesis of all the other supportive states of mind described and explored in the preceding exercises. It's a shorthand way of saying, "This is who I am when I'm prepared, ready, and capable of giving a blessing." In my classes, after we have reached a certain point of practice and understanding, I precede each exercise in blessing with the simple statement "Now go into your blessing place." By then everyone knows exactly what I mean and how to do it. But they have learned this not by following a recipe or my instructions but by observing who they are and what they feel like when they're giving a blessing. "What's the inner power, source, and presence from which I draw in order to come to the readiness to give a blessing, and how do I feel—who am I—as I do so?" The answer to that question, which is unique for each person, is the blessing place.

This exercise is only one way in which a person may come to this place. Please feel free to experiment and explore in order to find what's natural, integrated, attuned, and altogether right for you. But remember, the blessing place is dynamic. The more you bless, the more it will evolve, mature, and change. Be prepared to grow and to allow it to grow with you.

——————————— *Exercise* ———————————

Please make yourself comfortable and close your eyes. In whatever way you choose, go into the inner theater of your heart and mind, into the place where you daydream and fantasize, into the world of your imagination, into your imaginal space.

You're standing on a path that stretches ahead of you for a short distance. At the end of the path is a doorway, and the door is closed.

Alongside the path as you approach the doorway are three coatracks. On one hangs a pair of trousers. On another hangs a shirt. On the third hangs a headband.

You first come to the trousers. A sign on the coatrack reads "Your Empersonal Spirit." You take down the trousers and put them on. As you do, remember all that you've learned about your empersonal spirit and what it feels like to you. Putting on the trousers brings you fully and wholly into that feeling, into the power of being your empersonal spirit.

When you feel comfortable in these trousers, which, of course, fit perfectly, you walk on to the next coatrack. This one is labeled "Your Transpersonal Spirit." You take down the shirt hanging there and put it on. As you do, remember all that you've learned about your transpersonal spirit and what it feels like to you. Putting on the shirt brings you fully and wholly into that feeling, into the power of being your transpersonal spirit.

Standing there wearing the trousers and shirt, an amazing thing happens. The two pieces of clothing flow smoothly and seamlessly together into one perfectly fitting, absolutely comfortable body suit. It's like a second skin, and you feel strong and light within it. As you move around, feeling the presence of the suit, you experience a fierce joy. You can hear profoundly beautiful music being played on the superstings that run through all creation, and you feel empowered.

Now you walk to the third coatrack. This one is labeled "Opening." You take down the headband and put it on. Although you still feel the power and energy of the body suit you're wearing, you also feel your awareness opening gracefully and receptively. You're enveloped in a rich glowing light that is in perfect harmony with all that is around you.

Attired in this way, embodying a receptive and poised power, filled with grace and harmony, you come to the door. An eye appears in the door and looks you over. Satisfied with what it sees, the door opens. Ahead of you is a vast, open, space. A sign by the door on the other side says simply "Your Blessing Place." You step into it, taking note of any impressions, feelings, insights, thoughts, images, or ·sensations that arise for you. You remember what this place feels like, for it's a place of re-membering. It's the place of blessing.

When you're finished experiencing this place, open your eyes and move from your imaginal space into awareness of your everyday world, taking as much of the feeling and spirit of your blessing place with you as you can integrate. If it's helpful, see yourself back on the stage in your inner theater of the heart and mind. See yourself stepping down off the stage and leaving the theater, consciously reentering your everyday life, grounded and balanced, with a feeling of being refreshed, regenerated, and in harmony.

—— *A Final Commentary* ——

The question came up in some of my classes of how a person can find, much less enter, their blessing place when they're feeling constricted and angry in their lives and experiencing a minimum of self-acceptance and self-esteem. There's no one answer to this. It's the function of many spiritual and psychological practices to address these issues of self-sabotage, obstructedness, and anger. One must find what works and practice it consistently in order for it to have practical value in everyday life. In the context of this Workbook on the Art of Blessing, the exercises on stillness and unobstructedness may be of particular value.

At the heart of this issue is choice. First I must wish to bless and choose to do what I must to make it possible, then I can discover and use tools and techniques to help me do so. But no technique will really work when in reality what I truly want is to feel my anger or sorrow or victimization.

Here I believe we must understand there are times when it's valuable and right to just be with our negativity, as long as it's not injuring or oppressing someone else. There are times when the right choice is to stand in our constricted place and feel and understand its contours. For I believe it's only when we have that kind of understanding that we will find a lasting way out. Every inner prison has a secret latch that will unlock and open a hidden door to freedom. But it may take time, silence, and exploration to find our latch. And then we must decide if we really want to use it. The smallness of our chamber, however uncomfortable, may seem safer and preferable to the unknown vastness of the world outside it.

So there are times when we just cannot find the unconditionality, the love, or the willingness to enter our blessing place—and should not fight that. But if we choose to enter our blessing place, can we take our anger with us? How wounded can we feel and still be in that place effectively? As one of my students asked, "Who am I to step into a sacred space when I'm not all sacred?"

Our blessing place *is* a sacred place, but it's also a human place. It has room for our human frailty as well as our human dignity and power. Otherwise, how could we ever bless? If with all our imperfections we cannot make a space sacred, either within ourselves or within our world, then how will we ever learn the nature of a sacred space?

To me in my spiritual practice, a sacred space is not an absolute. It does not demand that we be one way and one way only in order to enter it. We don't go in one great leap from being a lowly human being to being one with God. Instead, we enter a condition in which we acknowledge the essence of our sacredness and align with it as fully and as best we can, creating a space where God can do the rest. We're in sacred space when we're attuning to the superstring of ourselves, but we can only embrace as much of that string as we're able to at any given time. The superstring of my whole, sacred beingness may be infinitely long, and I may be able to grasp only an inch of it. But if I can pull that inch into my consciousness, I must of necessity pull the whole string towards me. And if I cannot fit it all into who I am in the moment, then God takes up the slack and holds what I cannot yet encompass.

That's the nature of sacred space to me: a place where you enter holiness as much as you're able, and God enters the rest of the way on your behalf, keeping the space open for you to grow into it. No sacred place is ever closed to you, whatever you're feeling, if you need or wish it to be open. Only you can make the choice to enter or not.

So if I'm feeling constricted, in pain, angry, wounded, tired, frustrated, depressed, and generally set upon by life (and who among us has not?), I'm not necessarily blocked from entering the sacred space that is my blessing place. Indeed, the choice to do so, the willingness to do so, the courage to do so, may be all it takes to shift my attention, to light myself as a candle, to be a beating heart of spirit, and to take me into that inner phone booth from which I reemerge clad in the blazing uniform of "Blessingman."

But heroes in the real world don't use phone booths anyway and rarely have any superpowers to draw on. They simply press on with the wounds, with the despair, with the anger and weariness to do what needs to be done. And when they do, sacred space can emerge all around them. If I can find no trace of anything resembling an empersonal or transpersonal spirit and if I feel about as open as an oyster at a walrus convention, I can still gather in my anger and weariness, depression, and woundedness and, in a spirit of self-forgiveness, enter my blessing place. And if I can do nothing else, I can still ask the sacred to do the blessing for me.

One participant in the original class on Blessing described an experience of being able to bless even when she was irritable and depressed. This was true even when in one exercise she found herself needing to bless another participant whom she had found particularly irritating. In so doing, she felt herself expanding and receiving a blessing herself. She learned that it was easy for her to fall into a trap of thinking in the moment that now was not the right time to bless because she did not feel centered, radiant, or loving enough. But this brought up a question for her. If she could bless when she was depressed or angry, who was the "I" who was doing the blessing?

There's no special I who blesses. The I who blesses is, when all is said and done, the I who chooses to bless and, through that choice, makes it happen. The choice itself becomes formative (or transformative) or, if you wish, "I-creating." Through my choice and action, I bring into being the I, expression of self that can do the thing I wish, even as other aspects of self are present as well.

Here I should point out, in case it's unclear, that the "empersonal spirit" and the "transpersonal spirit" to which I refer in the Art of Blessing are not "selves" or aspects of self. They're not I's. They're sources of energy and power—states of mind—that I can draw upon to enhance my ability to bless. For that matter, from my perspective the different I's alluded to in the question—the depressed I, the irritable I, the angry I, the happy or peaceful I—are not really selves either: They are energy states within which the essence of my personhood may manifest. Through imagination, as in the shifting exercise—and through choice and perhaps some degree of effort, depending on the situation—we can change our energy state. The I remains the same, but we're experiencing and resonating at a different "frequency." We've plucked a different note on the superstring of our being.

The mystery of the self, of who the I who chooses is, is beyond the scope of this book. The point here is that it doesn't matter if I'm not at my best as far as I'm concerned, or if my energy is low. To make the choice to bless, to make the effort to bless (which may simply be the act of getting myself out of the way), is to align with a higher energy state in which the blessing can "do itself," so to speak, and I'm energized, blessed, and raised up in response.

——— *Commentary* ———

How we see another person in our thoughts and feelings may seem to be a private matter, but every spiritual teaching of which I'm aware agrees that this is not entirely so. In some manner—whether as psychic energy we exchange, telepathic communication, the projection of images, a shaping of each other's fields of being, or some way we don't yet understand or cannot yet imagine—what we hold in our minds (especially if we hold it with feeling) does communicate and can affect others, even at a distance. Because of our inner psychic "immune systems," we do have some resistance to negative projections but will respond more positively if another sees us in encouraging, supportive, or loving ways. People also differ in their sensitivity to this inner communication, just as people differ in their sensitivity to the weather or to how spicy their food is. But even the most obtuse and insensitive of people can be affected by the thoughts and feelings others hold about them, especially over time.

Therefore, the place in which all blessings must start is our own minds and hearts. The simplest and most accessible way to bless another is in mindfully shaping how we "see" them through the inner eye of our thoughts and feelings.

I've included two exercises here, one to do solo in the privacy of your home and one to do when you're with others—in this case, either at work or with a family member.

——————————— *Exercise One* ———————————

Please make yourself comfortable and close your eyes. In whatever way you choose, go into the inner theater of your heart and mind, into the place where you daydream and fantasize, into the world of your imagination, into your imaginal space.

Go into your blessing place.

Picture in your mind's eye someone whom you know well and you like. As you do, just let your thoughts and feelings about this person, as well as any opinions and judgments that you may have, arise in a natural way from your memories and experiences of them. You observe, as you do this, though, that all your thoughts and feelings swirl around the individual like moths around a flame, and some of your stronger thoughts, opinions, and feelings actually stick to the person like little Post-it notes.

How dense does this cloud of projection become? Does it seem to you he has room to move within it, or is he bound tight? Can you see his own unique light shining through past all your own images of him? Can you see his creativity? Is there room in your expectations for him to be different, to surprise you, to transform? Can you allow him the freedom to do that? Are you taking him for granted? Are your expectations obstructions for him?

Go into your inner heart and begin to beat. Feel spirit quickening and circulating around you. As you watch, see this circulation swirl around your friend, dissolving and washing away all the Post-it notes and moths of your expectations. In your mind's eye, see him surrounded with his own open space, with room to move and stretch and grow, even in directions you may not anticipate or understand. See the light of the infinite within him, the creative power of the Source. In your own mind and heart, open up the space in which you hold him and release your expectations. See him unob-structed and able to expand and unfold as his own inner wisdom may dictate.

Bless him with the gift of the unobstructed world. Bless him by removing the obstructions that may be in your own mind. Through that subtle connection that exists between us all, this empowering openness will communicate itself to him and be a blessing in his life.

Now pick another person, this time someone you don't like or someone who has been obstructing or difficult towards you. Repeat this exercise. Are you willing to release him, to see him free from your own possible projections of hurt and anger, bitterness or re-venge? Can you extend the blessing of forgiveness, which is itself a creator of open space? Can you bless him unconditionally? If so, how do you feel? What freedom may come to you?

Take a moment to reflect on the two parts of this exercise. How were they similar? How were they different? Was one more difficult than the other? Make note of any impressions, ideas, insights, thoughts, feelings, or images that may have arisen for you.

When you're finished, open your eyes and step out from your imaginal space back into your everyday world. If you wish, see your-self back on the stage in your inner theater of the heart and mind. See yourself stepping down off the stage and leaving the theater, consciously reentering your everyday life, grounded and balanced, with a feeling of being refreshed, regenerated, and in harmony.

—————————————— *Exercise Two* ——————————————

When you're with someone else, either a family member or a co-worker, repeat the preceding exercise but with your eyes open. You don't have to keep staring at him, but keep him in your thoughts and look at him now and then. You're seeing him both outwardly and inwardly. Without saying anything to him, simply try to see him enveloped in a liberating, empowering open space. See his life becoming unobstructed. See him being freed from your own expectations and projections. Bless him through your sight.

What's it like doing this with a real person as contrasted with doing it imaginally? If you're working with a buddy or partner, have him or her do this exercise on your behalf. What does that feel like?

When we see someone, we shape him in our inner sight. Sometimes the shape we give him is not his shape at all, or is a shape that restricts and binds his possibilities. To bless him with unobstructing sight and an open mind and heart can be very powerful. It's one of the easiest ways to practice the Art of Blessing.

—— *Commentary* ——

This is the culmination of it all: the act of blessing. In this exercise, we go through a complete blessing, drawing on what we have learned and practiced in all the preceding exercises. I also assume you're blessing a person.

This exercise is designed to be done on your own as a solo reader, but it contains suggestions on what to do if you've found someone willing to be blessed by you. Adjust the exercise according to your situation and what you need. Once you have a sense of what you're doing, though—and it really isn't difficult at all—I do recommend you try it out with a partner. Then you can get them to bless you in return!

—— *Exercise* ——

Please make yourself comfortable and close your eyes. In whatever way you choose, go into the inner theater of your heart and mind, into the place where you daydream and fantasize, into the world of your imagination, into your imaginal space.

Go into your blessing place.

See the person whom you're going to bless. If you're working with a partner, open your eyes and look at them, but stay within your blessing place. If this is difficult, then do this exercise with your eyes closed, opening them only when necessary to orient yourself. If you're working solo, then picture the person in your mind's eye.

Take a moment to attune to the power and receptive openness of your blessing place. You're a superstring aligned with the infinite, aligned with the Source, aligned with your humanity, the earth, your own earthiness, and your embodied personhood. Feel the energy of your empersonal spirit. Feel the energy of your transpersonal spirit. Feel them blending and becoming one, filling you with a presence of connectedness and wholeness. Feel the energy and light of this presence filling your blessing place, infusing it with unconditional love.

Now, attune to the person whom you are blessing. Decide how you wish to connect with them. You might visualize energy streaming to them from your blessing place or from specific parts of your body such as your heart and your hands. You might imagine yourself drawing them into the openness and presence of your blessing place, as you might gather a person into your arms. You might imagine the field of your blessing place expanding outward to surround and include them. But whatever image or technique appeals to you or seems intuitively right in this moment, connect with the person you are blessing.

As you do so, the energy of your presence and all its connections to earth, to Source, to your own power, and to the person's presence as well moves from you to the blessee. You may imagine this in any way that is meaningful to you: as energy coruscating over and around this person, as liquid light surrounding and bathing him or her, as an enfolding field and presence of light and spirit that the intelligence and wisdom of the person's own body and soul can appropriately absorb, direct, and assimilate.

You'll instinctively know when you're finished. It doesn't take long to transmit a blessing, though, hardly more than a minute or two. When you begin to feel the energy wane or your body becomes restless, it's time to stop. Depending on the images that you are using, pull the energy, the field, or your presence back into yourself, back into your blessing place. If you're working with a physical partner and were touching them during the blessing, take your hands off their body and step back about a foot or so, so that you're outside the immediate range of their bioenergetic field.

Now, step out of your blessing place by letting the energy and presence you have invoked absorb into your body and become integrated. Picture the energy soaking into your body and becoming balanced and stabilized within your center of gravity, then moving out to be absorbed by your cells. Direct any surplus you feel down through your legs and feet into the earth, or offer it to spirit to be used wherever there's need.

Finally, take a moment of silence. Give thanks for the blessing that has occurred. Then open your eyes if they're not already open. Give yourself a physical shake or wiggle and move around a bit. See yourself consciously reentering your everyday life, grounded and balanced, with a feeling of being refreshed, regenerated, and in harmony.

Take time to note any sensations, images, feelings, impressions, thoughts, or intuitions that occur to you while doing this exercise.

——— *Final Commentary* ———

Please remember that there are many ways of giving a blessing. This exercise is intended simply as an example. But as you practice the Art of Blessing, be sensitive to finding your own particular style.

Remember, too, that the most powerful blessing need not be anything complex. A moment of caring or support offered at the right time can be more powerful and effective than the invocation of the most elaborate ritual. A blessing really is the product of a dynamic relationship between you, the person or object you are blessing, and the overall situation. This means also that a style of blessing that worked once may not do so as effectively, or even at all, the next time, because the situation and timing have changed, and the people—including yourself—have changed too. Be sensitive to this dynamic factor; it requires mindfulness and discernment.

Also, as you become familiar through practice with the Art of Blessing, you'll find that you can move in and out of your blessing place with ease and rapidity, and that giving a blessing becomes less an act that you perform and more the radiance of your very being. One thing is for certain: You'll find the Art of Blessing to be a practice that evolves with you and that offers you an ever-changing opportunity for exploration and adventure.

—— *Commentary* ——

This final exercise is optional. In it we'll be invoking spiritual help from non-physical beings who act as spiritual allies. Such beings mediate forces and energies, fields and presences, that we may not be able to contact or express on our own. It's a common thing to do when giving a blessing; many blessings the world over involve some specific specific invocation of spiritual forces in order to give the blessing greater power than a person feels capable of doing on his or her own.

Some people may be nervous about working with unseen forces. Books and movies often portray the non-physical worlds as filled with evil entities waiting to pounce on the unwary. This may be good for creating thrilling fiction, but it's far, far from the truth. Each of us possesses a fairly strong inner immune system, as I talked about in the exercise on seeing on page 255. Given that we're leading a reasonably moral life and demonstrating through our attitudes and actions a sense of caring for the well-being of others, this immune system will protect us well. And in my experience, the forces of benevolence and helpfulness far outnumber those of darkness and obstruction.

But when dealing with inner forces and experiences, one should always take care nonetheless, not so much because of encountering anything evil but because of invoking more energy than one can properly integrate and assimilate in the moment. Here one's own intuition should be a guide. Also, sensations of discomfort, irritability, or restlessness in the body can be a good indicator to go slowly; I've always found my body to be a good alarm system when I'm wading into deeper waters than I may be ready for.

If you feel such discomfort or simply don't wish to deal with spiritual beings of any kind for whatever reason, then (as this whole book has amply stated) you have plenty of resources within yourself and your own spiritual presence to marshal in offering a blessing. And you can always bless by invoking the sacred.

In fact, the greatest spiritual ally available to us is the sacred itself, which, as Christian tradition puts it, is "closer than hands and feet." For millennia, countless people in all lands have offered blessings by calling upon the sacred, whether they name it Lord, Father, God, Krishna, Brahma, Christ, Buddha, Allah, the Goddess, the Lady, or some equivalent image and presence of divinity.

Calling upon the sacred is the simplest blessing technique of all. All we need do is ask its presence and power to be part of the act of blessing. But this invocation should be more than just in name alone; the most powerful invocation is through the resonance of our hearts. It's when we feel that sacred presence as a reality and invite it daily into our lives that we draw it most easily and fully into our blessing place. Indeed, it's already there.

But in this exercise, I'm looking at a different step, which is working with specific spiritual allies. Whether we call these allies saints or angels, our departed relatives or spiritual guides, nature spirits or shining ones, makes little difference. The point is that we're interacting in a positive, co-creative way with the larger ecology of being of which we're a part.

Why we should wish to work with spiritual allies instead of going directly to the Source is a matter beyond the scope of this book. Sometimes it's a matter of personal preference or spiritual understanding, sometimes a matter of intuitive guidance, sometimes a matter of weaving together specific energies or presences who have some direct relationship to a particular blessing: like calling upon a healing angel when performing a blessing for someone who is ill. Of course, as my friend Peter Caddy, one of the founders of the Findhorn Community, used to say when presented with a choice between two good options: "Why choose? Take both!"

So, although the focus of this book has been on the power we have within ourselves to bless, I present this exercise as an illustration for those who wish to involve other spiritual allies in the process. After all, you can build a house by yourself, but it's also nice to have help from the neighbors.

———————————————— *Exercise* ————————————————

Please make yourself comfortable and close your eyes. In whatever way you choose, go into the inner theater of your heart and mind, into the place where you daydream and fantasize, into the world of your imagination, into your imaginal space.

Go into your blessing place.

Imagine yourself standing in a space that represents holiness for you. Before you, you see a symbol that represents for you the presence of the sacred. As you watch, this symbol begins to glow with light until it becomes Light. This Light surrounds you, filling you with a sense of the sacred. Within it, you feel loved, protected, and empowered.

Now, in your mind's eye, you see an image of the person or object you're going to bless. Hold this image steady. As you do so, invite assistance from the spirit that dwells within the presence of the sacred that surrounds you. If you're used to working with a particular angel or saint, guide or inner teacher, then invite their assistance specifically. As you make this invitation, one or more beings begin to emerge out of the Light, as if the Light itself condensed into their shape and substance. Thank them for their assistance and tell them the objective of your blessing. Open to them and ask if they have any specific guidance to offer. Listen within your stillness and be aware of any images or impressions that may arise.

Then turn your attention back to your own blessing place and to the person you're going to bless. Using whatever style you prefer, let the energy and presence of the blessing flow to and around the person or object you're blessing. As this happens, see those spiritual allies joining their presence and energy with yours. In effect, they become part of your blessing place, adding their wisdom, intelligence, and spiritual power to your own.

Allow the blessing to proceed in its natural way, and when it seems that the energy is waning, the work has been done, or you're becoming restless, pull back into your blessing place and separate appropriately from your blessing. Specifically thank your spiritual allies for all their contributions and ask them for their blessing upon yourself. Then allow them to depart, seeing them in your mind's eye reentering the light of the sacred.

Take a moment to be still and pay attention to any impressions, thoughts, feelings, images, or sensations that may have arisen during this blessing.

When you're finished, open your eyes and step out from your

imaginal space back into your everyday world. If you wish, see your-self back on the stage in your inner theater of the heart and mind. See yourself stepping down off the stage and leaving the theater, consciously reentering your everyday life, grounded and balanced, with a feeling of being refreshed, regenerated, and in harmony.

EXAMPLES OF
BLESSINGS

INTRODUCTION

In order to have examples of something, we need a definition of what that something is. If I want to present you with examples of how a duck behaves, I need to know what a duck is and how to recognize one when I see it.

The challenge with blessings is that they can look like so many things. Over the years I've asked people for their blessing stories. I've had them tell me about remarkable healings they have witnessed or experienced, about incredible, synchronistic manifestations of money, resources, or help at times of need, or simply about nice and happy things that have occurred for them, such as being given a puppy that brought joy to their family. In their minds, all these things are blessings—and who am I to suggest otherwise?—but these stories often have little in common except that they all end happily. This is true even if the story began tragically, as, for example, with the death of a loved one whose passing set in motion a train of events that ultimately brought a deeper sense of attunement and joy into that person's life.

In giving examples of what a blessing may be like or of how to bless, though, such stories, while inspirational, are not always helpful. Shall I say, "If you wish to bless, give a person a puppy," or "Fire your employee and watch how adversity brings him the blessings of deeper wisdom and strength?" Should I advise you to become ill so you can experience the blessing of being healed? Of course not! Yet, the fact remains that in almost any circumstance of life, we can find a blessing—or we can create one.

To avoid being lost in such an abundance of possibilities, I use three criteria for defining a blessing in the following examples. First, a blessing enhances the life of a person or other living creature, or enhances the functionality of an object. Because of the blessing, he, she, or it has access to more of what it needs to fulfill its potential. Second, a blessing is unobstructing in some way. It opens up a space in which we can see and move in new directions. It gives us an experience of the unobstructed world. It makes us less constricted. Third, a blessing connects us in a deeper way with our world, allowing us to feel a greater sense of belonging and wholeness. It connects us with the circulation of the blood and breath of spirit amongst us all.

One could pick other criteria as well, and I encourage you to adjust this definition of blessing in whatever way you wish or need to fit your experience. Only remember that if you make your definition too broad, it may not serve you as well.

You'll notice that I didn't say anything specifically about the sacred. In a way, this is a fourth, unspoken criteria for me: that in some manner, the presence and love of the sacred is part of a blessing. But I take this as a given, that a blessing is a relationship in which at some level of awareness we celebrate and experience the sacred within us, between us, and around us in the world. It's that experience that underlies our sense of enhancement, unobstructedness, and connection.

However, for my purposes, particularly in this book, to say that a blessing must bring a person explicit experience of the sacred—or that the sacred must be called upon to make a blessing possible—is paradoxically too limiting a criterion. For one thing, not everyone agrees on the nature or definition of the sacred—or even that there is such a thing. In my observation, such disagreement or disbelief has never proved to be an obstacle to the giving or receiving of blessings. And for another, as I've repeatedly remarked, I'm focusing on the Art of Blessing as an element of spiritual practice in which, by discovering within ourselves a personal power with which to bless, and by expressing that power into the world, we both deepen and unfold ourselves in fulfilling ways. We become mindful and deliberate agents in increasing the joy and wholeness we feel and increasing the unobstructedness in our world. In the process, in a way unique to each of us, our activity as blessers can lead us to an appreciation of and unity with the Source, however we may imagine it or name it.

In this context, I should add that there is a whole class of blessings that can be thought of as prayers, and invocations that are requests that the sacred perform a blessing. For example, while I was writing this book, my father sent me a delightful little book compiled by Ray Simpson called *Celtic Blessings: Prayers for Everyday Life*. This book contains prayers invoking blessings on a variety of everyday events such as taking exams, giving parties, traveling, gaining a promotion, and anniversaries, as well as for weddings, baptisms, the saying of grace at mealtime, and holidays. Indeed, the book fully embodies the Celtic spirit of giving blessings for everything in life, no matter how seemingly trivial. In many ways, it captures the love and grace at the heart of blessing.

The use of invocations and prayers in a blessing is a matter of personal preference and style. I use them sometimes, and when I do, I almost always create them out of the inspiration of the moment. However, as I said above, I'm interested in the spirit that emerges from us as spiritual beings working in partnership with each other, with the world, and with the sacred, so I don't include specific invocations or prayers as part of my teaching of the Art of Blessing. By equating a prayer or invocation with a blessing, we can limit our appreciation for and participation in the process.

The real value of books such as the one my father sent me lies, not in having a set of pre-packaged blessings to pull out and read at the appropriate occasion, but in using the prayers and invocations as contemplative images that lead to a deeper sense of the *spirit* of blessing. It's that spirit we wish to embody when we practice the Art of Blessing, and anything that helps us do so can be, well, a blessing!

The following examples are drawn both from my own work and from stories told to me by students. They're only examples, and limited ones at that, and not recipes. I encourage you to experiment and to explore. In the examples from my own life, the blessings reflect my particular style. For example, touch is an important sense for me, so I like to lay my hands upon whatever I'm blessing. I may say a few words, usually in the form of a prayer, but more often than not I do the work in silence.

The key thing about my approach, and it's what makes giving examples difficult, is that I always bless as if I'm doing it for the first time, so no two blessings are ever exactly alike. I never look back to see how I did it before in a similar situation. I cultivate a feeling of walking naked into a situation, confident in my own spirit and its alignment with the Source to clothe me with what's needed. I open to the situation and allow it to call forth the shape of the blessing, and I trust in the combination of my own mindfulness and the presence of spirit to inspire me appropriately. It is just such a trust and alignment within yourself that I encourage you to practice and to develop.

Also, in the following examples, I use terms like *radiating* and *subtle energies* freely and for simplicity's sake, with no additional elaboration or conditionality. I use them to create a picture in your mind of one way of describing the non-physical relationship between you and your world. In the main text and in the exercise commentaries, I've shared my reservations about these and similar terms and emphasized the need to keep an open mind about just what's happening at this supersensible level and how best to describe it. With these reservations in mind, though, there's no reason not to use such terms to facilitate our imaginative and intuitive grasp of what's going on.

As a final observation, some of the following examples may seem trivial—on the level of "We received a puppy and it brought so much joy into our lives that we felt blessed." The fact is, the majority of the blessing stories and examples I've heard over the years are very simple and, as seen from the outside, not dramatic at all. No miraculous healings, no pulse-pounding promulgations of powerful presences, no visitations from on high.

But I believe this is how it should be. We can be seduced and misled by the need for glamor and a sense of the dramatic fostered by our culture. Real blessings in everyday life are more like peasants than nobles; they move and mingle within the commonality of our daily experiences, sometimes going unnoticed or unrecognized for what they are. The casual loving touch of your significant other may not seem like a blessing; yet, in the love and solidarity it conveys, it communicates a moment of enhancement, unobstructedness, and connection. The soul will notice even if the mind does not.

Indeed, the ultimate objective is for blessings to *be* normal and commonplace because we have all learned to support each other in a state of grace and unobstructedness as the customary way of being. There may be no drama or glamor in this, but there's certainly joy and liberation.

So there's no hierarchy of blessings, with dramatic visitations and boons from angels somewhere near the top and the rompings of ordinary puppies at the bottom. Any act of blessing, born of compassion and love, is neither shallow nor deep, trivial nor dramatic. It manifests in ways appropriate to serve the need and spirit of the situation.

After all, the flame of a match looks different from the flame of a blowtorch, but they're both fire. If I'm lighting the candles on a birthday cake, I need that fire, but a match is more appropriate for the job than a blowtorch. The blessing of an archangel that gathers the world up into its cosmic heart is different in degree but not in kind from the blessing a mother gives her child who is off to school for the first time. Both emerge from love, but for the child, all the celestial light there is may not equal the embrace of her mother's arms and a kiss for good luck.

Nor are some people more qualified than others to give blessings. A door does not care if the person who opens it is thin or fat, rich or poor, happy or irritable, a saint or a sinner, a light-hearted optimist or a curmudgeonly grouch; its task is simply to become an open space through which someone or something may pass. A blessing is a portal, too, through which the sacred may pass—or through which we may pass to embrace each other in new and co-creative ways; the important thing is that the way be opened, however narrowly or however hesitantly and skillfully we do so.

So appreciate the ordinariness of some of these blessings and realize that when you give blessings, they can be very ordinary as well. What is the ordinary after all but the extraordinary in familiar clothes?

BLESSING ONESELF

Blessing oneself is every bit as important as blessing others. The nice thing is that the opportunity to do so is always present! Blessing oneself is part of an overall program of self-maintenance, which would include also being kind to oneself and seeing that, where possible and appropriate, one's needs are met.

Of course, there can be limits to how fully or appropriately I can lavish kindness upon myself. I may feel that I really need two weeks in the Bahamas but not be able to afford it, or feel that I would be doing myself a kindness to have another helping of chocolate cheesecake but know that it would be harmful to my health. A real kindness may be to get up a half hour early every morning to exercise or meditate, in spite of wanting to stay in bed. So being kind to ourselves, as we all know (or eventually find out) is not the same as indulging in anything and everything that may bring us pleasure.

Blessing oneself, though, can be done without limits, anytime, anywhere. It does not cost money; it does not add calories. It's an action that may not directly satisfy any of my personality's needs or wants—it's not like having that extra piece of cake—but it nourishes my soul, which, in the long run, is like investing in a blue-chip stock that will pay handsome dividends.

The trick is to put yourself in blessings' way. Whatever connects you to the world, to others, to the Source, or to yourself in wider, deeper, empowering ways can be a source of blessing. Whatever enhances your life's energy and the flow of your creativity, insight, vitality, and joy can be a source of blessing. Whatever gives you a sense of being unobstructed and unobstructing—or actually diminishes obstructedness in your life—can be a source of blessing.

For some people, this can be immersing themselves in fulfilling work or in a creative activity. For others, it may be spending time in nature or taking time for spiritual study or meditation. And many find blessing in the company of others.

Perhaps the deepest way to bless oneself is by loving oneself, for nothing brings a state of spaciousness, vitality, and unobstructedness quite as powerfully as love.

One of my students, when asked how she blessed herself, said, "I bless myself with permission to make mistakes and by giving love to those parts of me that are hurting." Another said in a similar vein, "I bless myself by giving myself permission to be myself, rising above my feeling that I must always be pleasing others even when it robs me of energy and leaves me exhausted."

Some class participants expressed very practical and down-to-earth ways of blessing themselves. One said, "I bless myself by taking care of my body through exercise and nutrition and taking care of my spiritual needs through daily meditation." Another remarked, "I bless myself by working reasonable hours, by taking time to see friends and family, and by finding good cappuccino!" All excellent ways of keeping one's energy flowing, open, and lively (though personally, I would choose hot chocolate . . .)!

Then there are those who bless themselves by engaging with the sacredness of life in some manner. "I bless myself through an ongoing reflection on my purpose within the flow of the sacred," said one participant. "I explore the infinite ways in which God has blessed the universe through gifts of spirit and life, and I know I share in those blessings." Another said, "I bless myself by standing in my power and essence, which ultimately come from God." Others found blessings in nature—"being surrounded by the elements," as one woman put it.

Some people use images to put them in a state of feeling blessed. A friend of mine, especially when she's feeling constricted, pictures herself "curled up in the bowl of a great vessel or Grail," which is a wonderful image of receptivity, "allowing my greater 'I' to bless me"—in effect, seeing herself immersed in an outpouring of love and energy from the superstring within her. Other friends of mine have used similar imagery. One man pictured himself stepping under a waterfall of light, feeling the flow of spirit cascading upon him and uplifting him.

The efficacy of imagery depends on whether or not the individual is able to make a real connection between the image and the deeper reality it represents. Such images are usually shorthand for an experience, the way picturing a loved one brings to mind all the richness and depth and memories of the relationship. Imagery that's simply conjured up can only be fantasy unless it's linked to something experiential. Therefore, if I'm going to use images of waterfalls or showers of light, then at some level of my awareness, I must have a sense of just what that light represents. If the image of light represents the sacred to me or a vitalizing presence of spirit, then what have I done or what can I do to actually experience that sacredness or spirit right down to my blood and bones?

In short, I need to build up an inner vocabulary of experiences and related images. For example, if I want to have an experience of the sacred, where is this likely to happen for me, given my history, my preferences, my beliefs, and so on? Of course, the sacred can break through into our lives at any time in unexpected and remarkable ways, but aside from this, if I were going to seek out a sacred experience, where might I go? To a church, a mosque, or a synagogue? To a worship service? Into meditation practice? Out into nature? To a workshop on spirituality? Whatever the answer may be for me, I need to seriously pursue it and pay attention to what happens.

When I have an experience that for me at that moment says that the sacred is with me, I want to be very mindful of what it feels like—of what I feel like—and remember it. It may not happen again in quite the same way, for surely our relationship with the sacred or with spirit is an evolving one, but the memory serves as a good starting point. It gives substance and reality to any images I may use in order to invoke blessing or put myself in my blessing place. Then they're not just fantasies in my mind but links to very real experience.

As befits my somewhat improvisational and extemporaneous approach to life, I usually look for blessings wherever I am and take them "on the run, " so to speak. But sometimes I feel the need of something more focused and deliberate. In such an instance, I may create a ritual for self-blessing.

I like to keep rituals simple and short, seeking just the right amount of symbolism and activity to accomplish my purpose. When rituals become elaborate and complex, it may enhance the energy of the event but it can also disperse it; we become so intent on the ritual itself and on doing everything correctly that we forget to fully appreciate and experience the spirit we're actually invoking. We end up doing a performance rather than a ritual.

Usually for my purposes I use candles. The simplest ritual is to light a candle, invoking the presence of the sacred and making the psychological shift into an inner space of attunement. Then I enter my blessing place and spend time enveloping and filling myself with the energy of its presence.

If I want to do something slightly more elaborate, I arrange four candles in a traditional cross, one at each of the cardinal directions of east, south, west, and north, and I sit in the center of the circle that's thus created. I sit for a time with the candles unlit, simply appreciating my surroundings and my presence within them, pulling all my attention to the moment. As I do so, I seek my inner stillness, as in Exercise 2. When I'm feeling centered, present, and still, I light the candles as in Exercise 3, lighting each one with the invocation of a protective, enveloping, nourishing spirit. Thus, by the time I've lit all four, I'm enclosed in a sacred space. (It's also possible to reverse this procedure, using the creation of the sacred space through lighting the candles as a way of focusing yourself and finding stillness.)

After the candles are lit, I open myself to the flow of spirit and ask that I be aligned with the sacred and filled with the blessing and grace of the Source. I usually feel a rush of energy and a sense of joy and peace filling my being, but even if I feel nothing, I still sit in silence for a while, just enjoying the stillness. Then when it seems to me that nothing more is going to happen or I become restless, I give thanks and extinguish the candles, asking that the energy of the sacred space be released into the world to carry bless-ings wherever they may be needed.

I can add to this simple ritual by having an altar in the sacred space on which I would place objects that represent for me both my empersonal spirit and my transpersonal spirit. For example, I have a pewter figure of Merlin holding the baby Arthur, which repre-sents for me the magic, wonder, and delight of fatherhood, which is a very important and uplifting part of my everyday experience, and hence of my empersonal spirit. I also have a Celtic cross and a fig-ure representing the feminine aspect of the sacred, both powerful images for me of my transpersonal spirit. So I would have these three figures on my altar, and their presence would act as reminders of aspects of my being that I might wish to invoke as part of creat-ing my blessing place.

An alternative ritual I perform is very similar but involves a glass of water. Instead of me being in the circle created by the four lit candles, I place the glass there. I then ask that the spirit within the sacred circle fully enter, charge, and unconditionally bless the water for my highest good. I leave the glass in the circle for a short period of time, no more than five or ten minutes. Then I give thanks, ex-tinguish the candles—asking that the energy of the sacred space be released into my life and into the world to be used however and whenever needed—and remove the glass. I then drink the water, feeling as I do the spirit within that water entering my body and bringing blessing to all my cells and outward to all the subtle parts of my being as well.

Because I use this ritual to bless the water for my well-being, I don't use it for other purposes. However, a similar ritual could be performed to bless water for more general purposes should you feel the need to use the water for some other acts of blessing, such as blessing a room by sprinkling consecrated water around in it.

These are simple rituals. If you do them, I ask you to pay attention to what you feel in the process. If you understand the process and gain a sense of invoking and interacting with the spirit and energies involved, then, just as you internalized the lighting of the candle in Exercise 3, you can internalize these rituals as well. You can, for instance, shift yourself into a sacred space or into a blessing space simply by imagining yourself surrounded by the lit candles or imagining yourself in the presence of your evocative altar. In time, the felt sense of that shift will become so familiar that you don't even need the images to bring it about. Likewise, you can bless any water that you drink just by holding it for a moment and directing your intentionality into it, along with the felt sense of what the ritual of water blessing was like for you.

Remember always that you're a living ritual. All the things you do in a formal ritual only externalize and represent qualities and powers that already exist within yourself. Once you understand and experience this, then anything you do can take on the power of ritual, invoking and evoking spirit in the midst of your daily activity.

One thing to keep in mind is that as you do this—as you work with subtle forces—you'll develop an increased ability to participate in the flow of those forces that can be a blessing to you in itself. It may bring you empowerment and greater creative power and control over your life. With the growth of your skill at inner work, though, comes more responsibility to act with integrity. You must be particularly mindful of the moral aspects of your life and your dealings with others. In working with subtle energies, the possibility of using them in selfish, manipulative, and invasive ways is always present. Thus it requires mindfulness and a commitment to harm-lessness and a personal morality that always seeks the highest good of others and sees yourself as a servant. In developing inner power and skills, which is what the Art of Blessing is all about, every step forward in power needs to be accompanied by two or three steps forward in moral and ethical awareness as well.

Ultimately, to bless yourself is to shift yourself into your blessing place. For that's where you experience the presence of your com-bined personal and spiritual power and attunement and place your-self into the flow and circulation of spirit from the heart of the sacred.

For this reason, the heart of my spiritual practice is to take mo-ments throughout my day just to shift into my blessing place and feel myself as a "lit candle" or a "beating heart." Then I discover that the ideal way to bless myself is to participate, through blessing oth-ers, in the flow of spirit and blessing that circulates from the Source. For when I do, I stand in a stream of love and power from which I cannot help but draw nourishment. By offering it to others, I find my own place in the unobstructed world.

One of my students put it very well: "I bless myself by asking for what I need to have in order to continue to serve and bless others. Then I bless myself in accepting the answer."

Finally, perhaps the greatest blessing for ourselves comes from the fact that we can bless at all. A friend of mine, Michael Lipson, expressed this thought in a letter to me: "[The idea that we can bless] is extremely inspiring. It has to do with the absolute avail-ability of our connection to the Divine, which only awaits our good intent and act of will to manifest in some form. The idea that bless-ing is so available makes of us something very different from what we normally think ourselves to be: participants instead of isolates."

BLESSING A PLACE

How do people bless the places in which they live and work?

"I bless my home by appreciating it and caring for it," said one friend of mine. "I take care in how things are arranged and put my creative spirit into how it looks. Being in my home is to me what walking in a beautiful forest might be to someone else."

Another friend took a different approach. "I don't care so much what my home looks like, though I want it to be clean and cared for. But I really want my home to be lived in. My home is blessed when my children and their friends feel welcome in it, when it's a place of love and comfort for them, like an old shoe. I don't necessarily like the messes they make, but messes can be cleaned up. What I want is a lively home filled with laughter and a happy spirit."

A third friend wrote me: "I work in cubicle city, where every employee has his or her own little space separated by a wall, just like in *Dilbert*. It's pretty sterile. But I bless my space by having a little altar on my desk. It's not a religious thing but just a place where I put little toys and flowers and pictures that inspire me and give me a sense of spirit during my day. While I wouldn't choose to work in a cubicle, when I see my altar, I'm reminded to fill this space with my love. When I do, it really does come to feel like a very open, sacred space to me."

Blessing a place is attuning it to a state that's vibrant and aligned with spiritual energies that in turn can bless and sustain everyone who enters it. It's a way of making a place inwardly spacious so that there's nothing to obstruct or constrict the circulation of spirit. Sometimes when I think of this, I'm reminded of the strategic use of mirrors in a small room to make it seem larger. A blessing likewise reminds us that the inner space of a specific physical area and the spirit it may contain can be very much larger and more powerful than the physical surroundings and characteristics may suggest.

The energy of a place is a combination of the natural radiation of the elements and materials from which it's constructed—with natural materials such as wood and stone being the most inherently "alive" and vibrant—and the quality of subtle energies that soak into it from human thought, feeling, and activity within or around that place.

We all radiate a subtle energy that more or less reflects our inner states as well as our physical vitality. If we're angry, fearful, depressed, or hostile, then that's the quality of energy that impacts our environment, with greater or lesser effect, depending on just how strongly we embody these psychological states. If we're feeling very needy, we can become a hungry vortex that sucks energy from the environment, draining what we need from others. However, when our energy reflects such positive states as an inner attunement, an optimistic disposition, a warm and welcoming presence, and a compassionate heart, then it's a radiance that can vitalize and bless an environment without our having to think about it. I call this an "automatic blessing." Its impact is directly proportional to how strongly and coherently we're experiencing these psychospiritual states. Of course, if we're in the integrated presence of our blessing place, then the effect can be much stronger.

So we can bless places simply by being in them or walking through them, depending on the quality and intensity of presence we embody at the time. On the other hand, unless we're radiating in a particularly strong way that imprints itself deeply upon our surroundings—or unless we're attuned to the place in a powerful way because we have an ongoing relationship with it and a personal resonance built up over time—the energy of an environment can change again when the next strongly radiating person comes by. Consequently, "automatic blessings" may not be particularly long-lasting and generally affect only the surface energies of our surroundings, like a wind setting up waves on a lake. The depths of the lake are unaffected, and the wave pattern will only last until the wind shifts.

To have a stronger effect, we must mindfully work with the qualities of a place. One of the simplest ways to stir up and remove stagnant subtle energies in a room or building is to clean it. One student said to me, "When I want to uplift the energies in my home and give it a blessing, I do a thorough housecleaning from top to bottom. I get rid of clutter that's accumulated and reorganize my rooms. I may even rearrange my furniture. I don't mind the work. I put on happy music, and I visualize waves of sun-kissed water washing through everything, sweeping away whatever is old and stagnant. Whether I'm scrubbing the floors or the walls or dusting my shelves, I do everything with love, for that's the energy I want in my home."

In a similar vein, I once met a realtor who told me that when she was trying to sell an empty house, she would light a candle in each room, invoking a blessing upon it and asking that the atmosphere of the house be cleared and turned into an inviting open space. Then when prospective buyers came in, their own energies were not "crowded out" by those of the previous inhabitants and they could more easily imagine their own life-energy filling that space. She found it to be a very successful technique.

A similar way of blessing a place, as my friend working in "cubicle city" discovered, is to place an altar in it. The simplest form of such an altar may be simply a clear space with a candle on it. It need not have any overtly religious themes. An altar may contain objects that only have a personal significance, representing happy experiences or items that have an archetypal significance for you. It may not look anything like an altar we would find in a religious setting, but it still represents an empowering focal point for remembering the spirit in one's life.

For example, I have a shelf in my office that contains a great many objects that act as spiritual icons for me. Some are obviously religious in nature, such as a little figurine of Quan Yin, the Chinese goddess of healing and compassion, and a Celtic cross. Some come from popular culture, such as a figure of Yoda, the Jedi master from *Star Wars,* while others have a purely personal significance. I've already mentioned my figure of Merlin holding the baby Arthur.

Of course, these objects themselves don't, in most cases, have a spiritual energy of their own except what we may bestow upon them through our own thoughts and feelings. Their power lies in their ability to remind us of a deeper world and to inspire us to align with it. As we do that, we imbue our altars with a spiritual force that in turn can radiate back to us as well as become a focal point with which spirit itself can resonate and flow through into our world.

In my classes over the years, I've often had my students create altars in class to explore this technique for focusing spiritual energy within their homes or places of work. In particular, I have them create altars using non-religious icons or objects, like brooms and toasters, car keys and washcloths, in order to emphasize the potentially sacramental power of the ordinary things we encounter and use in our everyday lives. If you're interested in exploring this technique further, an excellent introduction to "altar-making" as a way of blessing is a book by Denise Linn called simply *Altars.*

However you go about blessing a place, whether you're a house-cleaner, an altar builder, or use some other technique, a place may be blessed at two levels. The first is simply a generic blessing that fills the space with qualities of energy that are uplifting, nourishing, spacious, and flowing with the circulation of spirit. One way to do this, as I've mentioned in the text, is to step into your blessing place, draw the spirit of blessing into yourself, and let it flow through into the space around you. You might, for example, imagine yourself as a tuning fork sounding a note that fills the space and sets it vibrating in resonance with you.

Another technique which I've found helpful uses the quality of seeing that I discussed in Exercise 16. It's very simple and can be done anywhere. Basically, when you're in a place you'd like to bless, let your vision travel over the walls, the ceiling, the floor, and everything within them. Look at everything appreciatively, without judgment. Imagine that your eyes have an unobstructed channel to the source of blessing and love within yourself. As you look over the room, imagine this blessing and love pouring out through your eyes into everything you see.

How well a generic blessing works depends on the quality and tenacity of the energies already present in a place as well as the depth and strength of your own spiritual attunement and the power of your intentionality. If you're trying to change the quality of energies that have built up over a long period of time, then much more work will probably be needed. Still, such a generic blessing always has some beneficial effect and is not to be underestimated.

The second level of blessing addresses the specific spirit and intentionality of a place. In other words, if a room is used for healing, then you bless it in a way that specifically aligns and supports healing work. If it's a schoolroom, you bless it for the purposes of teaching and learning. If it's an office, you bless it as a place where a particular kind of work with a particular purpose and intent is being done. If it's a home, you bless it in accordance with the character and life of the family who lives there.

Of course, some places are the locations of activities that are negative or harmful in nature. In such places, your blessing would not be to support that activity but to support the presence of redemptive, healing, and transmuting forces. Here, you'd be supporting restoration of health and wholeness, not furtherance of the hurtful activity.

Care must be taken here, though, not to confuse an evil energy with one you simply don't agree with. I've been in places where people were working towards political, economic, or social goals that I didn't happen to support; yet, the activity was well motivated, the people were open and happy, and the quality of the spiritual energies within the place was healthy and good. I have, for example, found powerful and uplifting spiritual presences in churches whose congregations have religious beliefs that I don't share. I'm quite happy to bless such a place towards the furtherance of the spiritual efforts of the people who use it. While I may not share their particular path, I certainly share the value of being on a path and of orienting one's life to the highest spiritual values of which one can conceive.

In blessing a place specifically for a particular use or purpose, I enter into my blessing place. Then I perform a generic blessing as a way of making preparation. This usually entails just being quiet in the place, standing in a flow of spiritual energy and allowing it to spiral out and around me, filling the space I'm in. I may also use the blessing-through-sight technique I mentioned on page 255.

Once the energy is moving and I have a sense of attunement to the place, I go more deeply, asking that I be in touch with the intent of the spirit within this place. If I'm successful, then I usually have a sense of a presence moving in a particular way with specific characteristics that relate to the purpose of the place. At this point, I always ask permission to connect with that presence. If I feel blocked at that point, then I back off and bring the blessing to a close, simply asking that whatever is for the highest good of all concerned unfold within this place. Otherwise, if I continue to feel an easy sense of flow, I "step into" or blend with that presence, offering myself as a connection between it and a larger spirit that can embrace and bless its particular purpose or activity. In effect, I create a larger, shared blessing place with that presence. I stay in that state until I feel the energy begin to diminish or a restlessness arise within me. Then I step back, give thanks, and withdraw my own energy into my own blessing place and from there back into my everyday self.

Of course, there are other things one can do to facilitate a specific blessing, such as using invocations, candlelight, incense, water that has been blessed, and the like. I leave such choices to personal preference and to what seems appropriate in the moment. The key ingredient, however, no matter how many other tools and resources you use, is the clarity and alignment of your own being and the degree to which you as the blesser can stand as a representative of the unobstructed world within the specific place which you're embracing in your love.

BLESSING ANOTHER PERSON

At the end of one of my classes, my students and I had gathered in a circle for a final blessing together. Before we started, one of the women told the group that she and her husband had been trying for years to have a baby, with no luck. Both she and her husband were in good health and from all medical indications should have been able to conceive a child. Now, as we gathered for a final time, she felt a strong impulse to ask the group for a blessing that she might become pregnant. The response from the group was unconditional and positive, so we gave her the blessing for which she asked.

A couple of years went by, and I forgot all about this incident. Then one evening after a lecture, a woman came up to me whom I recognized as a former student from that class. She asked if I remembered the woman whom we had blessed in support of her having a baby. When I said yes, she told me that not quite a year afterwards, that woman had successfully given birth to a healthy baby girl.

Blessings are powerful things. Even something as trivial as saying "Bless you!" when someone sneezes can carry a momentary burst of spiritual energy. How much more powerful it can be, then, when the blessing is deliberate, mindful, and skillfully directed.

But it may be more accurate to say that we ourselves are powerful beings, even when we don't fully realize it, for a blessing is an extension of our own love, our humanity, and our inner alignment with the sacred. If a blessing is powerful, that's because it draws at least in part on a power within our own beings.

The daughter of a friend of mine had unexpectedly plunged into a depressed and self-destructive state and had come back to live in her parents' home. They tried to help, but she seemed caught in a whirlwind of previously repressed emotions and inner conflicts. One evening she complained of a migraine headache, and her father offered to hold her head in his hands as he'd done when she was a child to make the pain go away. As he did so, he felt inspired to give her a blessing. In the midst of this blessing, he felt something shift in the energy around them.

Her self-destructive behavior began to diminish after that, and over the next couple of months, she completely turned her life around, achieving happiness in a new marriage and discovering a healing power within herself as well. She had to do a lot of inner work to make this change possible, but as her father put it to me, "With that blessing, I could feel that a deep connection was made and a turning point initiated."

I said at the beginning of this book that there are many ways to give blessings, probably as many ways as there are people. When I asked a new class of students how they blessed people, I received a wonderful variety of answers:

"I bless others by visualizing a stream of golden light coming through my fingers towards their heart," one person wrote.

Another said, "I bless another by visualizing and connecting with the "Guardian Angel" of that person. When I get an image or sense of this presence and I can align with its energy, then I get a better understanding of the work that person is doing, the challenges they face, and the beauty they can express." This person went on to say that he let that understanding then guide the nature of his blessing.

A third person said, "When I bless, I envision Christ's energy flowing through a situation or a person. Sometimes I put my hands on the person and see energy flowing from above, through me, into them."

Of course, blessings don't have to be visualized or projected as energies. They're often very concrete actions—and wonderfully so. One of my students had flown to Washington, D.C., on a consulting job and rented a car at the airport. Her plane had been delayed, so night was falling as she drove into the city to her hotel. It also began to snow. Never having been in Washington, she inadvertently took a wrong exit and ended up in a neighborhood that did not appear terribly inviting or hospitable. Then, to cap it all, one of her tires went flat. So she found herself stranded in the middle of an unfamiliar city in a run-down neighborhood with a flat tire in a snowstorm at night! A man came by walking his dog, and she asked him if there was a pay phone anywhere nearby where she might call for help. He listened to her story, then invited her to his nearby apartment, where he fixed her a cup of tea while she called both her hotel and the car rental company, which immediately dispatched a driver with a new car to come pick her up. As she said to me later, "I felt truly blessed by this man who helped me out. Going to a strange man's apartment at night is normally a dangerous thing to do, but he projected such a sense of reassurance that I felt completely safe."

I've been blessed in so many ways by so many people during my life, sometimes through very concrete actions and sometimes purely through an extension of their spirit in subtle ways. As I said in the main text, in any way that we can unencumber and unobstruct another and enable his or her energy to move with greater vitality, freedom, and wholeness, we're offering a blessing. How we do it is less important than the quality of spirit and alignment that we bring to the process.

In blessing another person, the key is to act in an unconditional way. There's a strong ethic around the proper use of subtle energies. When you set out to bless someone, you need to see yourself as a servant of the spirit and integrity of that person, able to relate to them without projecting your own will upon them. A blessing is not the act of a superhero demonstrating his special inner powers; it's not the province of a magical adept or spiritual initiate. It's the inherent ability within any of us to connect with another person with love and goodwill, linking our spirit with his, enabling both of us to remember the love and spaciousness that lives within us.

I've described in Exercise 17 one way I would go about giving a blessing. However, there's one thing I didn't share in my description of that exercise. That's the tremendous sense of privilege I feel in making that deeper connection with another. When I bless someone, I feel that I'm entering the holy ground of their being, and I can do so only if I'm harmless and hold their highest good in my heart. Within each of us is a place where the sacred dwells, and it's to that place that a blessing is directed (or perhaps I should say that it's with the cooperation of that place that a blessing unfolds). To go to that place within another is to realize the beauty and pricelessness of each of our lives. To serve that place, to be able to nourish the sacredness within each other (and within ourselves), is a privilege beyond any other. It's joyous and humbling at the same time. It's what makes the Art of Blessing the wondrous and powerful practice that it is.

BLESSING THE NON-HUMAN WORLD

The basic principles of blessing something in the non-human world—a piece of land, an object, an animal, a plant—are the same as for blessing people or places. You enter into your blessing place, you honor the integrity and identity of that which you're going to bless, you open to it and connect with it, and in the relationship you form you allow the blessing to unfold. You're enhancing the nature, the functioning, or the life of that which you're blessing so it can fulfill potentials of expression or connection that are inherent in it.

The primary difference is that you're dealing with something whose fundamental nature is not human and towards which you may have certain expectations. For example, we're used to using tools, animals, plants, and the land as resources. Whereas we no longer believe in owning humans (although sometimes we act towards each other as if we did), in our culture we can claim ownership over non-human entities. We own our land, our cars, our pets, our livestock, our fields of grain. And when you own something, you may fail to see it as something separate from you, something with its own life, its own identity, worthy of respect and love as a fellow participant in the wholeness of creation.

Yet, the art of blessing requires that when we bless someone or something, we respect that person or thing's unique integrity and identity, or at least the unique manner in which spiritual energies configure themselves around and within him or it. At the very least, everything that exists is rooted in the Source and is a manifestation of that mystery. At the most, from a shamanic point of view, everything in the world is alive and participates in the mystery of consciousness even if in a way so different from our own that it's unrecognizable to us. Either way, when we deal with the things and entities that surround us, we're dealing with much more than appearances may suggest.

For example, I did an exercise with one of my classes in which I asked them to bless an inanimate object of their choice out of several I had presented to them. Here is what one of the participants had to say afterwards: "That was a radical experience! I was blessing the bell. I could imagine its atoms and the craftsperson who made it. But then, in treating it with respect—omigosh! If I allowed respect for all the objects and non-human things in the world, there are huge implications for living differently, managing material things differently. I know this intellectually, but daring to open to that awareness was powerful!"

Yet, this is exactly the awareness to which we open in blessing something from the non-human world. In doing so, we must drop our thoughts and feelings of ownership, even when dealing with an artifact that we've purchased or created, and approach it with the same openness and respect that we would a fellow human.

At the same time, we must be careful not to anthropomorphize it. We don't enter into the blessing of a thing as if it were a human being in a different shape. Rather we focus on our awareness that it is what it is—a rock, a cellular phone, a ferret, a pine tree—and that what it is is not lesser than we but simply different. Like you and me, it's also a part of the sacred.

And it's also part of its own world, the world of minerals, animals, and plants. So, like an ecologist who comes to know an animal or a plant by studying it in its natural habitat, we want to bless a thing in the context of its natural habitat. If it's an animal, then as part of the blessing, I want to attune to the nature of "animalness," just as in invoking my empersonal spirit, I attune to the nature and spirit of my humanness. If it's a rock, then I want to attune to the earth and to its "mineralness." I'm, after all, not blessing it to be like me but to be what it already is in a deeper and less obstructed way.

This requires me, when I'm in my blessing place and opening to the integrity of what I'm blessing, to take an extra step into a part of me that's open to the non-human aspects of the world. At first this may be difficult, and my tendency may be to anthropomorphize, but with practice it can be done. The results can be quite powerful in terms of deeper insight into the nature of the connect-edness we have with the world and with the true meaning of life.

Of course, to achieve this, we may need to begin in the theater of our hearts and minds, imagining ourselves as a plant, an animal, a stone. This is not difficult. Actors do it all the time as part of their training, and it's an integral part of shamanic training the world over as well. In fact, good trackers and hunters, as well as good naturalists, may do this automatically, using their imaginations to "get inside" the animals they're following or the plants they're try-ing to understand. What's important, though, is to move beyond the images into the sensations and intuitive connections that are behind them. You want to develop enough empathy with what a rock is like or a crow is like to be able to connect with their essence as you bless them. Otherwise, you may simply project human energies and images upon them, which won't have the same effect as a blessing.

I was once asked to bless a stone. As I remember it was just an ordinary stone, the kind you could pick up from the ground in al-most any field. As I held it in my hand, I took myself into my bless-ing place and began to love this stone. I admired it, I attuned to its hardness, its earthiness, working my way down into it through my love for it. As I did, the spirit of the stone began to open and I found myself in touch with what I could only describe as the spirit of the earth or at least of its mineral nature. It seemed I could trace a line of connection from that stone right to the earth's molten core. At the same time, another line of connection ran out into space, into the ubiquitousness of stone throughout the universe. In short, this little stone had become a portal for me into a vast community of spiritual beings who embodied the qualities of the mineral king-dom and its molecular and atomic structures throughout creation.

Holding this stone in my hand, it felt just like a small living creature, particularly as I felt the energy coming from this larger community of "mineral beings," and I proceeded to bless it just as I would any other living being. I attuned as best I could to the larger community from which it seemed to come, inviting its combined energy into the process, using myself as a vessel with which to receive and focus the blessing. Then I added my love and energy and enfolded the stone in the resulting mixture of energies, asking only that the essence of the stone be blessed so that its own spiritual evolution might be heightened in whatever way was appropriate for its highest good.

Here I wish to make an important point. In the magical arts, there are techniques for turning something, usually an inanimate object like a stone or a crystal, into a talisman. This is different altogether from blessing. When you make a talisman, you're asking an object to serve as a battery, absorbing the particular subtle energies that you direct into it so that you can draw on those energies later by tapping into that object. With a blessing, you're empowering that object to be more of itself, to experience itself within the context of a larger wholeness. You're not projecting energies into it or using it to store anything. You're working with its energies and your energies in an act of love and mutual enhancement. If anything, you're reminding it of who it is in the context of the sacred and unobstructed world.

So in the blessing of the stone, I wasn't trying to "charge" the stone with higher energies. Instead, I was using my energy to bring it more fully into the presence of its own spiritual sources, into the deep essence from which it had emerged. I was reminding it of its own connections with Source, just as in blessing a person, I would perform the same act of re-membering that connection.

In blessing plants or animals, or even parcels of land, I use the same principle, but I attune to a different aspect of life. I attune to the spiritual source of the animal or plant, for example, and to the larger community of being of which it is a part. For all blessing is fundamentally an act of community and connection. In blessing, I'm just remembering that connection and the community it creates and from which it emerges. In working with a piece of land, I seek to attune to the essence of all the lives that live within it or use it, to the way in which that land is part of a larger ecological system, as well as part of the earth. The principle is the same, but the direction of attunement and the images involved may be different.

It does no good for me to describe what I experience in all these cases; for one thing, the visual imagery often differs from one time to the next, although certain basic qualities of soul and energy remain consistent. When I have a truly good connection with spirit, the imagery falls away anyway. In any event, what I experience in blessing an animal or a plant, at least in the way of imagery, may be very different from what you experience; the last thing I would want is for you to use any descriptions of mine as a guide to what you should be seeing or experiencing if you're successful. So what's important is that you understand the principles and the intent involved; then you can take it from there.

The key thing is that as a blesser, you're there to enhance and vitalize the essence and spirit of what's already there. You're the servant of the life before you and its quest to embody the Source in ever more effective ways. To attune properly to this life, you must inwardly meet it on its own terms, just as you would a fellow human being. In the process, you may have to push your boundaries beyond your customary way of seeing and understanding things.

Of course, there are rich traditions in both eastern and western spirituality to draw upon for help in this process. In the Christian tradition there are men like Saint Francis of Assisi whose love for and connection with nature is legendary. In the east, there's the rich tradition of Taoism, which looks upon each thing as just what it is and blesses it for being so. And more ancient still, there's the legacy of the shamanic perspective, which is reemerging and evolving in our society as we enter the twenty-first century.

When blessing an artifact made by human beings, another element enters the picture, for now you have natural materials that have been assembled and crafted with human imagination and purpose. So you're dealing with a human/non-human hybrid, something that's half from one world and half from another.

The core element to which you must attune, though, is the purpose for which the object was made, the nature of its functionality. In a blessing, you connect with this purpose just as you'd connect with the soul of a living being. It's this functionality—the "life" of the object—that you wish to enhance.

When I was living at the Findhorn Community in the early seventies, I had my first experience in blessing a machine. I was part of a singing group, The New Troubadours, that performed locally (and eventually performed in the United States as well). We wrote most of our own songs and eventually produced a series of tapes and records. The first of these were recorded at Findhorn under conditions that would have given a professional sound engineer gray hairs, but Chris Cathles, the man who was our recording engineer, was a true wizard of his art who was more than up to the task. The biggest problem was that his equipment was prone to breaking down. When it did, I would leave the group and go and bless his machinery, and it would start up again.

Doing a blessing of the sound control board, for example, was different from anything I'd ever done. I had to attune to the purpose for which it was built. It was around this purpose that the coherence of its energy field was organized. I had to reach into that field, attune to its purpose, and then "remind" it of the joy of fulfilling the purpose for which it was made. I invoked energy for its functionality and aligned it with the spiritual presence of a larger wholeness embracing both of us, just as if I were blessing a person. I have no idea what was actually going on within its electronic circuitry, but it felt to me as if I were waking it up and giving it a loving, appreciative pep talk, asking for its cooperation in the process of making our music. The process worked and the control board came alive again, much to my delight and, I admit, to my surprise. After that, I was able to bless it back into working each time it broke down—which I think was twice more—until we completed all our recording work.

The printer at Findhorn, a young man named Victor, had a very similar relationship with an old print machine that had been given to the community for producing its books and other literature. He was literally the only one who could use the machine—not because others didn't know how, but because he had an inner rapport with it to which it responded. When he was in the room working with it, it operated like a Swiss watch. When he was away and someone else, who knew just as much as Victor about the machine, tried to run it, it sputtered, jammed, shook, and generally worked poorly and reluctantly if at all.

This is not an unusual phenomenon. Most of us have experienced it at one time or another, most often, I think, with automobiles. It's not so amazing if we think that we're all energy fields of one kind or another, so it's not too far-fetched to imagine that these fields interact with and affect each other.

In blessing something from the non-human world, then, you proceed just as if you were blessing a person. But in creating your blessing place, you include an act of attuning to the essence of that which you're blessing, entering into the world from which it comes and into its "point of view," so to speak, so that you can feel that essence within you. In this process, your greatest tool is your love and respect for this essence and the material forms it can take. Then, once you have a sense of unity with this essence, you can connect more deeply with the object of your blessing, removing any obstructions that may be there because you're human and it's not.

As I go through my day, I certainly make it a practice to bless the things I work with and enjoy in my everyday life. They contribute so much to bringing beauty, comfort, utility, and pleasure into my life that the least I can do is to acknowledge them and invite them to share in the loving presence of the sacred as I discover it in the depths of my own spirit.

Blessing an Activity

From time to time I've been asked to bless what I can only describe as "activities," things like a new business venture, a project already in operation, a particular community, or a group. There are also plenty of examples of this kind of thing in the world around us. In fact, some of the most familiar blessings are blessings for activities: A chaplain blesses the proceedings of the United States Congress; a coach asks for blessings on his team before the big game; we ask blessings on our meals; we ask blessings for victory in warfare.

Unlike blessing a particular person, place, or thing, blessing an activity may mean blessing something that only exists as an abstraction. For example, two friends of mine recently asked me to bless a new business that they were starting. This business, an online school for spiritual teaching and development, does not exist except in their dreams and hopes, and in their considerable efforts to bring it into being. It's an abstraction living only in the imaginations of those who know about it and support it. Blessing them and their efforts is not the same thing as blessing this idea.

Once one begins to accept the reality, or at least the possibility, of subtle energies, spiritual beings, invisible realms, and the like— all the concepts that in one way or another enter into the art of blessing—it's not such a great leap to accept that something like an idea, if held clearly and strongly with emotional energy over some duration of time, could come into existence as an "imaginal" entity. This is just how this business exists, as something living on an imaginal realm, drawing the energy of its existence from the minds and hearts of those who share it and believe in it.

Eventually, if it's been shaped and energized clearly and strongly enough, it may take on an existence independent of those who originally conceived it. It may begin to live in the natural human equivalent of cyberspace that is the imaginal realm of the shaman, the astral realm of the occultist, or the collective unconscious of the psychologist. Weeks, months, or years later, others may pick up on it through some inner resonance, draw it into their mental sphere, and claim it as their own, fully convinced that they have "thought it up" or have been "inspired." (All of which could lead into an interesting exploration of "where do our thoughts come from?")

But it's precisely this imaginal reality of an idea that can be blessed. Doing so is like blessing a humanly created artifact like a car or a cell phone. The idea of the business in this example has a

life force emanating from my two friends who are creating it as well as from others who are supporting it, and it has an intent and a functionality. The business has a purpose to accomplish and a way of going about achieving that purpose.

In giving this idea a blessing, I go into my blessing place, just as I would for any blessing, and in my mind's eye I call forth the imaginal reality of the idea. This reality comprises all that my friends have shared with me about their goals, their dreams, their vision, what the business seeks to achieve, how it will go about it, how it will present itself to the world, how it will deal with customers and employees, and so forth. In the world of the imagination, this business is already gestating, interacting with the human world to invoke and organize all the elements that will give it birth and concrete substance.

What this idea does not have that a living entity does is a soul. It does not have a natural connection to the wholeness of life. Even a stone has more "life" and connection than this idea does, for the stone is part of an ancient community, perhaps the oldest community in all creation, while the idea is only newly formed. The exception to this, of course, is an idea that was directly inspired by a spiritual presence. Such an idea will have a connection to that presence, but even that's not the same as a soul.

Here I'm using the term *soul* to mean the specific link between the particularity of the entity itself—whether that's a person, an animal, a plant, a nation, or a business—and the universality of the spirit. The soul is the continuum between the particle and the wave; it lives in both worlds. It receives and holds in a specific way the life force, the spiritual power, the intentionality, the love, that flows from the Source and makes it available to its embodied individuality. In return, it receives the specific learning and experiences

and energies arising from that entity and distills them into an essence that enriches the spirit and becomes part of the universal. So in a way the soul is the lung that breathes between the human and the sacred, the membrane of transformation, transmutation, and exchange where the sacred becomes the human and the human becomes sacred.

So, in blessing this idea, I cannot give it a soul. It will eventually develop its own out of the contributions of all the people who help to create it and from the spiritual forces that they invoke. But in the meantime, I can lend it my own. Like a surrogate mother, I can take this idea into the womb of my own inner being and hold it there, bringing it into contact with my own spiritual connections and energies.

In the act of blessing, then, I see the imaginal reality of this idea being drawn into my own soul and exposed to the influences of the spiritual forces to which I'm attuned. So my own attunement, again, is the key. Equally important is the question of whether I can in fact attune to this idea and draw it into the integrity of my own being. It may, after all, be an idea or project with which I have no sympathy, one that my soul would reject or seek to transform, particularly if it were harmful or divisive. I could bless a person with whom I disagree or for whom I may feel antipathy because of their actions by using love to carry me into connection with their soul. But since something like an idea for a business doesn't have a soul, there's no deeper place for my love to take me, no place of shared unity with the Source where I may make contact.

I must also be careful not to confuse blessing an idea with molding that idea and therefore becoming one of its creators. I may have that option, but then again, I may not. The business idea that my friends have created happens to be one with which I feel fully

aligned, but it's still their idea. I can contribute to it creatively and have done so, but it's arising from their life force at the moment, not from mine or anyone else's.

So again I return to the principle that a blessing creates an open space in which something may unfold and thrive and, in contact with its own essence, discover potential new directions for growth and development. But a blessing does not set down that direction or tell that life what to do. A blessing can, however, enhance the connectedness that that life experiences, drawing it into a larger context and hopefully onto the dance floor of the unobstructed world.

That's what I do in blessing my friend's idea. Holding it in my blessing place, I lift it up to spirit and connect it to any spiritual presences whose resonance may be in harmony with its intent. In this case, because it's a business that will deal directly with people and has a mandate to provide a service, I link it in my blessing to the spiritual presence of humanity, asking that this idea be consecrated to human service and to advancing the cause of the human spirit.

So, as you can see, in blessing an activity, you're usually blessing an intentionality and the imaginal construct that arises from that intention. The blessing is both an act of drawing forth the inherent energy in this intention and aligning it with a larger context of life as well as the Source and whatever spiritual presences or allies seem appropriate. You can also bless the participants in the activity—the players on a team, the workers on a job, the members of a group—in my case my friends. In so doing, though, you need to remember that they're whole people whose lives and spirits encompass far more than just the particular activity in which they're engaged together. So you need to take this larger context into account and bless them for the highest good in the wholeness of their lives and not only for their success in this particular activity.

The blessing of an activity does not have to be purely an inner process. In the main text I told the story of the CEO who blessed his employees by getting out of their way and letting them redesign the whole factory floor as well as their own work process. In so doing, he was aligning the imaginal reality of his business with an organic image—he was connecting it to the power and vitality of the natural world and his goal of "growing his business like a plant"—but he implemented that alignment with very practical, down-to-earth steps that actually enabled the blessing to take shape in the lives of his workers and in the success of the business.

A business is an example of an idea that takes form by involving a number of individuals who then begin to act in concert with each other. It becomes a collective activity. A group or community is another example. Blessing a group or a community is like blessing a collective being. The question you must ask is: What's the soul of this group? Where is its collective coherency, its unity, its inner focus and centeredness? What's holding it together? In many cases, its coherency may not lie in the idea behind the group—its group identity or mission statement—but in how the group functions as a collective entity. A group is created by the relationship of its members, so what you're blessing is, not necessarily the idea of the group or specific people within the group, but the dynamic field of relationship that everyone is co-creating and in which they're participating. You're seeking to connect with, enhance, empower, and unobstruct the capacities of the group members to relate successfully with each other. In this sense, the blessing at a practical level may resemble a process of team building but one in which people are asked to go more deeply in connecting with and understanding each other than just dealing with surface appearances.

Of course, you can also bless a group by lifting its vision, enlarging its sense of who it is and what it can be doing, and by expanding its sense of connectedness with the world and with the circulation of spirit. You can help the group discover its own blessing place, a place of attunement, creativity, and mutual support; you can bless it by helping it learn how to "light" itself as a collective candle or "beat" itself as a collective heart within the circulation of spirit and love within the world. The principle works collectively as much as individually: If a group learns to be a blessing, then the group becomes blessed.

In supporting their particiular activities and supporting their collective spirit, a group can use blessings to identify and establish their specific identity. In a sense, the blessing is used to affirm the boundary between themselves and everyone else. We say, for example, "God bless America," not "God bless all creation" or "God bless Humanity." The blessing not only says to whom the spiritual energies should be directed but also marks us as part of the specific target group. While there's nothing wrong with identifying a specific group to be blessed, care must be taken about the attitude with which that blessing is invoked. Either by implication or even outright declaration, the blessing is seen as marking the specialness and exclusivity of that particular group. The subtext of the blessing is: "We're the ones who are being blessed and have a right to be blessed, not anyone else. We are the blessed ones and you who are not part of our group are not." In this context, the blessing becomes an instrument of separation and divisiveness.

The thing to remember about a blessing is that it is a bridge between the specific and the universal; it forms a connection between the two. Consequently, a blessing is not adversarial. It certainly acts to enhance the life and energy of the specific entity involved but not at the expense of others or of a larger wholeness. When someone attempts to use a blessing as a tool of competition to enhance one side over another, it fails to be as powerful as it could be because it has lost its connection to a universal context. Indeed, it may cease to be a blessing at all. A blessing is intended to draw the best out of a particular person, place, thing, or group, not diminish the best in someone or something else.

For example, if I'm a football coach and I'm going to bless my team before the game, my blessing—if it's a true one—cannot simply be that my team will win and the other team will lose. I can certainly bless my team to play their very best, to be filled with vital energy and team spirit, and to experience an effortless flow of grace, strength, and prowess in playing the game. But a blessing, by the very nature of the forces it's intended to invoke, spills over and embraces the wholeness of the game itself, which includes the participation and well-being of the other team.

It can certainly be said that both as a player and as an observer, the most exhilaration and fun in sports comes from a close game well played by everyone involved. Although it might be satisfying to our partisan ego to have our team crush their opponents in a one-sided show of strength, this doesn't make for a very good game. If the other team is no good or doesn't play at their best, what is there to draw out the excellence of your own team? What encourages your players to push the envelopes of their competencies and skills? While a coach wants to win, he wants his team to excel in a contest of equals or especially against a team that's considered better.

In the competitive atmosphere that surrounds so many of us in our lives, the goal seems to be the triumph and dominance of one idea, place, person, or group over another. The Art of Blessing offers a different perspective. The activities or groups we may be called upon to bless may be very specific, but they operate in a larger context of spirit and wholeness that nourishes and sustains all beings. We diminish that wholeness at our own risk. We must keep in mind that in giving blessings, we act as agents of connection. While working in a world of particulars, when we bless, we serve a greater wholeness that includes us all and whose only boundary is the sacred itself.

BLESSING AND INNER WORK

Blessing is a way of working with spiritual energies, but it's not the only one. Other forms of inner work include manifestation, healing, mediation, and the transmutation of negative energies. Each of these has its own particular focus, and there's considerable overlap between them. Until you become sensitive to the "feel" of different subtle energies within your own field and within your body, it may be hard to distinguish when a blessing merges into a healing or vice versa. And in most cases, except to a specialist, it may make no difference. In any event, I feel that examples of how the art of blessing relates to these other forms of inner work may be helpful.

Generally speaking, all forms of inner work draw upon your own presence and energy field, which in turn is aligned with larger sources of spiritual power and wholeness. In inner work, you want to integrate the particular and the universal, the personal and the sacred. Such integration requires personal stability and harmony as well as an ability to go beyond your own perspectives in service to another's highest good. It always requires the presence of unconditional love coupled with discernment and wisdom. The art of blessing involves the development and practice of exactly these qualities and conditions, so it can act as an excellent foundation for other types of inner work. Standing in the integration, power, and attunement of your blessing place is a good beginning for whatever work you wish or need to do with subtle or spiritual energies.

Likewise, such work as manifestation, healing and transmuting easily lead to a condition of blessing. Any of these activities can result in the spiritual enhancement of a person or place, a clearing away of obstructedness and stagnation, and a regeneration of flow and attunement. So blessing can be both the beginning and the ending of these other types of inner work; what's different is what happens in between.

A blessing can bring about healing, manifestation, or the purification of negative conditions, but it does so almost as a secondary effect. Its primary objective is to create a state of unobstructedness in and around whatever is being blessed so that energy can freely flow and vitality is restored or enhanced. The result of this greater energy and wholeness can certainly positively affect conditions of lack, illness, or negativity, but it does more than just that. It's an upliftment and re-membering of the whole person—a restoration of connectedness—and not just the correction of a specific problem within some aspect of that person's life or environment.

To explore the relationship between blessing and other forms of inner work, we can look specifically at the differences and similarities between giving a blessing and manifesting, healing, transmuting negativity, and engaging in prayer and mediation.

Manifestation

Manifestation is the process of using inner attunement, visualization, and one's own presence to bring into your life something you wouldn't be able to get through ordinary means. It's a way of inducing a synchronistic occurrence. You may read about an out-of-print book you'd like to have and then, using a technique of manifestation, later discover it seemingly by coincidence at a neighborhood garage sale. Another example is seeking to manifest the money for a bill you cannot pay, and then getting a check from an unexpected source for exactly the amount of money you need. Both events can look like coincidences, but through inner work, you have enabled them to come about. To explore this concept further and to learn a technique for manifestation, I can suggest my own book on the subject, *Everyday Miracles*.

But as I said, a blessing is not designed to bring something specific into your life in this manner. However, anytime your life's energy and presence are enhanced, they have a greater capacity to reach out into the world and shape the probabilities that in turn become the events and experiences of your life. A blessing can give you greater attunement and inner power, and that will help you work with manifestation.

Here is an example of an approach you could try. The thing you're seeking to manifest may be an object, a quality, or a new situation such as a new job or a new relationship.

Go into your blessing place. Centered in its power and alignment, picture in your mind's eye that which you wish to manifest. Don't just picture its surface appearance but try to grasp its essence and its connections to the world as clearly as you can. You want to see this image not only in relationship to you, or colored by your desire, but possessing a life or energy of its own. Then, in an unconditional way, extend a blessing to this image and what it represents. Hold it in the light and presence of the unobstructed world; hold it in a sense of spaciousness and freedom. See it unfolding to fulfill its own inner nature, whatever that may be. Honor it as something apart from you, yet connected to you through the presence of the sacred. Freely bless it with no sense of obligation or demand upon it. It doesn't have to be part of your life for you to bless it, nor does the blessing compel it to be part of your life.

Hold the sense of this blessing for a minute or two, then, with respect, invite this thing or person or situation into your life. Ask for its blessing, even as you extend your blessing to it. Again, do this without pressure or compulsion. Register the feeling of this mutual blessing as a felt sense or sensation within your body. Then release the image, allowing it to go on its way, as you do the same.

If you wish, you can follow this exercise with whatever manifestation technique you've been taught or have evolved on your own, drawing into it the power of the blessing you've just done.

Healing

Much of current research into the nature of subtle energies and their application is being done in the area of spiritual healing. Using spiritual forces for healing is an ancient practice that's increasingly finding its place again in modern society. More and more books on healing and the new field of energy medicine find their way onto the shelves of mainstream bookstores, not to mention the alternative ones. An excellent introductory book I recommend to people in this area is *Joy's Way* by Dr. Brugh Joy, but for further exploration I would also recommend the books of Dr. Carolyn Myss and Dr. C. Norman Shealy, a neurosurgeon who is the founder of the American Holistic Medical Association.

The line between a blessing and a healing is thin indeed and at times non-existent. Giving someone a blessing can result in a healing for that person, even though the blessing may not have been specifically directed towards that end. Likewise, if I'm healed of an illness, it's almost certain that I will feel blessed.

The primary difference here is that the healing use of subtle energies is usually directed towards a specific need and task, whereas a blessing creates a more general condition of connectedness and wholeness. A blessing is not necessarily or even primarily directed toward the recipient's body, emotions, or thoughts but toward the whole "superstring" of who they are. That said, though, a good healer will also always work with a patient's whole being within the healing process, with the goal being a restoration of wholeness.

Consequently, the overlap between these two forms of inner work is considerable, and they complement each other to a great degree. However, as I mentioned in the main text, working with *energies* is not the same thing as working with *soul*. Sharing spirit together is different from one person sending healing energies to another. A blessing is a portal into what's most real in life, into a remembering of Source and unity and the presence of the unobstructed world. A healing can certainly initiate this state, but it can also be, well, just a healing, a restoration of functioning within some part of us so that we feel better but without any deeper or fundamental change in how we relate to our world.

I do very little healing work. If someone comes to me and asks for a healing, I almost always refer them to someone else whom I respect as having more experience. However, there are occasions when it seems right to incorporate a specifically healing element into a blessing. Here's an example.

A friend of mine came for a visit from the East Coast. While carrying her luggage into the airport, she had pulled some muscles in her neck and back. Sitting for several hours in her narrow, cramped seat on the plane had not helped, so when she arrived, she was in considerable pain. Unfortunately, it was late in the evening, so there were no chiropractors or bodyworkers available until the next day. Knowing that I did not do healings myself, she nevertheless asked if I'd give her a blessing, and I agreed.

I went into my blessing place and, aligning myself with the felt sense of the unobstructed world, I held her beingness within the field of my inner presence. As I did so, I suddenly discovered I was seeing the inflamed muscle tissue in her body appearing like a brushfire just under the skin of her back and neck, glowing with redness and heat. Feeling prompted by this, I shifted the focus of the blessing from her to the tissues and cells in the inflamed area. I did not attempt to direct energy to them, nor did I attempt to "heal" them, but I held them in the same sense of remembrance, spaciousness, and attunement in which I had been holding her. I sought simply to enhance their life and the circulation of energy around and within them.

As I held them in this blessing, I could see the "fire" going out. The small flames dancing beneath the surface of her skin vanished and the red glow disappeared. When it was gone, I shifted the blessing back to her and then pulled my field of presence back into myself, bringing the inner work to a close. As she got up from the chair where she'd been sitting, she announced that the pain in her back and neck was gone. When I saw her the next day, she still felt fine and had no more muscle problems during the rest of her visit.

In this situation, I hadn't tried to actually heal anything in my friend's body. Instead, I had embraced her inflamed muscles in the wholeness and energy that I was feeling within my blessing place.

Most importantly, I didn't embrace them as "inflamed" or "sick" but as fellow living beings emerging from the Source and sharing with me the wonder of life. Just as I would not bless an individual simply as a doctor, a pilot, a housewife, or a salesperson, in using a blessing in a healing way, I wouldn't approach the tissues of my friend's sore back through an image of their sickness. Instead, I reached out to their essence, which a blessing is designed to evoke. A blessing is a relationship from soul to soul, spirit to spirit, and while I may never have thought of my cells as having souls, there is within them a light and presence of spirit as surely as there is within me.

Before I have a massage, I take a bath to relax my muscles. Then the tightness in my body is loosened, and the massage can have a deeper and more powerful effect. In a similar way, a blessing sets into motion forces of attunement and wholeness that can prepare the way for healing work by heightening the flow of energy around a patient. The art of blessing and the art and science of healing definitely support each other and, when used together, can create a synergy of positive results for the patient.

Protection, Cleansing and Transmutation

Any of us may encounter negative energies during the course of our day from the anger or jealousy of a co-worker, or the surliness of a stranger in a shop, to the depression or irritability of a loved one. Some of us may be in professions where we encounter much worse: hatred, malice, fear, pain, despair, cruelty, and other emotions that can disintegrate any awareness of wholeness within or around us. It's unfortunate, but painful and hurtful thoughts, feelings, and actions are part of our world at the moment, and no amount of denial or seeking escape into blissful fields of spiritual attunement is going to change this fact. We must meet these conditions head-on in ways that are protective and healing and that cleanse and transmute negative energies so that they are no longer destructive and harmful.

This is a major undertaking, and one we're all engaged with, if only in dealing with our own negativity and the ways in which we can become hurtful to others. In fact, internal cleansing is the most important aspect of this work, and however we pursue it—whether through self-understanding, therapy, a spiritual practice and attunement, or some other means—the negativity and evil in the world will only diminish as we transform it at its source, which for the most part is ourselves as human beings.

Not that we're inherently evil, a position I don't accept. For me, the core of the human being is rooted in the sacred, and love exists at the core of all of us. This is not to say that there aren't dysfunctional people in whom this core has been sealed off, whose connections with the whole have been broken or atrophied, whose relationships with others are defined by sociopathic attitudes. Such people do exist and can pose a genuine threat not to be underestimated. However, they don't for me define the reality of humanity itself. Nor do they constitute an argument that by virtue of being inherently corrupt and evil, our human nature fundamentally flawed, we're incapable of blessing or of being a source of spiritual energies. Anyone who thinks otherwise may profit from reading, as I suggested in the exercises on humanity, a book called *The Brighter Side of Human Nature,* by Alfie Kohn, a hard-headed, deeply reasoned examination of our inherent capacities for altruism and empathy.

Rather than being fatally flawed, we are people in the making, unfinished, still painfully learning the skills of mutual respect and empowerment, still discovering the deeper reality of connectedness and love. We act out of fear, selfishness, bewilderment, and ignorance. We create negative energy in the process, and when that energy is allowed to accumulate and fester like a wound, it begins to take on a power of its own that's demanding, corrosive, and at times seductive and attractive.

The issue of protection and of dealing with such evil is one that often arises around doing inner work with subtle energies. If you're interested in exploring this topic more fully, I suggest Dr. William Bloom's book *Psychic Protection* as an excellent place to start.

For our purposes, the best protection of all is a healthy subtle immune system, which, like our physical one, is kept in good order by everything we do to keep a flow of physical and spiritual energy moving through our lives. Our moral lives *do* matter, and how we treat others—as well as ourselves—not only outwardly but inwardly plays an important role in keeping us attuned to spiritual forces of balance and wholeness. In many ways, the health of our psychic immune system is directly related to the integrity of our lives as a whole; anything we do that goes against that integrity, that dishonors or destroys it, has an adverse affect on our inner protection as well.

In the art of blessing, the act of invoking the power of your empersonal and transpersonal spirits and aligning with the sacred that helps create your blessing place is also an act of inner protectiveness. The blessing place as a sphere of energy and power in which you stand is itself protective. Moreover, it protects by radiating. You're not locking yourself passively away from the world behind a mystic barrier. You're manifesting an inner (and outer) identity that's dynamic and cannot be overcome or invaded by anything less than what it is. If you don't resonate with the negative conditions around you, you can stand in their presence and not be harmed (though you may certainly feel their impact through your empathy and mindful awareness).

Anyone who works with subtle energies develops methods of self-protection, and in one way that includes all of us whether we realize it consciously or not. These may range from the classic attitude of seeing oneself "surrounded by Light," to looking for the positive in a situation, using humor to break up tension, or just taking a deep breath and centering oneself. Another classic method of cleansing oneself is by taking a shower, for the energy of the running water also helps to cleanse one's energy field. But any technique we may have learned or intuitively developed can only be synergically enhanced by doing it from within our blessing place.

One way to think about negative energies is that they are information. They are telling you something about the world around you or about your inner state. Your blessing place is also a form of information, in this case about the presence and power of wholeness, spirit, love, and connectedness in your life. This information can reinterpret and reorganize, and in effect erases and rewrites, the negative information you may be receiving. The energy of your blessing place and the information it contains can transform the negativity.

For this reason, blessings have also traditionally been used to cleanse and purify negative conditions in buildings or around people. This may be done ritualistically using candles, incense, or the sprinkling of consecrated water, along with invocations and prayers. It may be done, as I've already described, by physically cleaning out a place, scrubbing it down with soap, water, laughter, and high spirits. In the long run, the best way to transmute the energies of a place once an initial cleansing is done is to bring new life and activity into it that resonates with the qualities you want it to have.

Evil, on the other hand, is more than just the presence of negative energies. Evil from my point of view is a condition resulting from the implosion of negative thoughts, emotions, and intents into a dense, dark "black hole" of the spirit. I view evil as an actively obstructing and draining presence that has become disconnected from the larger wholeness of creation. It's a hungry presence that sustains itself on the life force around it. Like a black hole in space, it's a gravity well of inertia and selfishness that gives nothing back to the universe, a depressing, crushing force that seeks the cessation of activity rather than promoting a particular activity of its own.

To deal with such a force requires a powerfully vital and connected spirit, one rich in life that can use its own energy to embrace that deep, sucking inertia and set it in motion again—for once an energy is in motion, it can be redirected and transmuted. However, the act of getting it moving again can release all the energies of pain, anger, fear, isolation, hatred, and malice that created this black hole in the first place. The person doing the transmuting must be prepared to deal with all this, holding the released energies in containment so they don't escape to harm anyone, most likely by absorbing and transforming them within his or her own being with all the risks this entails. This is a vital and daunting task, one that almost always requires the intervention and assistance of spiritual allies.

Such work is not for everyone or even for most people. It's certainly beyond the scope of the art of blessing as I've presented it in this book. Yet, it's still an act of blessing. And as such, it's empowered and served by all other acts of blessing we perform. The more we discover ways to bless each other, to bless the places in which we live and work, and to bring the spirit of the unobstructed world into our lives, the more we raise the global conditions of the subtle energies in which we all live. And this provides invaluable assistance to any and all who undertake the work of transmuting and healing the conditions of evil in our world, creating resources of spirit and energy upon which they may draw.

If a person is inwardly drawn to such a work, then I believe from my own experience and observation that they will receive the help and training they need. One very vital issue is the avoidance of glamor or of identifying oneself as a "warrior of Light." Thinking of oneself in this way as being part of a great battle or as a fighter for God can actually become a hook that shifts one away from the compassionate yet detached inner stance that's required. Engaging with anything with an adversarial attitude creates a connection to it, which then interferes with the cleansing and purifying process. In spite of the glamor of being a spiritual warrior, cleansing a place, a person, or a situation that has been imbued with deep negativity is an act of ecological re-balancing rather than an act of spiritual warfare. Restoring the healthy, free-flowing energies of an environment whose energies have become constricted, stagnant, and dark is not an act of battle but one of reclamation and recycling. It's an act of healing. To approach such a task in a spirit of combat is to inspire resistance, counterattack and attachment, which will only make the work more difficult and risky.

Transmuting evil energies is an act of spiritual service requiring a person with a healthy, stable, balanced personality who also has a clear, strong alignment with powerful spiritual sources and allies and with the sacred. They must also be confident enough of their power to love and to forgive, as well as to remain emotionally and mentally unaffected by the negative qualities they're dealing with. And whatever other qualities and insights such a person may bring to the process, however, being able to create and stand in a place of blessing within themselves will greatly enhance their own protection and empower the success of their work.

Mediation and Prayer

Mediation is the art of linking with a spiritual presence or power and using one's own consciousness and being to "step it down" into a form that can successfully engage with the conditions on our world. The best way to do this is not through becoming a passive channel but by being a dynamic partner standing in your own blessing place and using the resonance of its energy and your connection with the world to "pass through" energies from a higher spiritual source.

The highest form of meditation—and, paradoxically, in some ways the simplest—is to open oneself to the sacred and to make oneself a willing and unconditional servant of its will to bring about the highest good in any situation.

The simplest way to do this is through prayer. Indeed, all of the forms of inner work I've discussed can be subsumed into prayer. Whether I need a blessing, a manifestation, a healing, protection from negativity, or the cleansing and transmutation of evil, I can ask for help from the sacred through prayer in achieving these things. And in one way or another—often in ways unexpected by us—there will be a response.

But there are so many ways that one may pray. For me, because my experience of the sacred has always been infused with the sense of an unconditional love, I have for over forty years referred to God as the Beloved. When I was at the Findhorn Community and I would give blessings and invocations, I invariably used this term, beginning each prayer by saying "Beloved." Although I never asked anyone else to use this terminology, it caught on in the community for a while. One day I was part of a group working in the kitchen, preparing the evening meal, and all of us were participating in a blessing under the leadership of an American woman in her eighties. Several times she tried to start her prayer by saying "Beloved . . ." but she would get flustered and stop. Finally, she turned to me in some distress and said, as if it made any difference to me, "David, I'm sorry. I just can't use that word, 'Beloved.'" Then she threw back her head and hands, gave a wonderful shout of "O Lord! Hallelujah!" and proceeded to lead us quite happily in the blessing.

Because prayer is such a personal thing, I offer no examples, other than to say that I like to keep my prayers short and sweet and to let the words evolve out of the spirit of the moment. I do, though, suggest that entering into prayer can be like entering into your blessing place—and why not? For the most powerful prayer is to be in the presence of the sacred, to unite with the Source, to be with that which is Most Real. Prayer is not just asking for things; that's the least, most superficial aspect of it. Prayer is a relationship. It's being in the Presence, and removing any obstructions between ourselves and the sacred. It's the very heart of blessing, the spirit and power of the unobstructed world in which nothing stands between me and the Beloved.

To step into one's blessing place is to step into prayer. To give a blessing is to make that prayer flesh.

BLESSING AND WORLD WORK

I'm out of my body and looking down on central Africa. Below me, I see a great volcano that's risen out of the land, its crater a gaping maw of fiery hot energy that's almost white in the intensity of its heat. From this opening, molten fire is pouring out into the land around, a yellow-red energy streaked with black. Looking at it, I can feel waves of fear, hatred, anger, and despair arising, for that's what the volcano really is: a symbolic representation of a caldron of human emotion as the nation of Rwanda is engulfed in genocidal killing.

I'm engaged in an aspect of what I call "world work," a form of blessing meditation (or meditative blessing) in which I enter into my blessing place and then, in my mind's eye, project my awareness and journey imaginally to some part of the world where there's suffering or difficulty. It's 1994, and in Rwanda, the suffering is monumental as extremist members of the Hutu tribe slaughter hundreds of thousands of minority Tutsis and moderate Hutus. It's to this situation that I've directed my attention.

As I do so, the vision of the volcano appears before my inner eye. As I watch this maelstrom of pain and hatred symbolized by the erupting volcano, I wonder what to do. Then I become aware of streams of beings coming from all directions. They seem made of ice, brilliantly shining blue-white beings, and they plunge unhesitatingly into the volcano, where they melt and disappear. As they do, however, a small part of the fiery energy is subdued and cooled.

I don't know what these beings represent; I suspect they're embodied prayers being sent to this horrific situation. They're certainly born of light, and their action is not to combat the situation but to absorb and lessen the energy that's there so that the volcano does not grow larger and widen the area of its influence. They're literally trying to cool the whole thing down.

It's clear I am not to plunge into the volcano myself. But I realize what I can do is to use the energy and presence from my blessing self to heighten the absorbing power of these creatures. I can, in effect, make them colder so they don't melt as quickly and can therefore affect more of the volcano. So I imagine that the field of my presence expands to form a lens over the whole volcano, a refrigerated lens through which these ice-beings pass en route into the crater, taking some of the energy flowing through me to "chill" themselves still more. I hold this for several minutes until I feel the image fading and my energy waning. Then I pull myself back into my body, sit for a couple of minutes in silence, feeling the energy of my blessing place flowing within and around me. Then I open my eyes, take a deep breath, and go about the business of my day.

How real was this experience? The visual part—the volcano, the icy beings, my refrigerated lens—were all imaginal and symbolic. They were tools helping my concrete, everyday mind to understand and to participate in what was happening. They were not the reality at all. But at the same time, another part of me was very aware of the energies and conditions involved, and I could feel an energy of blessing flowing from me to help in this situation, joining with the energy from perhaps millions of other people throughout the world praying and working on behalf of the suffering people in Rwanda.

This kind of blessing from a distance for situations in the world is important. We're all part of the world in more ways than we know. This actually gives us a great potential to help, for in the nonlocality of our spiritual presence—in its transcendence of the ordinary boundaries of time and space—we can be anywhere, participate in any event, and bring to it our blessings using the techniques and tools we've discussed in this book.

Two things are important here. We should never glamorize this work. We can be proud of what we do, but we should realize that in fact as far as spirit's concerned, it's just good-neighborliness, like bringing meals to a family who has just had a new baby or calling 911 if we see a neighbor's house on fire. To turn it into high drama and to feed our egos on it is to diminish the power of our blessing place and to reduce this world work into fantasies of our own creation.

The second thing is that we must always work from an inner center of peace from which we can act in a non-judgmental, non-adversarial way. When we bless, we become servants of the whole, not of some faction of it. In the experience I described above, my work was not to spiritually zap the "evil" Hutus but to empower an activity that was attempting to liberate all involved from a rampaging flood of emotional and psychic energies that had turned everyone into a victim. And while special attention was undoubtedly being given to the Tutsis who were directly being abused, murdered, and tortured, in the long run the healing and restoration of wholeness has to encompass the Hutus as well. The often unrecognized and, for some people, unwelcome and difficult realization is that God does not take sides. All beings are embraced in the compassion of the sacred, for if any being can be denied the hope of redemption, then ultimately all of us could be so denied.

So if we're going to be partners with the sacred in our acts of blessing, then we must learn to see as the sacred does and love unconditionally. This doesn't mean that we must accept all behaviors or abandon all discernment, but even as we act to bind what's evil and protect what's innocent, we cannot cast away our love or fail to realize that as long as any are bound, even for the protection of others, we're bound as well. Ultimately, the source acts for the liberation of all, and it's that spirit of liberation and reconnection that lies at the heart of all blessings.

In doing this kind of work, you enter into your blessing place and then, in whatever way feels comfortable, attune to some event or condition in the world that you wish to bless. Because world events or problems are often complex, you may wish to translate this event into a symbol that represents its essence to you, offering you a form of imaginal shorthand. Hold that event or condition in your mind's eye, drawing it into that inner spaciousness and place of love and remembering that is your blessing place. Draw it into the space of the unobstructed world as you experience that world in yourself. Then proceed with the blessing in whatever way seems appropriate. In your inner eye, for example, you may see the situation bathed in the light of the unobstructed world, allowing that light to work as it deems best. (I should say here that I rarely get visual images while doing this; the experience of the volcano and the angels was unexpected and unusual for me.) Then bring the meditation and blessing to a close as you've learned to do when the energy begins to wane.

Because the context of this kind of blessing work is planetary, there are two spiritual allies on whose resources I regularly draw. These are the soul of humanity and the world soul. The majority of our problems in the world today are either ecological in nature, in which people's interests or ambitions are pitted against the total well-being of the earth in some way, or involve one part of humanity in conflict with another, a civil war within the human family. For this reason, invoking the spiritual presence of the world soul or of humanity's soul seems highly appropriate. It can be done as simply as saying, "I now invoke the spirit of humanity that includes and cherishes all people to join and empower my blessing," or "I invoke the soul of the world that nourishes and loves all life to join and empower my blessing."

In order to invoke these great presences, it's important to understand that you do not take sides, nor are you asking them to. They represent the wholeness to which we aspire. They are not partisan. From the perspective of spirit, all conflict—whether of people against people or people against the ecological balance—is a rending of the body of life against itself. The desired outcome appropriate to an act of blessing is not the victory of one side against the other but the reconciliation and healing of the whole.

World work does not have to address itself only to crises. You can bless any kind of activity that works for the well-being and wholeness, as well as the advance and unfoldment, of humanity and our world. You can bless scientific and technological research and discovery. You can bless positive political efforts to develop a sense of world community. You can bless efforts at discovering new ways of integrating our human needs and objectives with the needs and balance of the natural world. You can bless humanity as a whole and the world as a whole. In so doing, you seek to add your inner contribution to keeping the positive energies of life, discovery, growth, and connection moving and dynamic in our world.

You can do world work by yourself, of course. But this kind of work also lends itself very well to being a group activity. Great power can be generated when a group of people get together to bless in concert with one another, creating a collective blessing place within which they can all participate. In such a blessing circle, each of you can draw on the power of this shared blessing place to focus individually on a number of situations or issues, as directed by your own inner intuition or interests. Or you can join together in a group blessing in which everyone focuses upon the same objective. In either case, all the principles of the art of blessing are the same, but the power can be magnified by your collective attunement and communion.

Because the focus of blessing as a world work is often on crisis situations, it is not unexpected that powerful emotions can be aroused. World crises can seem very overwhelming, often because of their scope. We can feel powerless. Naturally, we can feel distressed at the suffering that may be present. Whatever emotions are aroused can be magnified by the group setting as people share and echo each other's feelings. So in a group, it's especially important to cultivate being centered in the blessing place. It's important to be appropriately detached so as not to project the group's own emotional state into the situation in the name of giving a blessing. A key thought to remember is that when you bless a situation, you're not trying to fix it. You are adding to the possibility that it can and will be fixed, but in the context of sending a blessing, you are not taking on that responsibility yourself.

Any kind of world work can be taxing. It's important not to exceed either your own energy level if you are working alone or that of a group if you are working collectively. It's not the length of time you spend doing spiritual work either individually or in a group that makes a difference; it's the quality of energy you can bring to it. If either you or your group is attuned, experienced, and focused on what needs to happen, a blessing can take place and powerful energies can be exchanged and transmitted in a matter of seconds or minutes.

I've participated in group work where the goal seemed to be to see how many projects one could get through in an evening, or how long the spiritual work could be stretched out. I can tell you from hard-won experience and observation, though, that when people's stamina begins to flag and their bodies become restless, the quality of inner energy can fall off dramatically. Then, by the end of the session, no one is really doing anything except massaging inner images and fantasies. In world work—or in any inner work, for that matter—it's good to have check points to see how the energy level is holding, and if it's not, then take a break.

Each group of people should establish their own protocols for managing their collective (and personal) energy while working together. Over time and with experience, this will come naturally. The principle that quality is better than quantity most of the time holds just as true for spiritual work as for things in the physical world. And, of course, this same principle should be applied when you're working solo in giving blessings. That's why in the exercises I often said to stop when you began to feel restless. Your body can be a good gauge of when your energy is beginning to wane.

When a group has finished with any inner work in which strong emotions have been present or powerful energies have been worked with, which is often the case in world work, some kind of restorative activity is important before going on about your daily lives. I find having a snack, sharing funny stories, and enjoying laughter together is very grounding and restores the energy of the people in the circle before they have to leave. A simple blessing of each other can help, too, as long as it doesn't become an elaborate exercise in using still more of your inner energies. The idea is to bring everyone back to a refreshed, balanced state at the closure of your time together. This is also true when you are doing solo work.

There's one final point to make about world work. Because each of us is a part of the world—more intimately so, in fact, than we may realize—any work we do to bless our own personal trouble spots and move them towards resolution and healing will add to the greater circulation of spirit within the world as a whole and bring the incarnation of the unobstructed world that much closer.

So, we return to where we were at the beginning of this section of the book. Because of the interconnected nature of all things, an essential part of world work is to bless yourself and to bless the other people, the places, the things, the creatures, and the activities with which you share your daily life. All blessings support and connect with all other blessings in the great circle of Spirit. All blessings serve to make our world a better place.

All these examples and suggestions are only that: suggestions. The wonder of the Art of Blessing is that it unfolds from each of you in a unique way that will honor and reveal who you are in connection with the Source, with others, with the world, and with your own being. Explore and be open to discovery. The process is really very simple. It is not so much a technique as an attitude, a perspective on yourself and on life. As a blesser, you become an agent, a servant, of the potential for love and wholeness within each of us and for the incarnation of the unobstructed world within and around us all. Beyond that, the path of blessing you find will be your own.

When you do, follow this path with joy and with honor. Have fun.

And walk in blessing.

FURTHER EXPLORATIONS

In the course of the text, commentaries, and examples, I've mentioned a few books that elaborate upon some of the issues I've discussed. While they don't discuss the Art of Blessing in the same way I do, they all complement it in one way or another. I want to list them in one spot so you can pursue them if you wish. Of course, there are other books out there whose material relates to or can supplement this one, and I encourage you to seek them out. This list is only a small beginning in that further exploration.

Reading List

BELITZ, Charlene, and LUNDSTROM, Meg.   *The Power of Flow.*
New York: Harmony
Books, 1997.

This is an introductory book to the whole psychospiritual state of "flow," in which an individual feels open, empowered, and able to achieve optimal performance. This is an excellent state in which to perform blessings!

BLOOM, William.   *Psychic Protection.* New York: Simon & Schuster, 1996.

This is an excellent introductory book on working with subtle energies. Written in everyday language with simple examples and techniques by a master teacher in this field, this book goes far beyond issues of protection and deals with the whole range of engaging with subtle energies in one's life. It also includes an excellent section on blessing.

The Endorphin Effect. London: Piatkus Books, 2001.

Based on more than twenty years of research and teaching in the human potential and spiritual growth fields, this book deals with the neurochemical side of invoking and embodying spiritual states such as those that help create blessings. It combines up-to-date research in biochemistry with the insights of one of the best spiritual teachers in the field. Simply and wonderfully written, it is filled with excellent and very practical exercises that can enable anyone to make use of the information William is presenting. I find this book a perfect complement for Blessing and recommend it highly.

CSIKSZENTMIHALYI, Mihaly. *Flow: The Psychology of Optimal Experience.* San Francisco: HarperCollins, 1993.

This is the pioneering book on the psychology of flow states. It presents the theoretical basis for understanding and achieving inner states of harmony and connectedness, in which all things seem possible and one is empowered by an effortless flow of energy.

DOSSEY, Larry. *Healing Words.* New York: HarperCollins, 1993.
Be Careful What You Pray For. San Francisco: HarperSanFrancisco, 1997.
Reinventing Medicine. San Francisco: HarperSanFrancisco, 1999.

These three books, which should be considered a trilogy, do not deal with blessing per se but with prayer and healing. However, blessing and prayer can fade into each other with no sharp boundary between them. These books, filled with spiritual insights as well as scientific evidence supporting their perspectives and conclusions, are excellent explorations of how we interact with each other in non-physical ways using subtle forces we have yet to fully understand.

JOY, Brugh.   *Joy's Way.* New York: J.P. Tarcher, 1978.

An introductory book on working with subtle energies, particularly for healing, Dr. Joy's personal story, his wisdom as both a doctor and a spiritual teacher, and the ease and lucidity of his techniques all combine to make this book the deserved classic it has been in its field for the past twenty-two years.

KOHN, Alfie.   *The Brighter Side of Human Nature.* New York: Basic
Books, 1990.

An objection that can be raised against the art of blessing is that human beings are inherently too corrupt and evil to be a source of spiritual energy and that human nature is flawed at its core, making us unworthy to bless. This wonderful book elegantly refutes this position in a hardheaded, closely reasoned, and engaging way.

LINN, Denise.   *Sacred Space.* New York: Ballantine Wellspring, 1995
Altars. New York: Ballantine Wellspring, 1999.

These two books both deal with invoking and recognizing a spirit of sacredness in one's own home and in other environments in which one works. They give wonderful examples of how to bring blessing into places, thereby turning them into sources of blessing for ourselves.

NEELD, Elizabeth Harper.   *A Sacred Primer.* Los Angeles: Renaissance
Books, 1999.

Subtitled *The Essential Guide to Quiet Time and Prayer,* this wonderfully rich, wise, and practical book is about creating our own unique spiritual practice. One of the best books I have found on the art of spiritually blessing one's own self while incubating a force of spirit within one that can be a blessing to others.

SINETAR, Marsha. *The Mentor's Spirit.* New York: St. Martin's Press, 1998.

All of Marsha Sinetar's books are outstanding, reflecting her compassionate heart and her wise, insightful intellect, but this one is particularly relevant to the Art of Blessing. Her description of the spirit of mentoring, although it is described using different examples and metaphors, complements my own work with blessing in a wonderful way. Mentoring is a form of blessing, and her book clearly shows how we can walk a mentoring path with each other.

SPANGLER, David. *Everyday Miracles.* New York: Bantam, 1996.

Of all my own books, this one contains material closest to that covered in *Blessing*. It's about using our inner presence and subtle energies to create synchronicities or manifestations, so that we may craft our lives creatively and purposively. (Of course, if you want to read my other books as well, I shall hardly object!)